Renita Boyle gained a BA (Hons) in sexual exploitation. She is a former a
Children at Risk magazine. Renita
book chapters to various publications
the Toybox, published under the Barnabas imprint in April 2002. She is an experienced children's worker and is currently, among other projects, producing issues-based curriculum for CURBS. Renita is married to Eric. They have one young son, Jude.

Kate Smith gained a BA (Hons) in English and American Literature from the University of Warwick. Kate has experience of poverty through her work with International Development agencies both overseas and in the UK. After gaining a TEFL qualification, Kate worked with under-privileged children in Mexico and taught adults in Sri Lanka. She has also participated in research exercises for a number of UK-based organizations. Kate now works for Compassion, where she is their Advocacy Network Manager. She liaises with and resources the large network of Compassion advocates within the UK and also represents Compassion at events nationwide.

Text copyright © Renita Boyle and Kate Smith 2004
The authors assert the moral right
to be identified as the authors of this work

Published by
The Bible Reading Fellowship
First Floor, Elsfield Hall
15–17 Elsfield Way, Oxford OX2 8FG

ISBN 1 84101 343 9
First published 2004
10 9 8 7 6 5 4 3 2 1 0
All rights reserved

Acknowledgments
Unless otherwise stated, scripture quotations are taken from the
Contemporary English Version of the Bible published by HarperCollins
Publishers, copyright © 1991, 1992, 1995 American Bible Society.

A catalogue record for this book is available from the British Library

Printed and bound in Great Britain by
Bookmarque, Croydon

Understanding Compassion

A biblical exploration seen through the eyes of child poverty

Renita Boyle and Kate Smith

ACKNOWLEDGMENTS

Henry David Thoreau once said, 'How vain it is to sit down and write when you have not stood up to live.' I have been keenly aware of my own hypocrisies in the process of writing this book: how often I have mistaken pity for compassion, a few hurried coins for generosity, and random involvement for sustained servanthood. Despite this, however, I commend it to you. I pray that you will be as deeply influenced in the reading of this book as I have been in the writing of it; that you will love God more, serve others better and seriously consider the work of Compassion International. Indeed, the completion of this book marks the beginning of our own child sponsorship. I would especially like to thank Kate Smith for so ably and sensitively bringing the vast work of Compassion International to these pages, the Bible Reading Fellowship for its vision in taking on this project and Sue Doggett for her support.

This book was written during difficult personal circumstances. While I may have written about compassion, I am deeply humbled by the many people who daily define it for me. Special thanks to: Eric, you sharpen and soften me. Jude, you inspire me to love. Mum, my Naomi. Mom, my encourager. Dawn, sisters by birth and bond. Aunty Alice, Dad is smiling. Fiona, Isobel, Isabelle, Lisa and Rose: friends always love. Julie and Ruth, you bring the Spirit with you. Hazel, Karen and Rebecca: any friend of Jude's is a friend of mine. Amy, Anne, Agnes, Bill, Eunice, Evelyn, Hazel, Janet, Mike and Sheelagh: prayerful and practical. The families Brackenridge, Campbell, Dickson, Fleming, Gowler, Irvine, Kirkman, Krueger, Kynaston, Neal, O'Malley, Paulson, Proudlove, Rose, Sargeant, Sherry, Thompson: faithful in little and in much. Margaret, our Martha. Ruth and Ruthven, thanks for bringing us nearer heaven. Jill, Carey and Joanne: Borders anyone? Special thanks to The Crossing and the churches we call home in Bo'ness, Lenzie, Reddick and Reeve.

Renita Boyle

Contents

Foreword 7

Introduction 9

Chapter 1: Compassionate worship 19

Section One: Our compassionate God: worshipping the Tri-unity 20
Section Two: Our compassionate God: worshipping the Father 27
Section Three: Our compassionate God: worshipping the Son 34
Section Four: Our compassionate God: worshipping the Holy Spirit 41
Section Five: Our compassionate identity in Christ 49
In-depth reflection: What is poverty? 57

Chapter 2: Compassionate life 61

Section One: The compassionate life: in community 62
Section Two: The compassionate life: in solidarity 70
Section Three: The compassionate life: in servanthood 77
Section Four: The compassionate life: in obedience 85
Section Five: The compassionate life: in hopeful expectancy 92
In-depth reflection: Is it our responsibility? 100

Chapter 3: Compassionate prayer 103

Section One: Compassionate prayer: abiding in community 104
Section Two: Compassionate prayer: abiding in solidarity 112
Section Three: Compassionate prayer: abiding in humble servanthood .. 120
Section Four: Compassionate prayer: abiding in obedient response 128
Section Five: Compassionate prayer: abiding in hopeful expectancy 136
In-depth reflection: What is holistic development? 145

Chapter 4: Compassionate word 149

Section One: Compassionate word: in common unity 150
Section Two: Compassionate word: in solidarity 158
Section Three: Compassionate word: in humble servanthood 166
Section Four: Compassionate word: in obedient response 174
Section Five: Compassionate word: in hopeful expectancy 181
In-depth reflection: Why children? 189

Chapter 5: Compassionate community 193

Section One: Compassionate community: in common unity 194
Section Two: Compassionate community: in solidarity 203
Section Three: Compassionate community: in humble servanthood 212
Section Four: Compassionate community: in obedient response 220
Section Five: Compassionate community: in hopeful expectancy 228
In-depth reflection: Why partner with the Church? 236

Chapter 6: Compassionate witness 239

Section One: Compassionate witness: in common unity 240
Section Two: Compassionate witness: in solidarity 249
Section Three: Compassionate witness: in humble servanthood 257
Section Four: Compassionate witness: in obedient response 265
Section Five: Compassionate witness: in hopeful expectancy 273
In-depth reflection: How can we be changed? 281

Bibliography 284

Foreword

To those who say that you can't change the world, the answer is 'You can change the world for one person.' That is what *Compassion* is all about. It is about changing the world, one child at a time.

I have seen first-hand what *Compassion* does for children. They are fed, clothed, educated, evangelized, given hope and lifted from dismal futures through the sponsorship programme. Furthermore, support is given to the sponsored child's family, so that brothers and sisters also may share in the blessings that your gift provides. This is evident in the short stories contained within this book.

One day, during a visit to a government school in Zimbabwe, the children of the school were lined up to entertain the other visitors and me. One little boy (there was no way of guessing his age, because undernourished children experience retarded growth) was in incredibly dire straits. As he tried to sing the national anthem of his country for us, his little body swayed back and forth. Before the end, he simply collapsed. A teacher picked up his little body and carried him out of the classroom. I learned that later that day he died.

It is to prevent such horrors that *Compassion* exists. This book will introduce you to their ministry and its biblical foundation. It will help you to explore God's word and its practical application, giving you the insight and guidance to respond personally or introduce others to the work. After you read what follows, you will have to decide for yourself if you can turn your back on some child who might be rescued through your giving.

In 1 John 3:17 we read, 'How does God's love abide in anyone who has the world's goods and sees a brother or sister in need and yet refuses to help? To me, that's a good question. Loving God requires loving and giving to those in need.

Tony Campolo
Professor Emeritus, Eastern University, St David's, Pennsylvania, USA

Introduction

Compassion: the origin of our ministry

In 1952, during the Korean War, Everett Swanson, an American evangelist, was invited to preach to the American troops in Japan and South Korea. One morning, as Everett was nearing the end of his stay in Korea, he observed a truck rumbling through the streets of Seoul collecting rags from the doorways and alleys of the city. Everett watched the city workers kick each pile of rags, presumably to ensure they were free from rats, before throwing them on to the truck. It was only when he saw a small arm extending from one of the bundles that he realized the workers were not collecting rags from the streets, but the bodies of street children who had died in the night.

Everett was horrified by the inhumanity he saw, and shocked that this treatment of the street children was considered acceptable. Orphans of the war were considered to be vermin and treated as such; even if they survived the crossfire of war they could never escape the cultural disgrace into which they were born.

The silent faces of these innocent victims would never leave Everett and on his return he used his preaching engagements to raise funds for orphanages in Korea. In time, the need for ongoing support and individual encouragement for each child became apparent and the *Compassion* sponsorship programme developed. The name came from Matthew 15:32: 'I have compassion for these people... I do not want to send them away' (NIV). This verse is a promise that holds true; Everett did not run from those in need and neither must we. Embracing children in need is the heart of *Compassion*.

INTRODUCTION

Compassion: the quest for humanity

It would seem that children are as expendable today as they were when Everett Swanson first witnessed city officials discarding the bodies of dead street children in South Korea. Consider the following statistics:[1]

- 35,000 children under the age of five die every day from easily preventable causes.
- 300 million children are orphaned or homeless.
- 360 million children are illiterate, with little hope of staying in school—if they have access to school at all.
- 250 million children work for a living—120 million full-time.
- At least one million children are lured or forced into prostitution each year.
- Between four and five million children are infected with HIV, most of them through their mothers.
- Tens of millions of children have lost both parents to AIDS.

How many of us could remain untouched by the human suffering behind statistics like these? Which of us would not feel anger, sorrow and astonished disbelief? Who would not feel compelled to act helpfully even while feeling hopeless? We are stirred with passion, overcome with the desire to do good and intent on action, but is this compassion?

The English word 'compassion' is derived from the Latin *patior* and *cum* which together mean 'to suffer with'. It is used to describe the kind of sorrow and concern so aroused in us by another's suffering that we suffer too and use our every means to stand alongside and to help. In the Old Testament, the word 'compassion' is used in place of the Hebrew words *chamal* and *racham*. *Chamal* emphasizes an emotional response to a person in need, *racham* an extension of love or mercy to a person in need.[2] In the New Testament, the word 'compassion' is most frequently used in place of the Greek words *eleeo* and *eleos*, stressing 'mercy' by assistance.[3]

It is also used in place of *oikteiro* and *oiktirmos*, highlighting the feeling of 'tender mercy' or distress at the sight of suffering.[4] *Sympatheo*, *sympathes* and *matriopatheo* focus on compassion as an empathetic suffering with.[5]

The overwhelming intensity of compassion is particularly captured in the Hebrew words *racham* and *rachamim*. Both convey a cherishing felt as deeply as for a foetus in the womb, and the latter is most often used of God.[6] The Greek word *splanchnizomai* conveys a wrenching pull of the emotions so strong as if coming from the entrails. It is frequently used to describe the compassion of Christ toward both the multitudes and individuals.[7] These words in particular communicate compassion as a deeply personal and painful experience of undeniable force—like a contraction or urge—that cannot be contained or constrained. Hudson Taylor once said, 'Before I had children of my own I used to think, "God will not forget me"; but when I became a father I learned something more. God cannot forget me.'[8] The strength and beauty of God's parental compassion is stressed by his own affirmation of it through Isaiah. 'Could a mother forget a child who nurses at her breast? Could she fail to love an infant who came from her own body? Even if a mother could forget, I will never forget you' (Isaiah 49:15). Surely this deeply moving image of God's compassion from his own lips can only nurture our love for him and promote deep healing in those who have indeed been forgotten or wounded by their earthly parents.

The words 'compassion', 'pity' and 'mercy' are often used synonymously throughout scripture. However, 'compassion' offers the fullest understanding of the depth of emotion that causes us not only to act, but to act in a way that involves profound personal sacrifice. Compassion does not only suffer for, but suffers with. In fact, the words 'passion' and 'patience' have the same root. Hence, compassion is not only 'suffering with' but 'long suffering with'. Compassion is fundamental to God, a core quality of his divine nature. God the Father 'suffers long with' us, standing alongside us in the life and death of Jesus, God the Son. God continues to 'suffer long with' us in the ongoing and indwelling presence of God the

Holy Spirit. God's compassion is consistent and continuous. It never loses its intensity and it never stops.

Scripture reflects a deep awareness and awe of God's undeserved and unreserved compassion. The majority of biblical references to compassion relate to God's compassion for us as human beings. The rest focus on our responsibility to express to others the compassion we have experienced ourselves. This is particularly true in relation to those who are vulnerable: those who are orphaned, alien or widowed, in poverty or in peril.[9] The weight of scripture is unequivocal. God expects us to show compassion not only to each other, but to anyone in need. This point was made even more forcibly in the life and teaching of Christ. We can be disciples in name, only if we are disciples in deed. Like the good Samaritan, we are to make those in need our neighbours. Like the Lord we love, we are to love. 'We know what love is,' says John, 'because Jesus gave his life for us. That's why we must give our lives for each other' (1 John 3:16). We are made in God's image.

Compassion is the quest to be human as God intended. It is not a means to an end. We are not compassionate in order to make converts or as an end to poverty itself. Neither is compassion motivated only out of a sense of common humanity. The purpose and motivation of compassion are one and the same—to be like God. Compassion is respecting and restoring the dignity with which we were created. We are image bearers of God, meant for community with each other even as God the Father, Son and Holy Spirit are in community. In that community we uphold one another in equality and complement one another, benefiting each other with our strengths. When we trust God as our Father, look to Jesus as our pattern and rely on the Holy Spirit as our compass, compassion will be our central concern, not an optional extra. Compassion will be the overflow of our newness in Christ, not a virtue to be exercised. Compassion, like Christian faith itself, will be a way of being, not of doing. When we reclaim our human identity in Christ, compassion becomes a truly human response to human suffering. To lack compassion is to lack humanity and deny the divine.

Jesus captured the essence of Christian living and worship in his summary of the commandments. 'The most important one says: "People of Israel, you have only one Lord and God. You must love him with all your heart, soul, mind, and strength." The second most important commandment says: "Love others as much as you love yourself." No other commandment is more important than these' (Mark 12:29–31). We are to return God's love and reflect it to others, particularly the many millions of children in greatest need.

The ancient world of the Bible and the world we live in are not as different as we might expect. Infant mortality was high and those children who did survive often found themselves in the daily family struggle to stay alive. Crippling poverty left children open to mistreatment of every kind. Infanticide and abandonment, particularly among girls and those born with deformity, were common, as were abortion and sexual abuse. Strict discipline often contradicted parental tenderness and descended into assault. These 'Gentile' practices were abhorred and legislated against by Jewish law, but were still in evidence among Jewish communities. Despite children being regarded as a sign of God's blessing, and childlessness as a sign of God's disapproval, children were still treated more like property than persons. Their value rested largely on the size of their economic contribution, the guaranteed care they would provide to elderly parents and the part they would play in continuing the family legacy.

It is surely an act of deepest significance and compassion that God chose to come among us not as a fully grown human, but as a foetus in a womb. When God the Son became Jesus the babe, he entered fully into the process of childhood and, in so doing, affirmed the worth of all children. He dignified every child's experience of growing up, including our own, by growing up himself. He matured physically, mentally, emotionally and spiritually. We have a Saviour who is uniquely able to *suffer with* not only every human, but with every human child. Jesus understood children because he had been a child himself.

INTRODUCTION

Today nearly 80 per cent of children globally never hear or have the opportunity to respond to the gospel of Jesus Christ. How much more challenging and meaningful, then, are his teachings on the compassionate treatment of children: '"Let the children come to me! Don't try to stop them. People who are like these little children belong to the kingdom of God. I promise you that you cannot get into God's kingdom unless you accept it the way a child does." Then Jesus took the children in his arms and blessed them by placing his hands on them' (Mark 10:14–16).

The arrival of God's kingdom was a key theme of Jesus' ministry. Although his Jewish contemporaries believed that God already ruled creation, they were expecting God's final intervention in history, waiting for God to break in and deliver them from sin, suffering and their enemies. Jesus professed in word and deed that the kingdom of God was already present among them, in and through himself. Although God's rule was still to come in its future fullness, God's kingdom could be entered now through the invitation of his Son. Jesus' inclusion of children both in his teaching about the kingdom and in the kingdom itself was not a series of isolated incidents. Rather, such inclusion was an integral part of his ministry, a ministry that embraced the most marginalized people of his day, including children.

Though Jesus' references to children informed adult discipleship, Jesus did not lose sight of real children themselves. His teaching is a constant challenge to remember the child in each of us and to reclaim the spirituality of childhood. It is also of vital importance in the kingdom of God to care earnestly for children and their faith. Jesus welcomed children into his kingdom and into his arms. He touched them with his compassionate hands and upheld them to touch our hardened hearts. It is impossible to describe how strongly God feels about the protection and development of children, how angry he is when they suffer. 'When you welcome one of these children because of me, you welcome me,' said Jesus. 'It will be terrible for people who cause even one of my little followers to sin. Those people would be better off thrown into the deepest part of the sea with a heavy stone tied around their necks!' (Matthew 18:5–6).

We are now faced with permanent and absolute poverty in a vast number of countries across the globe. Over one billion people live in poverty, while tens of millions die of it—twelve million pre-school children among them—each year. Poverty doesn't affect pocket books but people. It stunts development, blunts intellect and causes poor health in those it doesn't kill. Poverty is more than starvation. It is inadequate shelter, unhealthy environments and lack of access to basic health and education services. It is the balance of power, wealth and resources weighted unequally and unfairly. Poverty saps the body and the soul of individuals, families, communities and entire countries.

We can't escape the reality of poverty, even though most of us will never truly experience it. We see piles of human flesh, bulbous eyes and bulging bellies behind every civil war, earthquake, flood and famine. The exploitation of the weak by the strong is an issue so fundamental to human dignity that it is a recurrent biblical theme. God's compassion (*suffering with*) reveals itself in a constant, consuming commitment particularly to those who are poor and oppressed. Poverty is not a political issue to be left in the hands of special agencies. It is a personal, communal and spiritual issue, reflective of God. We cannot honour God's worth and dignity while denying it in those who bear his image.

Convicted of injustice and ingratitude toward God, Israel asks, 'What offering should I bring when I bow down to worship the Lord God Most High?' Micah replies, 'The Lord God has told (shown) us what is right and what he demands: "See that justice is done, let mercy be your first concern, and humbly obey your God"' (Micah 6:6, 8). We are never closer to God, never closer to keeping his commands, never closer to pure worship, never closer to our true humanity than when we are meeting the needs of the most vulnerable.

INTRODUCTION

How to use this book

Understanding Compassion is an invitation to explore both the nature of God's compassion as it affects discipleship and the work of *Compassion*, an organization dedicated to the nurture of children caught up in poverty.

The book is divided into six chapters of five sections each. Each chapter relates God's compassion to an area of discipleship:

- Compassionate worship
- Compassionate life
- Compassionate prayer
- Compassionate word
- Compassionate community
- Compassionate witness

A quick glance at the Contents page will show that the first chapter contains five sections exploring the compassionate nature of God and our own identity in Christ. The remaining chapters contain an exploration of five recurrent themes—community (common unity), solidarity, servanthood, obedience and hope. The material has been designed to accommodate those who want to dip into specific themes of interest as well as those who want to delve into the subject of compassion as a whole.

Several footnoted Hebrew or Greek words are followed by a four-digit number relating to the reference system of Strong's Exhaustive Concordance.

Each section ends with a story from *Compassion*; each chapter concludes with an in-depth reflection based on the work and experience of *Compassion*.

Group helps

'Group helps' are included for pastors and leaders who want to use the material in this book as a basis for sermons, speaking or Bible studies. 'Group helps' are also based around key areas of discipleship.

- 'Worship' contains ideas for hymns and songs taken from Songs of Fellowship Volumes 1–3.
- 'Word' contains Bible references for two focal readings.
- 'Prayer' contains a link to stories from *Compassion*.
- 'Fellowship' contains an exercise for building Christian community.
- 'Witness' contains an exercise about how we approach those who have, as yet, no faith in Christ.

For personal reflection

Those who are reading *Understanding Compassion* on a personal level are encouraged to make use of the 'For personal reflection' material. This includes topics for journal writing or exploration with a close and trusted friend. 'For personal reflection' is also found at the conclusion of each section.

Understanding Compassion not only addresses the theological implications of God's compassion for Christian discipleship, but also provides a concrete example of this through the ongoing ministry of *Compassion*. The material invites you to explore the work of this Christ-centred, child-focused, church-based agency dedicated to the world's poorest children. Those who would like to learn more about child sponsorship, the core ministry of *Compassion*, will find details at the end of the book.

NOTES

1. Compassion, *Shaping the New Millennium One Child at a Time*, p. 3.
2. W.E. Vine, *Vine's Concise Dictionary of Bible Words*, Thomas Nelson, p. 62.
3. *Vine's Concise Dictionary: Eleeo* (1653).

INTRODUCTION

4 *Vine's Concise Dictionary: Oikteiro* (3627).
5 *Vine's Concise Dictionary: Sympatheo* (4384), *Sympathes* (4835) and *Metripatheo* (3356).
6 *Vine's Concise Dictionary: Racham* (7355, 7365) and *Rachamim* (7356).
7 *Vine's Concise Dictionary. Splanchnizomai* (4697).
8 R. Backhouse, *1500 Illustrations for Preaching and Teaching*, Marshall Pickering, p. 502.
9 The fatherless, widow and foreigner are often listed together (Deuteronomy 10:18; 14:29; 16:11; 24:19; Jeremiah 22:3), with those in poverty and affliction (Job 6:14; Proverbs 19:17; Zechariah 7:8–10).

CHAPTER ONE

Compassionate worship

SECTION ONE

Our compassionate God: worshipping the Tri-unity

'Tell me how it is that in this room there are three candles and but one light,' said John Wesley, *'and I will explain to you the mode of the divine existence.'*[1]

The word 'Trinity' is not in the Bible but describes biblical teaching about who God is. It comes from the words 'tri' meaning three and 'une' meaning one and literally means 'Tri-unity'—three and one. God has revealed himself as the Tri-unity since the beginning of human history. He is one God eternally existing in three equal persons, Father, Son and Holy Spirit.

Although God has many perfect qualities in equal measure, holiness and love best define him as God—distinct from everything he created. He is completely holy and completely love in each person of the Tri-unity. It is because God is holy—so pure, so entirely free from moral evil—that he can't look on evil or overlook wrong. It is because God is love—so utterly the definition of love with all its commitment and devotion—that he is compassionate, suffering with us himself to reconcile us and renew his image in us. God's love is completely unalterable despite the wrath we deserve in light of his purity.

It is impossible to overemphasize the love and compassion of our triune God. All three persons of the Tri-unity are involved in the activity of any one for our benefit. Consider God in creation. God is self-sufficient and self-fulfilled, a community expressing mutual everlasting love. He is completely self-reliant. God doesn't need anyone or anything else. He alone is God, but he is not a lonely God. We weren't created because he needed someone to love, but because he wanted to express love. Like the purest motivation behind human parenthood, God was so bursting with love that he almost couldn't contain it. We are expressions of triune love! The Father, Son and Holy Spirit created us and continue to sustain us.

A story is told of a boy who lovingly crafted a toy boat. One day it snapped free from its anchor and sailed swiftly away downstream. The heartbroken boy never stopped searching for his boat or longing for it. One day he happened to look into a shop window a few towns away from his own. There it was, his boat, battered and bruised among the bric-a-brac. He couldn't contain his delight when he announced to the shop assistant, 'That's my boat!' The assistant told the boy that if he wanted it back he would have to pay for it. The boy went home and set about raising funds any way he could, at great sacrifice to himself. When the sum was finally achieved, he returned to the store and redeemed his boat. 'Now you are twice mine,' he said. 'I made you and I have bought you back.' He took his beloved boat home and began the task of renewing it.[2]

The point of this story is obvious. God created us, and God has redeemed us. This truth is perfectly illustrated by the cross where Christ died for us despite our sin and, indeed, because of it. Through this one act we are reconciled, redeemed and renewed by God. We are no longer enemies of God, slaves to sin or image tarnished. God is love and showed it. As someone once said, 'What God's justice demanded, God's love provided.'[3] The Father sent the Son to be the sacrifice for forgiveness, and the Holy Spirit to restore our union with him and he with us.[4]

This supreme and sacrificial love (*agape*) is for those who have forfeited their right to it. In grace and compassion, our triune God bears the consequences of our sin himself. The cross is God's response to our need for forgiveness and rescue, the tomb for our freedom and renewal. The Father, Son and Holy Spirit, compassionately committed in singular purpose, act to rescue, redeem, release and renew us into relationship with him. 'God the Father decided to choose you as his people, and his Spirit has made you holy. You have obeyed Jesus Christ and are sprinkled with his blood' (1 Peter 1:2).

What security! Our standing with God doesn't depend on our grasp of him but on his grasp of us. We were guilty; now we are forgiven. We were rejected; now we are accepted. We were alienated; now we are intimate. We were dead; now we are alive. We were in bondage; now we are free. We were impoverished; now we are rich beyond compare. God's grace is not the work of any one member of the Tri-unity but comes from the compassionate co-operation of all.

In fact, God reveals himself in four ways through the Tri-unity—Father, Son, Holy Spirit and three-in-one. He expresses himself as three persons but also as one indivisible being who eternally exists in a union of perfect love. The most life-altering truth to understand about God is not that he is a personal God but that he is also a communal God—a loving community of equal persons. A little girl was once asked for a definition of God. 'He is all the love in the world in one place,' she said. She was right. John summarizes this profound truth in a simple statement: 'God is love' (1 John 4:8). Although Christian faith begins with a private and personal response to God's compassion, it can only be fully expressed in community. We were created in God's image to belong together in love as he is. The Tri-unity may be a mystery beyond our grasp but it is not beyond our reach, and reach for it we must. To know God—Father, Son and Holy Spirit—is to deepen our faith and worship and to know ourselves as God intended.

'Worship is a universal urge, built by God into every fibre of our being,' says Bob Gass. 'If we fail to worship God, we always find a substitute.'[5] The word 'worship' is Anglo Saxon and literally means 'worthship' or 'worthiness'. To worship God is an acknowledgment and affirmation of his *worth*. It is a response of honour, respect, adoration and devotion comparable to his *worthiness* of it.

To worship God in love is not only to acknowledge and affirm God's worth, but also to acknowledge and affirm the worth of all those he created, including ourselves. Inherent in the 'worthship' of our triune God is the affirmation of worth in his image bearers. Worship is not something we do together, but the way we are together, the way we honour each other, children included.

The abusive treatment of God's youngest image bearers continues to offend him and impede our worship of him. James makes this point quite forcibly when he says, 'Religion that pleases God the Father must be pure and spotless. You must help needy orphans and widows and not let this world make you evil' (James 1:27).

Here we see again that a holy life and a compassionate heart are inseparable. As we seek justice for those who are most vulnerable, we worship God. As we love mercy, we worship God. As we walk humbly, we worship God.[6] Worship is not coming into the presence of God but the awareness of God's presence everywhere. Jesus, speaking of the final judgment, says, 'Then the ones who pleased the Lord will ask, "When did we give you something to eat or drink? When did we welcome you as a stranger or give you clothes to wear or visit you while you were sick or in jail?" The king will answer, "Whenever you did it for any of my people, no matter how unimportant they seemed, you did it for me"' (Matthew 25:37–40).

There is an old Russian proverb that says, 'There is more light than can be seen through the window.'[7] How will we be windows to the greater glory of God today? How will we meet the needs of others to the worship of God—Father, Son and Holy Spirit? As we acknowledge and affirm his worth, let us also affirm the worth of those around us. Let us pray God's triune blessing for one another.

✷

Vision for the future

Menchit Wong, *Compassion* Philippines Director, has a vision for the children of her country. It is a vision born from her understanding and relationship with a loving and faithful God.

The Philippines is just one of the countries in which *Compassion* currently operates. The Philippines suffered under a military dictatorship until 1986, which perpetuated the divide between the rich and the poor. Now, with restored democracy, the country is struggling to cope with the poverty gap. City slums grow as rural dwellers seek a better lifestyle, but on reaching the city they are greeted with overcrowding, poor infrastructure, expensive education, slavery, alcohol and drug abuse, and sexual abuse.

The world they meet is far from the ideal community that a God of love planned for his people, however. Within this country of struggle, *Compassion*, under the leadership of Menchit Wong, is working to realize the vision that God has planned both for and with his people.

'My dream for the country is that the Lord will raise up an army from the young people and the children.' Menchit urges all those she encounters to see the children of the Philippines in a new way. She urges them not to see these children 'as poor kids, but [to see] them as change-makers and leaders. When we start to see the potential around us which God sees, then we can start to step into the future which he has planned.'

We need to start thinking outside the limitations set in place by the social structures of this world and start seeking God's will.[8]

Group helps

Worship

Father, we adore you, you've drawn us (SF1 97)
Heavenly Father, I appreciate you (SF1 156)
Holy, holy, holy, Lord God Almighty (SF1 168)
Immortal, invisible, God only wise (SF1 210)
Lead us, heavenly Father, lead us (SF1 306)

Word

Psalm 136
1 John 4

Prayer

- Pray that those in positions of authority will consider the needs of young people as they make plans for the future.
- Pray for the children who live in families where they are seen purely as another mouth to feed. Ask that they will encounter other adults who will tell them of their worth.
- Pray that children will be encouraged to have goals and ambitions for the future.

Fellowship

Use Psalm 136:1–9, 23–26 as the basis for a responsive reading. Choose a leader to recite each phrase aloud. The group then responds with 'God's love never fails.' Leader: 'Praise the Lord! He is good.' Group: 'God's love never fails.'

Witness

Affirm the worth of others by making simple contact with those around you. For example, chat to a person standing next to you in a queue or sitting beside you on the bus. Acknowledging a person's presence is the first step in affirming his or her worth and affords the opportunity to show Christ. It may also afford the opportunity to speak of him.

Personal reflection

Find three photographs of yourself—one as a child, one as a teen and one as an adult. Paste them on the inside front cover of your journal (any new notebook or blank book that you feel comfortable with). When did you first know that you truly believed in God? Where did your belief begin? Who influenced your coming to faith? Who has shown you love and compassion in this process? Who keeps you going now?

If you prefer, you may explore these questions with a close and trusted friend.

NOTES

1 A.P. Castle, *Quotes and Anecdotes: an Anthology for Preachers and Teachers*, Kevin Mayhew, p. 288.
2 Source unknown.
3 R. Backhouse, *1500 Illustrations for Preaching and Teaching*, Marshall Pickering, p. 101.
4 1 John 4:8–10, 13.
5 B. Gass, *The Word for Today*, August–September 2003, UCB, p. 52.
6 Micah 6:6, 8.
7 T. Castle, *A Treasury of Christian Wisdom*, Hodder & Stoughton, p. 144.
8 Interview with Menchit Wong, *Compassion* Philippines Director, taken from a *Compassion* 'It Works' trip, 30 June 1998.

SECTION TWO

Our compassionate God: worshipping the Father

A small boy eagerly awaited the arrival of a new baby. When his sister was born, his delighted parents told him that she was a gift from God. 'Quick, before you forget,' he said on first seeing her. 'What does God look like?'[1]

If someone were to ask us, 'What is God like?' how would we respond? Would we affirm what God says of himself through the prophet Joel? 'I am merciful, kind, and caring. I don't easily lose my temper, and I don't like to punish' (Joel 2:13).

What if the question wasn't 'What is God like?' but 'What is God like for you?' Would our answer change? If so, how? Would we now echo Asaph's doubt as written in the Psalms? 'Each night my mind is flooded with questions: "Have you rejected me for ever? ... Is this the end of your love and your promises? ... Do you refuse to show mercy because of your anger?"' (Psalm 77:6–9).

A little girl once wrote a letter to God. 'Dear God,' she said, 'I would like to know why all the things you said are in red.'[2] Perhaps she was wondering why the colour of Jesus' words in many Bibles is red. Perhaps she was thinking of her homework and wondering what God did to merit so much red ink from his teacher. We will never know. One thing, however, is certain. We are often like children who fear big red marks on the homework of our faith. Our energies are spent trying not to get the answers wrong rather than seeking God through our questions. For many, particularly those who have suffered abuse, the facts of faith clash with the experience of faith: God is an old man, blind to suffering, deaf to pleading and dumb with silence. He is a remote, vindictive 'Father' throwing his weight around like fists on flesh.

William Barclay once said, 'Truth that is discovered lasts a lifetime.'[3] We must uncover and shatter our own image of God as Father and continually discover the truth about him. Red may be the colour of God's anger, but it is also the colour of his love—the blood of Christ that cleanses us and makes it possible to love and worship the Father without fear.

As we have previously discussed, to worship God is to affirm his worth in a measure comparable to his worthiness. God alone is worthy of our worship and God alone is to be worshipped. Many of us, however, have unwittingly fallen into idolatry by possessing a mental and emotional image of God as Father that is completely unworthy of him. We are like the little boy who held on tight to his father's leg and said, 'I've got all of Daddy', when we should be like the little girl who nestled in her father's arms and said, 'Yes, but Daddy's got all of me!' Idolatry is essentially an issue of image, not images. God hates idolatry because it slanders his character, a character he is jealous to protect. How we approach God confirms what we truly believe about him. Worship that is worthy of God the Father is born from being held by him, not from holding on to him.

John Plomp says, 'The one thing children wear out faster than shoes is parents.'[4] Thankfully, this is not true with God. In a culture where parents, particularly fathers, were often stern and severe, Jesus revealed God the Father to be loving, approachable and compassionate. He enriched the existing understanding of God's fatherhood over a nation—based mostly in wisdom, power and holiness—by emphasizing his intimate and universal love for individuals. Like the father of the prodigal, God watches and waits, forgives unreservedly and celebrates us with abundant goodness.

Although Jesus called God 'Father', this title isn't intended to identify God as masculine. It is an analogy used to describe God's nature. Jesus brings the quality of God's paternity into focus. The attributes of the Father are clearly understood through the Son. Jesus said, 'If you have seen me, you have seen the Father' (John 14:9).

Jesus' approach to the Father flows from intimate trust. He prays to God as Dad (Abba) and teaches us to do the same. How the Father loves us; how compassionate he is! He is our creator. He sent Christ to make us his children and the Holy Spirit to live in us and help us. We owe him our existence, borrow his likeness, trust in his forgiveness and become his heirs. Though Christ suffered for us, he didn't *suffer with* us on his own. The Father and Spirit felt the full agonies of the cross as sin, guilt and separation were experienced by our sinless, guiltless God. No wonder the sun went out and the earth shook. These are expressions of near-unbearable grief within the Tri-unity. How sweet the victory of compassion! The stone was rolled, the veil was torn and Christ arose. And there's more. The Father who, with Christ, sent the Holy Spirit at a point in history (Pentecost) now ensures his constant presence in our history. This eternal process reminds us of the Father's eternal compassion. Can there be a deeper love? God *is* love.

We will never be beyond God's love. Nothing we do will make him love us more or make him love us less. God's love is eager, urgent and compelling; absolute, eternal and all-embracing. In Jesus, God's love is literally self-sacrificing. Where human love ends, God's love continues. It extends beyond life and death, present and future. It is stronger than any power known or unknown. It is more resilient than trouble, suffering and hardship; hunger, danger and death. It is so overwhelmingly secure that Paul asks rhetorically, 'What can we say about all this? If God is on our side, can anyone be against us?' (Romans 8:31). Everything about God demonstrates compassion—how tenderly and patiently he suffers with us.[5] He didn't abandon Israel's children to their desert and he won't abandon us to ours. God is not blind, deaf, dumb or vindictive. He disciplines, but never abuses. The Father gives us life, love, protection, provision and guidance.

Jesus showed us what the Father is like. How poignant it is that he reflected the love of a human father as well as the heavenly Father in the blessing of children.[6] Jesus enables our adoption into God's family and nestles us into his heart. How wonderful, then, to see ourselves at any age as the children he embraced.

It is amazing to think that the same love that flows to us from the Father flows through us to others. We are commended to express the Father's compassion just as we have experienced it. We love God because God loved us first. 'The commandment God has given us is: "Love God and love each other!"' (1 John 4:21).

What is God like for us? What lurking doubts do we have about his character? What image do we hold of the Father that needs to be shattered on the truth of his compassion? Idolatry is not about molten metal, wedges of wood or the struggle to keep things off God's throne. These are secondary. Idolatry is the worship of any image of God that is other than himself, and it always begins with our inner picture of what God is like. What will we recall of God the Father in our own lives that reminds us of how incomparable and worthy he is?

✶

Compassionate Father

To know that you have a heavenly father who loves and values you can be quite a hard concept to grasp if you are a small child abandoned by your own earthly parents. It is through an understanding of the love of God in all its fullness that we can share that delight with others.

Giovanna Martinez was born in one of the many slum areas of Lima in Peru. Raised solely by her mother, after her father abandoned the family, her early childhood was an incredible struggle. At the age of twelve Giovanna was quite literally starving. As this small girl scavenged for food, she found herself at the doors of her local church. The sheer desperation of Giovanna's situation was evident to the staff at the church, who immediately registered Giovanna into the *Compassion* project.

Eight years on, and Giovanna stands as evidence that the love of God can change lives. As a confident young woman she is overflowing with the love of God. Her work as a Sunday school teacher in the *Compassion* project enables Giovanna to share the love she has received with others. Far from feeling bitterness or anguish about the experiences she's had in her life, Giovanna recalls, 'I have many experiences in my life that can help me to help the children. I want to give them all the love I feel.'[7]

Giovanna is a channel for God's love. Just as her life has been transformed from one of helplessness to hope, so she can reach out with empathy and understanding to others in need.

Group helps

Worship

Father God, I wonder (SF1 92)
Father of the fatherless (SF2 950)
Great is thy faithfulness (SF1 143)
How deep the Father's love for us (SF2 780)
O worship the King (SF1 428)

Word

Psalm 145
Romans 8:31–39

Prayer

- Ask that God will provide positive role models for children who have been mistreated by those close to them.
- Pray that children who are in need will know where to turn to for help.
- Ask that churches will stand out in their communities as places of help and generosity.

Fellowship

Write a note, letter or e-mail to the significant children in your lives this week. This correspondence should include something that is appreciated about the child's character, an affirmation of love and an offer to spend some quality time together. For example: 'Dear Rebecca, I just want you to know how much I appreciate your cheerful spirit. I love you and am proud of you. What would you like to do on Saturday? Love, Dad.'

Witness

Make eye contact with those around you this week. This simple gesture will make an incredible difference to those who may be feeling invisible, including yourself. Next time you are approached by someone begging or trying to pass out leaflets, don't ignore them. Look them in the eye, even if you are saying 'No thank you'. Better still, offer them something warm to eat or drink, or stop for a chat.

Personal reflection

Think about yourself as a child. (Refer to the childhood photograph you pasted on the inside front cover of your journal.) Using as much emotional and sensory detail as possible, describe a time when you felt safe in the arms of your mother, father or guardian. Describe a time when you felt abandoned or frightened.

Think about yourself at any age. Describe a time when you felt that you were holding on to God. Describe a time when you felt God holding on to you.

Read Romans 8:31–39. Do you believe that God is a compassionate and loving parent? If not, how will you challenge this belief?

If you prefer, you may explore these questions with a close and trusted friend.

NOTES

1 P. Mason, *Out of the Mouths of Babe*, Monarch Books, p. 10.
2 S. Hample and E. Marshall, *Children's Letters to God*, Workman Publishing.
3 A.P. Castle, *Quotes and Anecdotes: An Anthology for Preachers and Teachers*, Kevin Mayhew, p. 285.
4 Castle, *Quotes and Anecdotes*, p. 157.
5 Psalm 145:8–9.
6 It was common for a father to pass his blessings on to his children (Genesis 27:38). How moving that Jesus reflects the love of our heavenly Father by blessing children, and does so intimately through the laying on of hands (Mark 10:14–16).
7 Source article by Angela Little, *Childlink*, Summer 2002.

SECTION THREE

Our compassionate God: worshipping the Son

'The central miracle asserted by Christians is the incarnation,' said C.S. Lewis. 'They say that God became a man.'[1]

The belief that God became human in the person of Jesus Christ is indeed central to the Christian faith. Never is the word 'compassion' so apt a description of God's love as in the incarnation. John, the disciple whom Jesus loved, must have fought fiercely with the limitations of language to express what he saw in Jesus. 'The Word became a human being and lived here with us,' he said. 'From him all the kindness and all the truth of God have come down to us... No one has ever seen God. The only Son, who is truly God... has shown us what God is like' (John 1:14–18). And should we have any doubt about the definition of love, John says, 'God showed his love for us when he sent his only Son into the world to give us life. Real love isn't our love for God, but his love for us. God sent his Son to be the sacrifice by which our sins are forgiven' (1 John 4:9–11). God became one of us and this solidarity became the way of salvation for us.

Despite the consequences of corrupted dignity, God has never abandoned humanity. In fact, God continually intervenes to help. The Old Testament provides clear testimony of God's salvation history.[2] Indeed, he is so closely associated with the rescue of his people that he is depicted as the author of salvation, his name and the title 'Saviour' being understood almost synonymously. In the Old Testament, to know God at all was to know him as a saving God.[3] In the New Testament, the English word 'salvation' is derived from the Greek word *soteria* and encompasses the idea of being delivered from imminent danger and dread and returned to a state of peace.[4] The New Testament fully honours the salvation history of the Old Testament and reveals the true extent of God's compassionate intervention on our behalf—Jesus Christ, God the Son.

Jesus' very name means 'God saves': 'he will rescue his people from their sins' (Matthew 1:21). Through his death and resurrection we can be forgiven for our rebellion against God in thought, word and deed. God has revealed himself to us in Jesus Christ and offers to rescue us, no strings attached. Salvation is ours through faith, repentance and confession. We radically shift from sin to God, put our confidence in what Christ has done for us and confess him alone as Saviour.

No amount of wisdom, merit, morality, religious technique or political liberty can deliver us back to the dignity with which we were created. God grants immediate and eternally ongoing deliverance only to those who accept his Son. As William Temple once said, 'I can contribute nothing to my own salvation except the sin from which I need to be redeemed.'[5] As someone else put it, 'The reason salvation is free for you is because someone else paid for it',[6] and that person was Jesus Christ, God become human.

When asked about heaven, a little boy remarked, 'Only your soul goes to heaven. They're not interested in the rest of you.'[7] Thankfully, this perception is not true. The incarnation is not only about being in God's presence after death. It is also about God being present with us through life. Although Jesus' sacrifice is central to our salvation, his solidarity is the beginning of it. The cross is meaningless without the cradle. Jesus is also called 'Immanuel', which means 'God with us' (Matthew 1:22–23).

There was never a time when Jesus was not fully and perfectly God and fully and perfectly human. Out of compassion, he freely emptied himself to become one of us and submitted himself to our limitations. From the womb to the tomb he dignified every age and stage of humanity, even taking it with him, wounded but glorified, into glory.[8] Although God, who is Spirit, can never change his personality, through Jesus the Tri-unity experienced humanity in a deeply profound and permanent way. He shared our flesh, vulnerabilities and temptations. His identification was so complete that he often referred to himself as the Son of Man.

'When Jesus was moved to compassion,' said Henri Nouwen, 'the source of all life trembled, the ground of all love burst open, and the abyss of God's immense, inexhaustible and unfathomable tenderness revealed itself.'[9] God cares about our selves, not just our souls.

David McInnes said, 'Jesus Christ is not the truth because he meets our needs; Jesus Christ is the truth and so meets our needs.'[10] These needs are not entirely met in the here and now. Salvation does not promise material wealth, physical health or protection from hardship, danger and tragedy. Neither does it necessarily liberate us from injustice and ill-treatment. Jesus felt gut-wrenching compassion for those who were confused and helpless, diseased, wounded and sick, hungry, blind and grieving. He often, though not always, healed. He loved without exception.

As we have seen, Jesus' view of children was in stark contrast to the majority view of his contemporaries. He keenly welcomed and observed his youngest followers and was so deeply moved by their suffering that several children are counted among those he healed. However, the focus of the miracles, including our own redemption, is not that God heals or saves but that God is so full of compassion that healing and salvation overflow. We too have hope for a cure, because of the compassion that carries it—the same compassion that led God to become one of us.

Jesus' entire experience of humanity was one of identification with those who had the least, and he invites us to fulfil prophecy and worship with him through our compassion. 'I'll tell you what it really means to worship the Lord,' says Isaiah. 'Remove the chains of prisoners who are chained unjustly. Free those who are abused! Share your food with everyone who is hungry; share your home with the poor and homeless. Give clothes to those in need... Then your light will shine like the dawning sun, and you will quickly be healed... your darkest hour will be like the noonday sun' (Isaiah 58:6–10; cf. Matthew 25:31–40).

How often have we been guilty of limiting the incarnation to a manger on Christmas day? Surely we must agree with John Robinson who says, 'Advent reminds us that Christ is always coming. We may be waiting for the Second Coming but Jesus is never absent.'[11] We must release the incarnation from dusty disuse and rely on its daily impact in our lives. The author of Hebrews writes, 'We are people of flesh and blood. That is why Jesus became one of us. He died to destroy the devil, who had power over death. But he also died to rescue all of us who live each day in fear of dying' (Hebrews 2:14–15).

What troubles us today? What miracles are we seeking? God's compassion isn't in the resolution of our problems, questions or doubts—though final and full resolution will come. God's compassion is in his presence, his standing with us where we are. Healing and deliverance emerge from this. Jesus—'God saves'. Immanuel—'God with us'. Where do we find God in Jesus? He is lying in a manger, blessing children, hanging out with the humble and keeping company with the questionable. He is healing those most in need of divine help and looking for God. Where is God in Jesus? He is being spat at and abused, hanging on a cross, buried and dead, risen and glorified. Where is God in Jesus? He is with us always. Through the solidarity of Christ we understand by experience that 'the most High God', as Howard Snyder says, 'is also the most nigh God'.[12]

*

A friend to the children

Rosa Hernandez, a teacher at *Compassion*'s Fuente de Jacob student centre, in Tegucigalpa Honduras, knows all about the struggle of life in the city. As a project worker, Rosa is on the front line in the war against child poverty. Rosa lives alongside the children she serves, and is aware with acute detail of the circumstances of each child in her class.

Rosa sees herself as a teacher and an advocate but above all a friend to these children. She takes time between classes to visit the children's homes, to listen to their troubles and to pray with them. She aims to stand alongside the children in all they do because she knows how powerful and precious they truly are.

Seven years ago, Rosa's four-year-old next-door neighbour pestered her to attend the church where the small girl was performing in a play. Rosa tried to excuse herself but the persistence of the child was too much and she found herself at the church. During that service, Rosa experienced God and began upon her journey with Christ. Her experience of Christ through a child has given her a real heart for young people.

Rosa is driven by a vision that is greater than the boundaries put in place by the web of poverty. Her knowledge of her community, her realism about the challenges that face children, and her own experience of the power of a child make her an ideal advocate for children in desperate circumstances. In the eyes of every child in her class Rosa sees incredible potential.[13]

*

Group helps

Worship

In Christ alone (SF3 1346)
Come, see the Lord (SF3 207)
From heaven you came (SF1 120)
Isn't he beautiful (SF1 228)
Love divine (SF1 353)

Word

Isaiah 53
Luke 4:14–22

Prayer

- Thank God for the dedication and unfailing love of those who have committed their lives to helping children in desperate circumstances.
- Pray that God will assist *Compassion* project workers to develop not only good relations with the children but also with their families.
- Thank God for the way he uses children to teach us more about himself.

Fellowship

Ask everyone in the group to bring a photograph and/or share a favourite story about themselves from childhood. Think about the humanity and deity of Jesus Christ. Discuss how he was both like and unlike you as a child. Discuss how this demonstrates God's compassion.

Witness

Think of a friend who has not yet found faith in Christ but is open to talking about spiritual things. Next time there is a natural opening, ask your friend if believing that God became human would make any difference to them. Don't push. Don't interrupt. Don't respond with answers. Just open the conversation, listen and see what happens. Perhaps you will be given an opportunity to share why God being human makes a difference to you.

Personal reflection

Find a photograph of yourself as a baby and paste it in a bottom corner of a new page in your journal. Think about your own physical, emotional, spiritual and intellectual development. Jot down several ways in which Jesus was like you in these areas of development. For example: Jesus had a tummy button, he cried, he learned how to pray and he learned how to read. What does this say about God's compassion? Write a letter in your journal thanking Jesus for his humanity.

If you prefer, you may explore these questions with a close and trusted friend.

NOTES

1. R. Backhouse, *1500 Illustrations for Preaching and Teaching*, Marshall Pickering, p. 53.
2. God who saved the fathers from Egypt (Psalm 106:7–10) and their descendants from Babylon (Jeremiah 30:10) is both the refuge and saviour of his people (2 Samuel 22:3). God is especially protective of those who are poor and needy and others who have no one to help (Psalm 34:6; Job 5:15). God saves his flock (Ezekiel 34:22). God rescues his people and is the only one who can (Hosea 1:7; 13:10–14). There is no Saviour other than God (Isaiah 43:11).
3. IVP, *The Illustrated Bible Dictionary*, Part 3, Tyndale, pp. 1372–75.
4. W.E. Vine, *Vine's Concise Dictionary of Bible Words*, Thomas Nelson, p. 325.
5. Backhouse, *1500 Illustrations*, p. 352.
6. Source unknown
7. E. Marshall, *Kids Talk About Heaven*, Kyle Cathie, p. 17.
8. Hebrews 2:14–18; 4:14–16.
9. H.J. Nouwen et al, *Compassion*, Doubleday & Co., 1982, p. 17.
10. Backhouse, *1500 Illustrations*, p. 50.
11. Backhouse, *1500 Illustrations*, p. 119.
12. Backhouse, *1500 Illustrations*, p. 63.
13. Taken from an article by Kate Smith in *Childlink*, January 2004.

SECTION FOUR

Our compassionate God: worshipping the Holy Spirit

A family was looking around a rather dark, imposing-looking church. 'Does God live here?' asked the boy. 'Yes, son,' replied the father. 'Oh,' said the boy, 'then why doesn't he move?'[1]

From the beginning, God chose to be among his people. He walked in the garden, wandered in the wilderness, rested in the tabernacle and filled the temple. In Jesus, God not only came among us but became one of us. Now, through the Holy Spirit, God is continually present in each of us—more proof of God's compassion if more proof is needed. God doesn't live in a building but in us. 'You know that your body is a temple where the Holy Spirit lives,' writes Paul. 'The Spirit is in you and is a gift from God. You are no longer your own' (1 Corinthians 6:19).

Jesus' relationship with the Holy Spirit was divinely and deeply intimate. The Holy Spirit was every thread and shade in the rich tapestry of Jesus' life. The Holy Spirit is credited with Jesus' human conception and participated in his childhood development. In a stunning affirmation of triunitarian commitment, the Holy Spirit accompanied the Father's audible declaration of love and delight in the Son by rending the heavens to descend like a dove at Jesus' baptism. This moving and powerful confirmation of Jesus' call to public ministry preceded his temptation in the wilderness, an exhausting 40-day experience that he could not have sustained without the compassionate guidance and filling of the Holy Spirit.

Jesus was equipped and empowered by the Holy Spirit

throughout his ministry. He attributed his miracles to the Spirit and modelled the fruit of the Spirit in his own life—love, joy, peace, patience, kindness, goodness, faithfulness, gentleness and self-control. In fact, Jesus experienced the indwelling of the Holy Spirit without measure or limit. This was equally true of Jesus' human nature as of his divine nature. In Jesus we see that humanity as God intended is dependent on the Holy Spirit for everything.

A story is told of Rossini, an Italian composer who was given a watch by the king of France. Rossini was very proud of his royal gift and carried it everywhere in his pocket. Many years later he showed it to a friend, who touched a secret spring inside the watch. An inner casing flew open to reveal a small painted portrait of Rossini himself. A stunned Rossini had never been aware of its presence.[2] How aware are we of the presence of the Holy Spirit at work in our lives?

Just as the cross is meaningless without the cradle, so is it an unfulfilled symbol without the empty tomb. Without the resurrection there would be no gospel to tell, no salvation to seek, no forgiveness for our wrong. There would be no hope for the future and no assurance for now. The Holy Spirit was actively involved in both the planning and execution of our salvation. He was not a spectator at Calvary but assisted Christ in the completion of his task. He used his power in both the resurrection and glory of Christ. Through the Holy Spirit, the Father accepted Christ's atonement—a single sacrifice for all people, for all sin, for all time—by raising Christ from the dead and welcoming him home. This same resurrection power is available to us. We must not be like Rossini who ticked over for years without knowing the true value of what was in his pocket. We are completely dependent on the Spirit. He leads us to Christ, transforms us into the image of Christ and empowers us to live like Christ. 'You are no longer ruled by your desires,' says Paul, 'but by God's Spirit, who lives in you' (Romans 8:9).

The Holy Spirit, known as 'the promise of the Father' (Acts 1:4), came at Pentecost where he appeared in a wildfire of tongues and filled the Church as a people, not just specifically chosen individuals.

Thus began a new era in human history. Peter tells his listeners that the Holy Spirit will be given to anyone who turns back to God in the name of Jesus Christ for forgiveness. This promise is for everyone in every generation everywhere. We need never fear that he will leave us. The eternally compassionate Holy Spirit who came at a point in history is now permanently and constantly present in each of us as a gift from God. The Father initiated the process of salvation and the Son carried it out on the cross. However, it is the Holy Spirit who brings us to faith in Christ and keeps us there.

No wonder Jesus called the Holy Spirit *parakletos*, meaning helper, comforter and advocate. It is a description that reveals both the depth and character of God's compassion for us. The Father and the Son sent us the Holy Spirit. He is another in nature (*allos*) like Jesus. As our helper, the Holy Spirit continues the work of the Father and the Son. He loves, protects, guides and gifts us. He faithfully helped Jesus and is faithful to us in the same measure. He completes the work of Christ by giving us not only new and unending life, but a life that is rich with quality. Indeed, the quality of life expounded by the Saviour can be executed only in the Holy Spirit. Paul prayed that the Holy Spirit would strengthen us with might equal to the immeasurable riches of God's glory.

According to an old Yiddish proverb, 'God's favourite place is in man.' As our advocate, the Holy Spirit continues the work of Jesus, who pleads to the Father on our behalf by helping us to speak for ourselves. 'For example, when we don't know what to pray for, the Spirit prays [intercedes] for us…' (Romans 8:26). How encouraging it is to know that our stumbling speech and jumbled thoughts are not problems for God. The Holy Spirit is such an able comforter because he can empathize with us. He knows everything, both what is deep in our own thoughts and 'what is deep in the mind of God' (1 Corinthians 2:10). He is not an unfeeling force; rather, he loves with deep compassion, and is joyous and peaceful. The Holy Spirit can be quenched like a doused fire that no longer burns, and grieves when sinned against. His suffering with us is so great that it spills into groaning prayer for us from within us. He experiences compassion with the same undeniable intensity and force as the Father and the Son. This compassionate intimacy is possible because he lives in us and is the source of all life, physically and spiritually. 'God's Spirit has given us life,' says Paul, 'and so we should follow the Spirit' (Galatians 5:25).

Jesus followed the Holy Spirit even in childhood. So can any child who knows and loves him. How wonderful is the universal and inclusive compassion of God. Jesus proclaimed himself the promised Saviour in his home town, Nazareth. There he not only confirmed that God is compassionate, but also revealed this compassion as the reason why the Holy Spirit came. 'The Lord's Spirit has come to me,' said Jesus, 'because he has chosen me to tell the good news to the poor... and to say, "This is the year the Lord has chosen"' (Luke 4:18–19; cf. Isaiah 61:1–2).

We too have been given the Holy Spirit in order to bring good news and freedom to those who are poor, imprisoned, blind and suffering—spiritually and physically. It is our job to proclaim God's love at this chosen time, in this day of grace, in this our generation. We too are led, filled, anointed, equipped and empowered by the Holy Spirit whose fruit is everywhere abundant in our compassion.

It was Jesus who said, 'God blesses those people whose hearts are pure. They will see him!' (Matthew 5:8). Sin renders us spiritually blind and ignorant of God. Jesus came to recover the sight of those who are blind—to restore in fallen humanity, through the presence of the Holy Spirit within, the purity of heart needed to see God and restore intimacy with him. A pure heart aims well. We will not miss in our worship if we are serving those who are most vulnerable. Carl Jung said, 'The central Neurosis of our time is emptiness.'[3] In the Sermon on the Mount, with children in attendance, Jesus affirmed that no one need be empty. Those who are oppressed, children included, are assured that God's blessings reach those who are least valued—those who are mourning, those who are meek, those who are merciful, those who are hungry, thirsty and poor, peaceful, pure and persecuted. Among these today are many children whom we are yet to welcome in Jesus' name.

Romano Guardini described the Holy Spirit as 'the living interior of God'.[4] In Christ, the Holy Spirit is also our living interior. We are called to worship him, honour him and let our relationship thrive. We need to ask him to draw us closer into his fellowship and produce his compassionate fruit in us. We need to embrace him and follow him. As Brother Lawrence once said, 'Those who have the gale of the Holy Spirit go forward even in sleep.'[5]

∗

Compassionate Spirit

God 'will give you another Counsellor to be with you for ever—the Spirit of truth' (John 14:16, NIV). In the knowledge of these words we know that we do not have to do anything in our own strength. The compassionate nature of the Spirit has been in evidence repeatedly in *Compassion*'s history.

In 1990 the small town of Gaba in Uganda was in turmoil. The town's fishing industry was in ruins, witchcraft had a strong reign in the town, and poverty and despair were evident everywhere. Against this bleak backdrop, Peter Kasirivu and his 15-strong congregation were working to bring the light of Christ to Gaba. Initially their efforts were met with stiff opposition, which frequently included physical violence, but the church did not lose heart. Their prayers were answered when Peter Kasirivu met Jacques Masiko, the *Compassion* Uganda Director. Jacques shared Peter's vision for the children of Gaba and so a project was established.

Thirteen years on, Gaba is a town with hope and a future. Gaba community church boasts a congregation of more than 1000 members, alongside a primary school educating 620 students and a high school with over 300 entrants. The dramatic growth in Gaba is evidence of a much greater power working through the human frames of the congregation in Gaba community church.[6]

✱

Group helps

Worship

Because your love (SF1 30)
Holy Spirit, how I love you (SF3 1284)
I'm learning to love you (SF3 1341)
Precious Father (SF1 456)
When I look into your holiness (SF1 601)

Word

John 14
Acts 2:1–21

Prayer

- Pray that those who are persecuted for their faith can feel the presence of the Holy Spirit.
- Thank God for the way he has worked through the church in Gaba, and pray that he will continue to inspire this community.
- Pray that the church will have more practical opportunities to show God's love.

Fellowship

Pass round a bowl of fruit. Talk about why fruit is so important to our diet. Think about the fruit of the Spirit as found in Galatians 5:22–23: love, joy, peace, patience, kindness, goodness, faithfulness, gentleness and self-control. Why is this fruit so important in our spiritual diet? How is it evident in compassion? Think of someone in your own life who displays one of these attributes. Make a point of giving this person a piece of fruit with a thank-you note for the fruit of the Spirit that you see in them.

Witness

Affirm the worth of others by exercising the fruit of the Spirit in your listening.

- Show love by keeping the focus on the other person. Use personal pronouns 'I', 'me' and 'my' as little as possible.
- Show joy by letting others know that you are happy to spend time with them.
- Bring peace by reflecting back what you have heard others saying.
- Show patience by letting others finish their sentences.
- Show kindness by using kind words or, if confronting, hard words in as kind a way possible.
- Show goodness by speaking and acting out of the best possible motives for the other person.
- Show faithfulness by keeping entrusted confidences.
- Be gentle: listen with your whole body, using physical contact where appropriate and with permission—a hug, a tear, holding a hand, eye contact.
- Be self-controlled by allowing the Holy Spirit to fill silences and prompt your responses.

Personal reflection

Focus on the presence of the Holy Spirit in your life. Go for a walk in a beauty spot, a park or around the garden. Read Acts 2:1–21 aloud in a whisper. Write about this experience in your journal. Were you aware of the Holy Spirit? If so, how? Did you feel uncomfortable? If so, why? What came to your mind? Write a prayer to the Holy Spirit reflecting on this exercise.

If you prefer, you may explore these questions with a close and trusted friend.

NOTES

1. P. Mason, *Out of the Mouths of Babes*, Monarch Books, p. 82.
2. A.P. Castle, *Quotes and Anecdotes: an Anthology for Preachers and Teachers*, Kevin Mayhew, p. 411.
3. R. Backhouse, *1500 Illustrations for Preaching and Teaching*, Marshall Pickering, p. 101.
4. Castle, *Quotes and Anecdotes*, p. 415.
5. Castle, *Quotes and Anecdotes*, p. 415.
6. Taken from an interview by Tony Neeves with Pastor Peter Kasirivu, 2001.

SECTION FIVE

Our compassionate identity in Christ

'Mirror, mirror on the wall, who is the fairest of them all?'

This question is asked every morning by Cinderella's vain and wicked stepmother. Most of us would not dare to ask the question, much less expect that we ourselves might be the answer. What do we see when we look in the mirror—perfect hair, perfect face, perfect body? Probably not. We are more likely to note our imperfections in detail. One glance tells us that we don't measure up to the ideal and never will—an identity that we put on with our underwear every morning. It is much the same with our inner selves. Though we are new in Christ, it is Adam who most often stares back at us in the mirror.

Scripture not only recounts the first sin in human history, but also presents the fall of humanity as personal to each of us. Adam, God's perfect creation, fell into rebellion and took us with him. Sin against God—with all its missing, erring and straying, stumbling, twisting and trespassing, failure, fault and wrongdoing—is now a common experience for us all.[1] Paul reminds us that none of us is good, not even one. We don't know what it means to understand God or search for him. We don't know how to live in peace or worship God. We have all fallen short of God's glory and the dignity with which we were created. Sin affects not only the whole of humanity but the whole of the human being—physically, spiritually, mentally, emotionally and intellectually. As Bruce Milne so ably puts it, 'We are wholly fallen and hence wholly in need of redemption.'[2]

At the end of the first performance of *Messiah*, the Earl of

Kinnoull came to Handel and thanked him for the 'magnificent entertainment'. 'My Lord,' replied Handel, 'I did not wish to entertain you. I wished to make you better men and women.'[3] Christ came to restore our true humanity. Paul uses the fall of the first Adam as the backdrop for discussing the redeeming perfection of the second—Jesus Christ. Once again, through all the compassionate intricacies of the incarnation, the perfect human being stands before God as God intended. The effects of the one sin of Adam are undone by the one sacrifice of Christ for all sinners. By our union in sin with Adam we are sinners. By our union with Christ in faith we are saved. As Paul says, 'Adam brought death to all of us, and Christ will bring life to all of us' (1 Corinthians 15:22).

Someone once said that 'in Jesus we see ourselves as God intended and God as he's always been'. If we want to see our true selves, we must take another look in the mirror—God's mirror. There we will see Jesus Christ, the fairest of them all. We will behold his image in us and reflect it everywhere. The more we seek him, the more we will reflect him. Even though our dignity was damaged by disobedience, it is renewed and remoulded in Christ. We can reflect God's qualities, like love and compassion, in a far greater measure than the old Adam will allow us to believe. In fact, says William Vine, 'God's grace in Christ will yet accomplish more than Adam lost.'[4] 'You are becoming more and more like your Creator, and you will understand him better,' says Paul. 'Christ is all that matters, and he lives in all of us' (Colossians 3:10–11). Anyone who is in Christ is a completely new person. Adam, though not completely gone from within us, is well and truly on his way out. The old has gone and the new has come.[5]

We are not what other people think, say or expect of us. We are not what we do or the awards we have won. We are not our looks or lifestyle. We are not the labels we wear or the lies Satan tells us. We are not our failures. Our sense of self is not dependent on what we do, but on who we are. We must stop trying to invent ourselves and accept the identity we have been freely given. We are saved by faith, not because we earned it but as a free gift. God has plans for us to do good things and to live as he has always intended. That's why Jesus came and makes us what we are.

Our identity is rooted in what God says about us, what God did for us in Christ, and what God is doing in us right now through the Holy Spirit. 'This is the mystery of the Christian life,' says Henri Nouwen, 'to receive a new self, a new identity, which depends not on what we can achieve, but on what we are willing to receive.'[6] It is in God's nature to be compassionate and it is in ours too. This was exemplified by Paul, who declared to the Philippians, 'God... knows that I care for you in the same way that Christ Jesus does' (Philippians 1:8). In Christ we are capable of loving and being loved with the same all-embracing, deeply stirred compassion of God.

Michaelangelo once saw a block of marble that was said to be of no value. 'It's valuable to me,' said Michaelangelo. 'There is an angel imprisoned in it and I must set it free!'[7] We may be unworthy of God, but we are worth everything to God. Lack of self-worth is surely part of the spiritual poverty that imprisons us all until Christ sets us free. As we lay hold of our identity in Christ, we can help others do the same. We become partners with Christ in the task of setting free those who are imprisoned within themselves. As has already been discussed, poverty affects people, not pocket books. It saps the soul as well as the body. Jesus repeatedly affirmed the worth of those least valued, children among them. Our affirmation of worth in those around us is an act of worship to the God who made us.

Compassionate living is an integral part of our identity and our destiny. Paul writes, 'God has done it all! He sent Christ to make peace between himself and us, and he has given us the work of making peace between himself and others' (2 Corinthians 5:18). We can be compassionate only as we look to and become like Christ—a continual process of the Holy Spirit within us. What a transformation! 'The Lord's Spirit sets us free,' says Paul. 'So our faces are not covered. They show the bright glory of the Lord, as the Lord's Spirit makes us more and more like our glorious Lord' (2 Corinthians 3:17–18).

We must see ourselves as God intended—image bearers living in community even as he does, and loving as he loves. We were created for community and as a community we witness to God's compassion in the world. In a society where people ground their lives on experience, we offer what is most needed—the incarnate love of Christ in you and me. Others will experience Christ first of all in our presence—the way we are in ourselves, the way we are with each other. We don't just preach the gospel; we are the gospel. We don't just preach Christ; we are Christ. 'We know what love is because Jesus gave his life for us,' says John. 'That's why we must give our lives for each other' (1 John 3:16). We must have compassion or else we can't say we love God. We show love not just by talking about it but by demonstrating it.

William Barclay once said, 'The surest way to paralyse a man's actions is to make him doubt his destiny.'[8] This is precisely the tactic that Satan tried to use against Jesus in the wilderness. Having been publicly affirmed in his destiny as God's Son, Jesus is now needled to doubt this destiny and act in ways unworthy of it. Twice Satan prefaces his temptation by attempting to undermine Jesus' identity: 'If you really are God's Son, then...' How often have we heard this same challenge ringing in our ears? Though Jesus' identity and destiny as God the Son are uniquely his own, his identity and destiny as a child of God are not. They are common to all those who accept the work of the second Adam on behalf of the first.

Jesus did not yield to doubt about his destiny and neither must we. We are children of God, accepted, secure and significant. God is our 'Father', we are in his family and we will, with Christ, inherit glory. Our identity is in Christ. 'All of you are God's children because of your faith in Christ Jesus,' says Paul. 'And when you were baptized, it was as though you had put on Christ in the same way you put on new clothes' (Galatians 3:26–27).

Who needs Adam's old underwear when we can put on Christ Jesus and clothe ourselves with the qualities of his compassion? Because of God's love we can be gentle, kind, humble, meek, patient and as forgiving as Christ. Despite every setback, we will never utterly despair if we believe that he who began a good work in us will complete it. We will look again and again to Christ and see in him what we are on our way to becoming—perfectly related to God and each other in love. Which Adam will we see in God's mirror today?

∗

Identity

Viewed as the property of their fathers, girls can command large dowries as payment when they get married. Their identity and worth are measured in terms of the financial benefits that they can gain in marriage. Five cows was the asking price to any man who would marry Mokonko, a *Compassion*-sponsored child in Kenya. When her father and brothers announced that they had found a husband for her, Mokonko had no say in the matter. They considered the financial gain from the union to be of greater worth than Mokonko's own happiness.

For Mokonko, marriage to a man she did not love would be virtual imprisonment. The frequency of physical, sexual and mental abuse is high in forced marriages. Women end up as domestic slaves who become financially dependent upon their husbands and lose their limited freedom altogether.

Mokonko refused the proposal, desiring instead to complete her education and shape her own future. She had learnt her own worth to God and did not want to be defined by the economic value placed on her by her family. Such defiance enraged her brothers, who forcibly took her 240 miles away from her home town, her friends and her project workers, to participate in the marriage ceremony.

Although Mokonko was on her own, a long way from her home, she was not alone in her fight against the negative treatment of women. Grace and Sandra were two project workers who felt passionately that women should be given the right to choose the direction of their future. Risking their own safety, they tracked Mokonko down and helped her escape the fate of forced marriage. Monoko was able to return to her studies but there are many who have been unable to escape.[9]

✱

Group helps

Worship

Above all (SF3 1151)
All hail king Jesus (SF1 6)
The price is paid (SF1 528)
We are heirs of God Almighty (SF3 1577)
Worthy, O worthy are you, Lord (SF1 624)

Word

Psalm 103
Colossians 3:1–15

Prayer

- Pray for positive role models for girls to aspire to in the developing world.
- Pray that the true worth of women will be recognized within the family home.
- Pray that women who are abused by their husbands will speak up and have a safe place to turn to.

Fellowship

Write out each truth and Bible reference from 'For personal reflection' below on a separate slip of paper, replacing 'I am' with 'You are'. Give one truth to each person in your group, doubling up if necessary. Turn to the person next to you and read the truth and the verse reference to them. For example: 'You are a new creation. "If anyone is in Christ, he is a new creation; the old has gone, the new has come!"' (2 Corinthians 5:17, NIV).

Witness

Affirm the worth of others by seeing God's image in them and treating them with dignity.

Personal reflection

Repeat this exercise, one truth per day, for a week. Stand in front of the mirror, look directly into your own eyes and recite one of the following truths along with its verse reference:

- I am a child of God (John 1:12)
- I am a co-heir with Christ and will share his inheritance (Romans 8:17)
- I am a temple, a place where God lives (1 Corinthians 3:16)
- I am a new creation (2 Corinthians 5:17)
- I am chosen of God, holy and dearly loved (Colossians 3:12)
- I will resemble Christ (1 John 3:2)
- I am born of God and Satan can't touch me (1 John 5:18)

Write about this experience in your journal. Which verse has become precious to you? Which truth do you find hardest to believe? Why?

If you prefer, you may explore these questions with a close and trusted friend.

NOTES

1. W.E. Vine, *Vine's Concise Dictionary of Bible Words*, Thomas Nelson, pp. 344–46. The Hebrew words *chatta't* and *chet* (2403) express the missing of a mark, or erring. *Chata* (2398) indicates moral failure against others as well as God and the guilt that sin produces. *Amal* (5999) refers to the self-inflicted suffering caused by sin as well as that inflicted on others. *Awon* (5771) relates to the twisting nature of sin. *Rasha* (7563) captures sin's inner turbulence and open hostility toward God and his people.

   The New Testament enlarges the concept of sin. The Greek word *hamartia* (266) depicts sin as failure, fault and wrongdoing. It also describes sin as the internal source of outward action and as a governing principle or power constantly at work in the body. *Hamartano* (264) is used of sinning against God, against Christ, against others, against the law and against one's self.
2. B. Milne, *Know the Truth*, Inter-Varsity Press, p. 104.
3. R. Backhouse, *1500 Illustrations for Preaching and Teaching*, Marshall Pickering, p. 39.
4. *Vine's Concise Dictionary*, p. 189.
5. 2 Corinthians 5:17 (NIV).
6. H.J. Nouwen et al, *Compassion*, Doubleday & Co., 1982, p. 21.
7. A.P. Castle, *Quotes and Anecdotes: An Anthology for Preachers and Teachers*, Kevin Mayhew, p. 111.
8. Backhouse, *1500 Illustrations*, p. 124.
9. Source article 'Angels with a Cause' by Hapi Wanje, *Compassion International*, 26 April 2002.

IN-DEPTH REFLECTION

What is poverty?

God has given us all the physical resources and spiritual gifts we need to live and enjoy life, and yet there is pain and suffering everywhere we look. In a search for the solution it is important to address the nature of the problem. What exactly is poverty?

Poverty is multi-faceted, and it comes in different shapes and sizes. You can see it in the swollen-bellied children suffering the effects of famine, in the parents who are forced to sell their children into slavery, in the refugees displaced from their homelands through war and in the limbless beggars by the roadside. Broadly speaking, though, poverty is simply a lack of choice. It is the presence or absence of something that prevents us from being and doing all that God wants. By its very nature, poverty stops us from being totally human and totally with God. It denies people the chance to live life in all its fullness.

It is easy to define poverty purely in terms of a person's financial or economic situation. The World Bank estimates that 55.6 per cent of the world's population live on less than two US dollars a day.[1] This gives us some idea of the scale of poverty, but it only shows us one part of the picture. It is not simply a lack of food, shelter and clothing that makes a person poor, it is the lifestyle into which they are forced as a direct result of their need to provide the necessities for their family.

Without sufficient education, well-paid and reputable jobs are out of the reach of most of the poor. Business owners across the world are wise to the desperation and, as a result, offer unskilled and low-paid jobs in frequently appalling conditions. In many cases, the desperation of a family is so bad that even the children are forced to work. It is estimated that 250 million children between the ages of five and 14 work; of these, 120 million work full-time.[2] As Wess Stafford, *Compassion*'s president says, 'It is desperation that so often conspires against the [poor] parents and results in their sons and daughters being exploited.'[3] Hours are long; conditions are bad and soul-destroying. Every year an estimated one million children are forced into the sex trade. These children are at great risk of further sexual abuse, sexually transmitted diseases and pregnancy.[4] Where exploitation occurs, the cycle of poverty continues.

Health is another factor that is both a cause and effect of poverty. The poor cannot choose where they live, the type of housing they have or the kinds of food they eat. Without adequate infrastructure, sanitation systems, access to a varied diet and facilities in which to cook and prepare food, the chance of getting ill are greatly increased. Doctors and simple medicines are hard to come by and too expensive for the majority of the poor, so illnesses such as sickness and diarrhoea are commonplace killers. Children are more susceptible to these illnesses and, as a result, many die unnecessarily at a young age.

Malnourishment is another condition that prevents children from being all that God intended them to be. Every single day, malnutrition is the leading cause of 30,000 preventable child deaths worldwide.[5] Malnourished children may not look as if they are starving, but an imbalance in their diet means that both their physical and mental development are stunted. Their inability to concentrate at school leaves them without the qualifications they need to secure good employment, so their choices in adult life are greatly reduced.

Perhaps the biggest health threat ever to be seen is that of HIV and AIDS. As the pandemic sweeps the world, the developing nations suffer most. A lack of education regarding sexual health, as well as the taboo that surrounds the issue, has led to an unprecedented growth of HIV and AIDS. The death of generations of healthy adults forces their children into positions of responsibility at an extremely young age. Children suffer emotionally as they watch a parent's health deteriorate, and often have to take on the role of a carer, looking after both sick parents and siblings. They are denied the opportunity of education and the freedom that childhood should bring.

Governments and those with power often make decisions on behalf of the poor. The poor do not own land or businesses and are not seen to contribute in any major way to the development of a country. As a result, they are overlooked in the decision-making processes. For example, major trading laws take into account the larger economic situations of a country but rarely involve those who work in the production process. These workers are at the mercy of larger companies and corporations whose concern is often for profit margins and not people.

The poor are rarely given any kind of identity or recognition within the society, making it extremely difficult for them to participate fully in the life of a country. In Honduras in 2001, death squads murdered over 1000 of the capital city's street children.[6] The only crime these children committed was that of being poor— a state inflicted upon them by situations and circumstances over which they had no control. Such social ostracision can breed further problems. Gang culture is rife the world over as groups of young people, who have not had the chance to participate fully in society, are seeking acceptance and respect elsewhere.

The continual struggle of daily life can breed an attitude of fatalism among some of the world's poorest people. It is easy for them to believe that there is nothing they can do to alter their personal situations. As they lose hope, they also lose their capacity and will to change. Alcoholism and drug abuse can become chosen escape routes for those in the grip of poverty-induced depression.

The lives of the poor are dictated not by the plans that God has for them, but by the plans that the world has for them. These flawed plans prevent the perfection of communion with God. We may not be directly responsible for the majority of the causes of poverty, but as followers of Christ who know the God of love and reconciliation, is it not then our responsibility to ensure that his plans and not those of the world are put into action?

NOTES

1. *The Millennium Goals*, World Bank Development Indicators 2003, p. 5, www.worldbank.org
2. *State of the World's Children* 2001, UNICEF.
3. *The Millstone Report* Sept/Oct 2002: 'Child Labour: A Discarded Generation' by Janet Root, *Compassion International*.
4. Madeline Eisner, 'Child Sex Linked to Spread of HIV/AIDS, Says UNICEF', African Church Information Service, quoting UNICEF executive director Carol Bellamy, http://allafrica.com/ posted December 7, 2001.
5. *The Millstone Report* Winter 2003, *Compassion International*.
6. BBC News country profile: Honduras: www.bbc.co.uk.

CHAPTER TWO

Compassionate life

SECTION ONE

The compassionate life: in community

There is an old Jewish proverb that says, 'Love thy neighbour even if he plays the trombone!'[1]

Those of us who have listened to a beginner practising or an orchestra warming up *en masse* know how grating disharmony is to the ears. It is almost a miracle that, once tuned and in the hands of the conductor, such discord is transformed into perfect unison and rich harmony. To live in harmony with one another takes practice too—the practice of compassionate love.

Compassion does not come naturally to our fallen nature. Instead, true compassion is the result of the unity generated among us by the Holy Spirit. Hence compassionate living in Christ is nothing less than a life devoted to this common unity. Christ acts as both our encouragement and our comfort as we look for ways to demonstrate God's compassion among one another. 'Live in harmony by showing love for each other,' says Paul. 'Be united in what you think, as if you were only one person' (Philippians 2:2).

Community is God's idea. As we have seen, God himself is a community of three equal persons—Father, Son and Holy Spirit—relating in love. This truth is the foundation for all our relationships. We are created in God's image and, as such, need loving community to thrive. Because of our sinful nature, we no longer live the way that God intended, but because of Christ, true community can be restored and flourish.

Stephen Neil says, 'Life is filled with meaning as soon as Jesus Christ steps into it.'[2] Our identity is in Christ and it is from him that we learn most about our own humanity and how to relate to each other in compassion. Jesus' words, works and ways were expressions of the intimate unity he shared with the Father and the Holy Spirit. We, too, are included in this intimacy: we are children of the Father because we are in Christ and the Holy Spirit is in us. The deeper our intimacy and union with God, the deeper will be our intimacy and union with each other. Fellowship with Christ is fellowship with each other.

There is a comic strip in which it would appear that a mother is trying desperately to persuade her hiding child to go to church. 'Give me one good reason why I should go,' says a voice from under the bedcovers. 'Because you're the minister,' comes the reply. We may smile, but even the most committed of us has, at one time or another, been dragged along to church out of duty rather than devotion. This will ever be the case until we shift our focus from *doing* church to *being* church. As a Christian community we are not driven together from fear, but drawn together in love. In fact, John argues that our inability to accept and exercise God's unconditional love is the basis of fear. Indeed, God's perfect love casts out fear. 'The thought of being punished is what makes us afraid,' says John. 'It shows that we have not really learnt to love. We love because God loved us first. But if we say we love God and don't love each other, we are liars. We cannot see God. So how can we love God, if we don't love the people we can see? The commandment that God has given us is: "Love God and love each other!"' (1 John 4:18–21). To be transformed by God's love is to be flooded with compassion. This is a persuasive incentive to live in devotion and unity with one another.

Compassion belongs in community and will always reveal itself there. To *suffer with* is not a personal attribute or talent, but a way of being together, a mutual communal vocation. Encouraged by the presence of Christ alongside us and the presence of the Holy Spirit in us, we are lifted out of our aloneness and into the togetherness that is community. We share all things in common. We reflect God's unity through the quality of our love and forgiveness, patience and peace, sacrifice and servanthood. We reject God's unity when rivalry and faction, pride and prejudice, selfishness and conceit divide us. To lack compassion is to deny our true humanity and destroy our witness. Disunity makes for dysfunction as it diverts and drains energy from the body. The more energy we expend fighting ourselves, the less we have to expand our self—for that is what we are, one body and one person in Christ. We witness to God's compassion in the way that we are together. We are on a common journey, with common goals, common faith and common passion —compassion.

A father, frustrated by his daughter's constant pestering, decided to give her something time-consuming to do. He cut out a map of the world from a newspaper, then cut the map into puzzle pieces. He challenged his daughter to put it back together. Five minutes later she called on him to inspect her finished puzzle. The father was amazed. 'How on earth did you do that so quickly?' He asked. 'That was easy,' she replied. 'I just turned the pieces over and on the other side there was a picture of a man. When the man was put together right, the world was right.'[3]

True spiritual unity is not imposed from the outside but comes from within as we are individually transformed by the Holy Spirit and bear his fruit. 'If you are guided by the Spirit, you won't obey your selfish desires,' says Paul. 'God's spirit makes us loving, happy, peaceful, patient, kind, good, faithful, gentle, and self-controlled' (Galatians 5:16, 22–23). The Holy Spirit also gives us complementary gifts to use for the benefit of the community. These include the gifts of prophecy, hospitality, teaching, encouragement, giving, leadership and doing good. Community results from our own personal fellowship with the Spirit and the common life produced by the Spirit in us as a whole. Unity is not to be confused with uniformity. We are of one Spirit and purpose, possessing common attributes but expressing different gifts. We are sometimes in unison but intended for harmony.

God's love is a broad love. So is God's community. It consists of people from every race, land and age who have been chosen by the Father, bought by the blood of Christ and made holy by the Holy

Spirit. We are many and different, but in Christ we are one and united.

Jesus demonstrated God's kingdom as an inclusive community, not as an exclusive club. A prime example of this is in his inclusion of children. Jesus treated children with tenderness and referred to them with respect. This sent a powerful message to a world in which children were often overlooked or treated with harsh cruelty and brutality. Jesus' own experience of violence was not limited to adulthood. He himself was the intended target of Herod's slaughter of countless male children under the age of two. Little may be specifically known about Jesus' childhood beyond his birth, but much may be safely assumed. Jesus brought to bear the experiences of both his deity and his humanity in demonstrating the priorities of God's kingdom—a kingdom in which children are not only included but provide the example for all adults who want to be admitted.[4]

One day an elderly lady sat next to a little girl. 'How are you?' she asked. 'Fine,' said the little girl. After a little while the elderly woman asked, 'Why don't you ask me how I am?' 'Because,' said the girl calmly, 'I'm not interested.'[5] It is imperative that we truly embrace the compassion of Christ if community is to be more than a Christian ideal. As disturbing as it is to look squarely into the face of global suffering, and even more disturbing to look into the eyes of those who suffer, we must. The compassion of Christ will not allow us to respond to poverty, disease, military conflict and inescapable debt with indifference and inactivity. We cannot refuse to know, abscond from awareness or claim ignorance as an excuse for maintaining the status quo. Through awareness, we can use the gifts that God has given us to strengthen the community in which he has placed us, locally and globally.

'One hundred pianos all tuned to the same fork are automatically tuned to each other,' says A.W. Tozer. 'They are of one accord by being tuned, not to each other, but to another standard to which each one must individually bow.'[6] As a community, we worship God in spirit and in truth. We seek solidarity with one another, to serve one another humbly and to respond obediently to God on one another's behalf. If there is any encouragement in Christ, if we have any comfort from his love, any fellowship with the Spirit, any tenderness and compassion—as indeed we have—we will be united with the same mind and motive, thought and purpose (Philippians 2:1–2). We can agree in the great things of God and keep the unity of the Spirit in our disagreements. We can, and must, find a way forward together.

Compassion is a 'suffering with'—a *metanoia* or complete change in our vision. Compassion allows us to look at each other with new eyes. We do not see in each other something new. Rather we behold in one another, remember and revere in one another, the dignity that has always been there but has somehow been damaged or forgotten. Compassion is transcendent. It yields a union that is powerful and deep, a union where we can, as Paul Keenan says, 'be on each other's side, not on each other's back'.[7]

*

Fragmentation of life

The family structure generally provides stability and love for a child as he or she grows and develops. In situations of war, any sense of normality and stability is ripped apart. This is evident nowhere more clearly than in the country of Rwanda.

As families and communities disintegrate, the fundamental basis of love and security upon which a child's life is built is destroyed. Not only do the family bonds of protection break down, but so too do the governmental and social systems that support communities. In Rwanda the continual ransacking of towns and villages saw migrant communities fleeing on a regular basis. The continual movement of populations made it virtually impossible for schools, churches and other community activities to function. Vulnerable children were therefore left without any support or sense of belonging.

The genocide of 1994 caused about 80 per cent of all children to lose at least one member of their family and about one third of all children to witness the murder of a loved one.[8] Children left alone in the world often internalize their distress and suppress bad memories and, as a result, convictions of anger and mistrust develop. Often unseen and unheard, this silent trauma is the most dangerous and debilitating effect of the war. It threatens to tarnish and prevent the development of a whole generation.

Although deep hurt cannot be erased, *Compassion* projects are developing across the country of Rwanda, offering structure and hope to the lost. They cannot replace the families and communities but, with stable love and support, they can help children to deal with their pain and shape a future for themselves. The common experience of war and pain can be moulded to a common unity and a common good.

*

Group helps

Worship

As we are gathered (SF1 24)
Bind us together (SF1 39)
Jesus, stand among us (SF1 290)
Salvation belongs to our God (SF2 992)
Thy loving kindness (SF1 556)

Word

Proverbs 29:7
Philippians 2:1–11

Prayer

- Pray for continued reconciliation and stability in the country of Rwanda.
- Pray that forgiveness will be upon the hearts of those who have suffered through the crisis.
- Pray that those who are responsible for atrocities will recognize their crimes.

Fellowship

Listen to a piece of classical or acoustic music together as a group. Discuss what would happen if everyone played out of tune or time. What is the role of the conductor? Apply this spiritually. Is your group in tune and in step when it comes to global compassion? How can the group show more compassion, and to whom—locally and globally?

Witness

Read Proverbs 29:7. Why is giving to charity not enough? Explore together some of the needs in your local community and identify some creative ways of helping to meet these needs. You could donate an assortment of Christian books (fiction, poetry, children's, biographies and so on) to the local library or promote the signing of a petition that will benefit the community, or become a befriender within the community.

Personal reflection

Either draw some musical symbols or paste a piece of staffed music paper into your journal. Choose a favourite piece of reflective music and listen to it with your eyes closed. Think about compassion and write from one of these prompts:

- In the orchestra of Christ's compassion, I play the…
- This is the rhythm of Christ's compassion…
- This is the tempo of my life…

If you prefer, you may explore these questions with a close and trusted friend.

NOTES

1. A.P. Castle, *Quotes and Anecdotes: An Anthology for Preachers and Teachers*, Kevin Mayhew, p. 100.
2. T. Castle, *A Treasury of Christian Wisdom*, Hodder & Stoughton, p. 143.
3. Castle, *Quotes and Anecdotes*, p. 235.
4. Mark 10:14–16.
5. M. Hodgin, *1001 Humorous Illustrations for Public Speaking*, Zondervan, p. 183.
6. www.christianquotes.org.
7. P. Keenan, *Heart Storming*, Contemporary Books, p. 193.
8. *Children in War: A Guide to the Provision of Services*, Everrett M. Ressler, J.M. and A. Marcelino, UNICEF, 1993.

SECTION TWO

The compassionate life: in solidarity

A story is told about a girl who went on an errand for her mother and was away longer than expected. When she finally arrived home, her mother asked why she was so late. 'I met a friend who fell down and scraped her knee,' she replied. 'Did you stop to help her up?' asked the mother. 'No,' said the girl, 'I stopped to help her cry.'

Such is the solidarity of the Tri-unity as expressed in Christ that he did not reach down to pull us out but came down to identify with us. The supreme price paid by the Tri-unity for this intimacy with us was separation from himself.[1] On the cross, God in Christ experienced the utmost depths of human sin, pain, anguish and confusion. He who did no sin, knew no sin and in whom there was no sin became sin to make us acceptable to God.

Jesus' solidarity in our suffering is not an interruption of his eternal deity. Rather, in the emptied Christ we encounter the tri-unity of God. Jesus claimed equality with the Father, forgave sins and accepted worship. He had power over nature, demons and death. He knew the future and what others were thinking, near and far. He was moved with compassion and, above all, it is Christ to whom we look for mercy. Jesus Christ was God set apart by his sinless nature. Jesus Christ was human apart from a sinful nature. As both God and human, Jesus showed us what the Father and the Spirit are like and how to live in the Father's will by depending on the Holy Spirit.

Dietrich Boenhoeffer says, 'A Christian is someone who shares the suffering of God in the world.'[2] Following Christ in his compassionate solidarity does not mean suffering as a goal in itself.

We have experienced God's compassion in Christ and in Christ we become compassionate. The goal of the gospel is to reconcile us to God, each other and ourselves. A gospel that doesn't reconcile is no gospel at all. Solidarity is not the outcome of hard work but the fruition of God's grace. Compassionate loving is part of our growing identity and a fruit of the Spirit in us. Paul says, 'God's Spirit makes us loving' (Galatians 5:22). Only we can offer what people need most—the incarnate love of Christ present in you and me.

Jesus proclaimed God's kingdom open to everyone, of any age or stage, who welcomed him. People who anticipated precedence in the kingdom based on their earthly status were given quite a shock. So too were those who had no status at all. Those people who were most open to Jesus and, therefore, to God's kingdom were often not the religiously respectable and revered, but the downcast and despised.

Indeed, even those in Jesus' closest company misunderstood the topsy-turvy solidarity of God's kingdom. In answer to a squabble over which of the disciples was greatest, Jesus said, 'If you want the place of honour, you must become a slave and serve others!' Then Jesus put his arm around a child and said, 'When you welcome even a child because of me, you welcome me. And when you welcome me, you welcome the one who sent me' (Mark 9:35, 37). When we welcome children into our presence, we welcome God. Jesus makes it clear that those who are weak and vulnerable are to be the foremost focus of our compassionate concern—a concern demonstrated by our presence with them.

As we have already noted, the words 'passion' and 'patience' have the same root. Hence compassion is not only 'suffering with' but 'long suffering with'. Perhaps this is why Thomas Aquinas says, 'I would rather feel compassion than know the meaning of it.'[3] In the story of Job, Job's worst possible fears are realized: he loses not only his health and everything he has but everyone he most loves. Job is so devastated and deeply broken that his friends, who arrive to comfort him, hardly recognize him. These friends come in for much criticism later in the story, but initially they respond to Job with compassionate solidarity. Job's friends are so deeply affected by Job's pain, so earnestly sorrowed, that they weep bitterly for him. They not only suffer Job's silence for seven days and seven nights, but 'suffer with' him in it by being silent themselves as they sit next to him on the ground.

It is unfortunate that Job's friends, having begun so well, eventually lose patience. Believing personal prosperity to be a proof of God's blessing, and suffering a proof of God's wrath, Job's friends advise him to repent of the sin that must have caused his suffering. In the process they make themselves judges and sin not only against their friend, who is indeed innocent, but against God who alone is worthy to judge.

We are witnesses to the compassionate God through our patient compassion with others. We don't seek suffering but will suffer because we identify with those who are suffering, God's presence becoming apparent in us. Comfort and consolation do not come primarily from helpful advice or action but from those who are humbly present with us, those who stop to help us cry and sit with us when words fail. Like Jesus, they demonstrate compassionate solidarity. They stick with us for as long as it takes to see us through. In so doing, those who bring compassion bring hope and help as well.

Solidarity is a mutual process. Through the power of presence we affect others and others affect us. In relationship we too find new ways of being and relating. Job's friends had much to repent of in their pious conduct, and Job had much to forgive. Ultimately all were restored to one another and deepened in their relationship with God. We too must be willing to repent and ready to forgive—to be deepened one in another through a compassion that 'suffers with' even in our mistakes.

Compassionate living is to relate to others as Christ has related to us. We love because he loves, we forgive because he forgives, and we serve because he serves. In heart, word and deed, Jesus reflected God's special concern for those who are poor. To 'love others as much as we love ourselves' is not to *wish* each other well but, through patient presence, to *make* each other well. We must not mistake sympathy for compassion. Suffering with others is not feeling sorry *for* them but experiencing sorrow *with* them. It is also being vulnerable enough to let others sorrow with us too.

It would be difficult to think of anyone more in need of our patient presence among them than children who must work through and recover from the wreckage of poverty and abuse. Compassion is a process, not a quick fix. We presence ourselves with those among us who hurt the most. Paul boldly states that bearing each other up under their burdens is more than just doing good; it *is* good. Compassion fulfils the law of Christ. Hence, says Paul, 'Don't get tired of helping others... We should help people whenever we can, especially if they are followers of the Lord' (Galatians 6:9, 10). We are like Christ when we are like him in the way he loves.

*

Hope in a letter

As much as we read, research and visit another country, it is virtually impossible ever to understand what it feels like to be a child born into the hopelessness of poverty. But these barriers and immediate differences should not prevent us from engaging actively with a child on the other side of the world.

Bill Clinton once raised the question of what is more important, 'our differences or our common humanity',[4] and what better way to show common humanity than by putting pen to paper and sharing a little of yourself with a child on the other side of the world? It is amazing how much we actually do have in common with our brothers and sisters when we think about it. Why should we be so surprised by this when we know that, at heart, we are all made in the image of God?

Children are inquisitive and desire to learn about what people in other countries do, where they live, what they eat. The best way for them to learn the real truth about another place is by engaging directly in correspondence with a person from another nation. When a child swallowed up by the slum of a Third World city receives a letter from thousands of miles away, then, in the words of a sponsored child, they 'feel loved'. It's not about writing in eloquent turns of phrase, but just about sharing a little bit of yourself with a child in need. Our money can go a long way but words of love are more powerful than we'll ever know.

*

Group helps

Worship

A new commandment (SF1 14)
God forgave my sin (SF1 126)
In heavenly love abiding (SF1 213)
O let the Son of God enfold you (SF1 403)
So freely (SF1 482)

Word

Psalm 35:9–10
Mark 9:35–37

Prayer

- Thank God for the opportunity we have to participate in the lives of those on the other side of the world.
- Pray that we will be open to learn from those in the developing world.

- Pray that our hearts will not be hardened by 'compassion fatigue' and that we never get overwhelmed by the size of the task that faces us.

Fellowship

Sing a medley of well-known children's songs. Some suggestions might be 'Jesus loves me', 'Jesus loves the little children', 'Jesus loves a little one like me' and so on. As a group, think of as many children as you can and name each one aloud by first name only. Identify and discuss what might be done to improve solidarity with these children and serve them to the glory of God.

Witness

Sing 'Jesus loves the little children'. Think of the children you know being embraced by Jesus. Suggest ways in which you can help Jesus embrace these children. Act on one of these suggestions by the end of the week.

Personal reflection

Read Mark 9:35–37. Refer to the picture in your journal of you as a child. Who served you in the kingdom of faith? With whom did you share your joys and sorrows? Think of the children you know. How are you serving them? Write about this.

If you prefer, you can explore these questions with a close and trusted friend.

NOTES

1. Matthew 27:46.
2. T. Castle, *A Treasury of Christian Wisdom*, Hodder & Stoughton, p. 227.
3. www.christianquotes.org
4. Dimbleby Lecture 2001, *The Struggle for the Soul for the 21st Century*. Bill Clinton 14 December 2001 available at www.bbc.co.uk/arts/news_comment/dimbleby/clinton.shtml

SECTION THREE

The compassionate life: in servanthood

Most of us will know the old put-down, 'He's so conceited that if he ever wrote a book he would entitle it, My Humility and How I Attained It.*' In truth, Jesus is the only person who could actually write such a book and get away with it.*

Compassionate living in Christ is not only a life of unity and solidarity, but also of humble servanthood. 'He gave up everything and became a slave,' explains Paul. 'Christ was humble. He obeyed God and even died on a cross. Then God gave Christ the highest place and honoured his name above all others' (Philippians 2:7–9).

In a 2003 national debate, the British public voted Winston Churchill the greatest Briton for his heroic leadership in World War II. At the end of the war, Churchill and Roosevelt had a chat about the newly elected Prime Minister, Clement Attley. 'He seems a very modest man,' commented Roosevelt. Churchill, also reputed for his wit, retorted, 'Absolutely true. But then, he does have a lot to be modest about.'[1]

Jesus is arguably the greatest man who ever lived. As both supreme being and supreme human being, Jesus had nothing to be humble about. However, it was Jesus' humility that affirmed his greatness. 'Whoever is the greatest should be the servant of the others,' said Jesus in response to the puffed-up Pharisees and scribes. 'If you humble yourself, you will be honoured' (Matthew 23:11–12). In solidarity, God became one of us. In humility, God came to serve us.

Rejecting royal robes for swaddling scraps, the Lord over all became the slave of all.[2] This he did without a hint of self-seeking personal ambition, all the way to the cross. On the way he contradicted all the acceptable models of greatness. He was truthful about his deity but not conceited. He rejected wealth, success and popularity. He used his power to serve and remained faithful to his call. Isaiah movingly depicted the coming Saviour as an unattractive, despised nobody whose life was full of sorrow and suffering—an abused, crushed and condemned innocent who did it all for us but was deserted as if deserving the punishment himself.[3] Perhaps Jesus so often quoted from the book of Isaiah because he found so much of himself there. 'The Son of Man did not come to be a slave master,' Jesus said of himself, 'but a slave who will give his life to rescue many people' (Matthew 20:28).

It seems strange that one so powerless frees us, so weak strengthens, so hopeless brings hope and so poor makes rich. It seems ironic that we are servants of the ultimate servant. Selfish ambition and conceit are so completely contrary to God's compassionate nature that he actively stands in opposition to everyone who is proud and helps everyone who is humble.[4] Indeed, James identifies selfishness as the root of all conflict in his confrontation of those who are quarrelsome (James 4:1–3).

A story is told of a little boy who kept staring at his father's bragging boss at the dinner table. Finally the boss demanded to know why the boy was staring. The boy asked, 'Are you really a self-made man?' The boss beamed his affirmation proudly. 'Well,' said the boy, 'why did you make yourself like that?'[5]

The word 'proud' is translated from the Greek *huperephonos*, which means to show oneself as pre-eminent above others. Pride is inseparable from arrogance and disdain.[6] In contrast, the word 'humility', translated from *tapeinophrosune*, means to have a lowliness of mind—not to think in terms of our own position at all, but to think often about the position of others.[7] Pride and humility are mutually exclusive. In fact, those who are proud are considered God-haters, always seeking out new ways of doing evil.[8] Pride is pretence, a form of self-idolatry and worship. It completely undermines the worth not only of our truly pre-eminent God himself, but also of those who bear his image. No wonder Proverbs says, 'Too much pride will destroy you. You are better off being humble and poor than getting rich from what you take by force' (Proverbs 16:18–19). Jesus took nothing by force but, through humble servanthood all the way to the cross, gained everything worth having.

Jesus revisited first principles at the last supper. In the absence of a servant and the presence of his followers, Jesus takes off his robe (deity), puts on a towel (servanthood), kneels in front of his friends (humility) and meets a common need by washing their feet (solidarity).[9] 'Do you understand what I have done?' he asks. 'I have set the example, and you should do for each other exactly what I have done for you' (John 13:12, 15).

Servanthood is the search for God, not just a desire to see change. The more intimately we know Christ, the more accurately we will reflect him. Paul reminds us to think the same way that Jesus thought.[10] There are no spiritual élites. We are all made in God's image and our identity is in Christ. Therefore, we miss the point entirely if we strive for inferiority. Rather, humility begins in the true estimation of who we are and what we have to give. Our unworthiness is understood in the light of our worth, our imperfections in the light of being perfected, our differences in the light of our sameness. Humble servanthood isn't thinking less of ourselves, but more of Christ. It isn't the neglect of our own concerns, but the exercise of a compassion broad enough to include the concerns of others. When we shift the focus from ourselves, we see others more clearly. We use our God-given abilities to meet each other's common needs without reserve or discrimination. Just before his ascension, Jesus promised his followers that he would be with them until the world's end.[11] We too must persist compassionately for as long as it takes to overcome human misery and reveal God's presence in our fractured world.

The word 'humbled', taken from the noun *ani*, means to be poor and meek. It took on a special significance for those being abused and exploited by the wealthy.[12] It should not surprise us that our compassionate and loving God has an especially soft spot for those who are humbled in this way. Jesus reflected this in his concern and ministry to those who were poor and meek. A pregnant and hope-filled Mary declares God's mercy and compassion for those who are physically humbled and spiritually humble. 'The Lord has used his powerful arm to scatter those who are proud. He drags strong rulers from their thrones and puts humble people in places of power,' she sings. 'God gives the hungry good things to eat, and sends the rich away with nothing' (Luke 1:51–53). It is worth asking, 'Who sings this song today?' Mary was not long out of childhood, poor and seemingly insignificant to all but God and those closest to her. Although there will never be another Mary, there are indeed many Marys expectant with the hope of physical and spiritual salvation among those who are young today. 'Mary's song is certainly a challenge to Christian action in the face of poverty,' says Leith Fisher. 'We must not think of money alone, but of all the wealth that surrounds us, of knowledge, power, comfort and security.'[13]

It is a lovely irony that one Mary should be prepared by God to deliver Jesus, the hope of all, in birth, and another Mary should prepare Jesus, God the Son, to suffer for us all in his death. In the midst of a tense, uncertain time, Jesus, his disciples and several followers huddled together in Simon's house. The threat of impending doom clung in the air. Suddenly, without warning or explanation, Mary broke her expensive bottle of perfume and began to pour it on Jesus' head and feet, which she wiped with her own hair. The sweet aroma of her offering filled the room and brought an unexpected moment of sanctuary. Not everyone, however, felt this way. Judas and some others became angry and accused Mary of wasting what might have been sold in aid of those in poverty.

Given Jesus' consistent and compassionate service among those in need, it is surprising, perhaps shocking, that he should respond thus: 'Leave her alone! ... She has done a beautiful thing for me. You will always have the poor with you. And whenever you want to, you can give to them. But you won't always have me here with you.

She has done all she could by pouring perfume on my body to prepare it for burial. You may be sure that wherever the good news is told all over the world, people will remember what she has done. And they will tell others' (Mark 14:6–9).[14]

It is a great disservice to Christ that his own words here have often been used as an excuse to neglect the needs of those who are poor and otherwise vulnerable. Jesus knew the hypocrisy of those who made the accusation, their lack of true compassion. He was not denying the priority of service among those who are poor but dismissing ill-motivated acts of charity as a means of meeting these needs or fulfilling God's requirement for true compassion. Mary is commended throughout the generations because she was the first to recognize what Jesus would suffer because of his servanthood. He would take on the mantle of humility and would give all on behalf of all. He alone is truly able to meet the deepest needs of those who are vulnerable, those with whom he had so strongly identified himself on earth. Indeed, we will always have those who are poor among us. How will we serve with humility and compassion among them?

*

A brighter future

Daniel Obrero is a young man overflowing with the love of God, which he seeks to impart to those whom he meets. Daniel's life used to be shaped by his circumstances in Laog City in the northern part of the Philippines. For a while, education seemed like a pointless exercise for Daniel: prospects were such that he could see no future for himself at all. He recalls a time when he was 'just dependent' rather than alive. This was before his encounter with *Compassion* and Jesus Christ. Now he proudly pronounces, 'I am thinking about my future.' He is no longer defined by the boundaries of his situation. While the world may see Daniel's future limited by the place in which he lives and the clothes that he wears, Daniel gets his sense of self-worth from God. He sees his own life as a vibrant 'river, flowing in a good and correct way'. It is no longer stagnant and pointless, but moving and developing.

Daniel wishes to share his new-found vigour for life with those about him and is currently studying to be a teacher. He proudly tells how 'it is part of my dream to be moulding the youth to become more rounded individuals, to be good citizens and builders of our country'. It is by changing the hearts and minds of individuals that circumstances can be changed.[15]

✷

Group helps

Worship

All to Jesus I surrender (SF3 1163)
Blessed assurance (SF1 41)
From heaven you came (SF1 120)
We really want to thank you, Lord (SF1 586)
You laid aside your majesty (SF1 638)

Word

Proverbs 16:18–19
Luke 1:46–55

Prayer

- Pray for more flexible educational opportunities for children who have to take on adult responsibilities at a young age.
- Ask for God's provision for families where the breadwinner has died.

- Pray for children who are in the care of extended families, that they will find love there.

Fellowship

Read the prayer under 'For personal reflection' below. Discuss these questions as a group:

- What are you complacent about?
- What are you ignorant of?
- What are you afraid of?
- Are there any forms of pretence in your service that need dealing with?

Read the prayer again before you part from one another.

Witness

Have a group re-think about how you distribute your resources for the purpose of mission or witness. Include all the ways in which you give your time, money, talents, energies and prayers. Ask the Holy Spirit to help you give with the right motive and redirect your resources in line with his compassion and priorities.

Personal reflection

Reflect on the lyrics of one of the songs under 'Worship' above. How can God come humbly into your life today? Write your reflections or, if you prefer, explore these questions with a close and trusted friend.

NOTES

1. M.A. Silver, *I Wish I'd Said That*, Robson, p. 108.
2. Philippians 2:7.
3. For more on the Suffering Servant, read Isaiah 53.
4. James 4:6.
5. Adapted from M. Hodgin, *1001 Humorous Illustrations for Public Speaking*, Zondervan, p. 86.
6. W.E. Vine, *Vine's Concise Dictionary of Bible Words*, Thomas Nelson, p. 294. *Huperephenos* (*huper*, 'above', and *phainomai*, 'to appear') (5244).
7. *Vine's Concise Dictionary*, p. 186. *Tapeinophrosune* (5012).
8. Romans 1:29–30; 2 Timothy 3:2–4.
9. Adapted from S. Bricscoe, *Bound for Joy*, Regal, p. 62.
10. Philippians 2:5.
11. Matthew 28:20.
12. *Vine's Concise Dictionary*, p. 186.
13. L. Fisher, *The Widening Road: from Bethlehem to Emmaus*, Scottish Christian Press, p.14.
14. See also Matthew 26:6–13 and John 12:1–8.
15. *One*, Celebrating 50 years of Compassion, *Compassion International*, 2002.

SECTION FOUR

The compassionate life: in obedience

Martin Luther says, 'If you want to understand the Christian message, you must start with the wounds of Christ.'[1]

Compassionate living in Christ is a life of obedient response. 'Christ was humble,' says Paul. 'He obeyed God and even died on a cross' (Philippians 2:8).

It is mind-boggling, but no less true, that God in tri-unity had a plan to save us before we were even created.[2] The cross wasn't an accident but the deliberate plan of the Father. The Son was to complete his given work on earth, enabled and empowered by the Holy Spirit, and return to glory where he would head the Church for ever. The Father promised that many would be added because of the Son's sacrifice.

Christ was not a passive participant in this plan. He willingly committed himself to the cross before the world began. He laid down his life, poured out his soul and offered himself up. He bore our sins and God's wrath. He bore the curse and the pains of hell. The Son wasn't coerced or conned into the cross: he chose it willingly and obediently. Referring to Isaiah 53, Peter says, 'Christ did not sin or ever tell a lie. Although he was abused, he never tried to get even. And when he suffered, he made no threats. Instead, he had faith in God, who judges fairly. Christ carried the burdens of our sins. He was nailed to the cross, so that we would stop sinning and start living right. By his cuts and bruises you are healed' (1 Peter 2:22–24).

Why is it that the very mention of the word 'obedience' causes many of us to cringe? Perhaps it is because we associate obedience with unquestioning, unwilling compliance. This, however, is not true obedience—not for Jesus and not for us. The word 'obedience' comes from the Latin *audire* which means 'to listen'. True obedience (listening) is an act of intimate trust. The one who obeys (listens) knows the mind and motives of the one who commands so completely that consent is natural.

Few of us respond to being scolded or harassed. A story is told of a boy with mental difficulties who accompanied his little sister to the shop. The boy took some bottles off a shelf, sat on the floor and began to play. 'Put those back!' barked the shop assistant crossly. The boy made no response. The shop assistant repeated his demand a second time. This time, the boy's sister went to the boy, put her arms around him and whispered something in his ear. The boy put the bottles back. 'You see,' said the sister to the shop assistant, 'he doesn't understand when you talk to him like that. You have to love it in to him.'[3]

In Jesus we witness the eager, attentive listening that flows from his intimate and loving relationship with the Father and the Holy Spirit. Co-equal and co-eternal, the Son knows all there is to know about the Father. Nothing is hidden. Theirs is such a close communion that Jesus could say, 'If you have seen me, you have seen the Father… I am one with the Father and… the Father is one with me' (John 14:9–10). In fact, Christ alone revealed the Father to us. 'No one has ever seen God,' says John. 'The only Son, who is truly God… has shown us what God is like' (John 1:18).

Jesus' obedience was a loving response to the loving Father even in the agonized questioning of Gethsemane. Jesus' public life was a direct response to his private life. He listened before responding and meditated before ministry. He knew and trusted the compassionate mind and motive of the Father. In Jesus we can too.

Obedience is central to compassionate living in Christ. It flows from intimate living, not human striving; the desire to hear, not the desperation to help. The relationship between Jesus and the Holy Spirit was so divinely and deeply intimate that every moment of Jesus' humanity was a moment shared by the Holy Spirit.

He is no less the same to us. It is through the Holy Spirit residing within us that the Father speaks. We must be still if we are to know God well enough to obey him. This is particularly true when we are in the midst of frenzied fear and confusion. 'God is our mighty fortress, always ready to help in times of trouble. And so, we won't be afraid!' says the psalmist. 'Nations rage! Kingdoms fall! But at the voice of God the earth itself melts… Our God says, "Calm down, and learn that I am God! All nations on earth will honour me." The Lord All-Powerful is with us' (Psalm 46:1–2, 6, 10–11).

God's voice both whispers and booms within us but it is always best to stay within whispering distance. We must come alive in our hearing if we are to help those children most affected by global turbulence. Ronald Dunn says, 'To live without waiting is to embrace humanism and wrap it in Christian trappings.'[4] Obedience that comes from listening produces a measured response, not a rash reaction. 'God calls everyone who is listening,' says Henri Nouwen. 'We must recognize the smaller calls hidden in the hours of a regular day.'[5]

Faithful stewardship of what God has given us is a recurrent theme throughout scripture and the central point in several of Jesus' parables. The sum of these is captured by Edgar W. Work, who says, 'The real tragedy of life is not in being limited to one talent, but in failure to use one talent.'[6] Whatever is in God's power to do through us, we must. Those who can't give materially must show the same generosity in other ways. We fail or succeed in our stewardship in proportion to how convinced we are that our lives belong to God.[7]

Longing for God to come makes us apprehensive about what he might bring. 'Light that will comfort and warm in the darkness,' says Janet Morley, 'may also expose what we would rather hide or not know about.'[8] Taken together, the world's neediest children form the largest unreached people group in the world today. Hudson Taylor's challenge for missionaries to China is equally true of ministry among children. 'It will not do to say that you have no special call to go,' he said. 'With these facts before you and with the command of the Lord Jesus to go and preach the gospel to every creature, you need rather to ascertain whether you have a special call to stay home.'[9]

A story is told of a little girl who was playing with her toys. Her mother noticed that her daughter's shirt was dirty and asked her to go and change. After calling her twice with no response, the mother yelled, 'Did you hear me, young lady?' The little girl answered, 'Yes. My ears heard you, but my legs didn't.'[10] Obedience is about responsive listening. There can be no mental consent to compassion without practical response.[11] How we respond will depend entirely on how intimately we listen, how well we know and trust God. Mark notes that Jesus drew his disciples closer into his hearing when he wanted to draw them closer to his cross. 'If any of you want to be my followers,' said Jesus, 'you must forget about yourself. You must take up your cross and follow me. If you want to save your life, you will destroy it. But if you give up your life for me and for the good news, you will save it' (Mark 8:34–35).

'Courage is what it takes to stand up and speak,' says Winston Churchill. 'It is also what it takes to sit down and listen.'[12] Faithful discipleship is as much about outer sacrifice as it is about inner spirituality. Obedience leads us into suffering not as an end in itself, but because God is compassionate. He will call us to respond compassionately where compassion is most needed. Says Peter, 'God will bless you, if you have to suffer for doing something good. After all, God chose you to suffer as you follow in the footsteps of Christ, who set an example by suffering for you' (1 Peter 2:20–21). Compassion is not a noble act of self-sacrifice. It is the listening obedience to the Father through the Holy Spirit. Even as a child, Jesus was about his heavenly Father's business, a business that took him to the cross.[13] Our obedience affirms that we do not take lightly what was so heavily laid on Christ. As David Livingstone says, 'Without Christ, not one step; with him, anywhere!'[14] We are most like Christ when we are like him in the way he obeys.

✱

Aftermath of war

War breeds prejudice and alienates communities and individuals alike, weakening the power of a people. Alexie is one of many children from war-torn countries who must suffer stigmatism for a crime which is not hers. In the aftermath of Rwanda's 1994 genocide, Alexie's mother was accused of war crimes and imprisoned. It is common practice for the young children of prisoners to be put in jail with their parents. Alexie's mother believed that her daughter deserved more from life and contacted her childhood friend, Rudasingwa Ruocah, and his wife to see if they would consent to be her daughter's guardians.

This placed Rudasingwa and his wife in a difficult situation. Taking care of a suspected war criminal's child would put them at risk of rejection and abuse from the community. But the family looked beyond the trappings of their world and stood firm on the word of God. They did not see the problem but the need and the opportunity to help.

Despite their own financial shortcomings, Rudasingwa and his family welcomed Alexie into their home and gave her the stability and love she needed to begin her life again. They leant on God and he provided. When Alexie was invited to join a *Compassion* project, her health, education, food and clothing were taken care of, so the financial burden on the family was relieved. Alexie's guardians could go on loving and encouraging her to be all that God wanted her to be.[15]

*

Group helps

Worship

How sweet the name of Jesus sounds (SF1 194)
It is the cry of my heart (SF2 832)

Jesus Christ is waiting (SF3 1381)
There is a home (SF2 1033)
Teach me to dance (SF2 1013)

Word

Psalm 46
Matthew 25:31–46

Prayer

- Thank God for those who stand up for the rights of the persecuted. Ask that they will be blessed through their actions.
- Pray for a wider network of support for those who stand up for the marginalized.
- Ask that the actions of love will speak into the hearts of those who witness them.

Fellowship

Explore the following questions together:

- How convinced are you that your life as a faith community belongs to God?
- How does the life and witness of your faith community reveal the answer to this question?

Witness

Play a game of telephone in which one person whispers a message in the next person's ear, which is then repeated to the next person, and so on. Ask the last person to repeat the message they received. Did the message change in translation? How can we help each other to be true to the message of compassion that God has given us to proclaim in life and witness?

Personal reflection

'My ears heard you, but my legs didn't.' Write about a time when you heard God but struggled to obey God. How has this situation been resolved between you?

If you prefer, explore this issue with a close and trusted friend.

NOTES

1   R. Backhouse, *1500 Illustrations for Preaching and Teaching*, Marshall Pickering, p. 101.
2   1 Peter 1:19–24.
3   M. Hodgin, *1001 Humorous Illustrations for Public Speaking*, Zondervan, p. 77.
4   R. Dunn, *Don't Just Stand There… Pray Something!*, Alpha, p. 42.
5   H.J. Nouwen, H.J. McNeill, D.A. Morrison, *Compassion*, Doubleday & Co., p.74.
6   A.P. Castle, *Quotes and Anecdotes: an Anthology for Preachers and Teachers*, Kevin Mayhew, p. 110.
7   Adapted from Pearl Bartell, www.christianquotes.com
8   J. Morley, *Bread of Tomorrow*, SPCK/Christian Aid, p. 14.
9   www.christianquotes.org
10 S. Hughes, *My Favourite Stories about Children*, CWR, p. 93.
11 There can be no mental consent to compassion without practical response (James 2:15–16; 1 John 3:17).
12 Source unknown.
13 Luke 2:41–51.
14 www.christianquotes.org
15 Source article, Janet Root, from *Compassion International* website, 2002.

SECTION FIVE

The compassionate life: in hopeful expectancy

A story is told about a boy who didn't know what to get his sister for her birthday. When asked, she responded, 'Just surprise me!' So when the day came, he crept into his sleeping sister's room, put his mouth next to her ear and shouted, 'BOO!'

Sometimes we just don't get what we expect. This is surely how the disciples felt in the dark days after Jesus' death. They had expected an invincible Messiah who would carry them to victory over their enemies. It was surely an impossible mistake that they would, instead, have to carry his cross and forgive their enemies. They did not yet understand that victory could come no other way. Do we?

God loves people but hates sin. 'If you want to know how much God hates your sin,' says Stuart Briscoe, 'look at the cross. If you want to know how much God loves you, look at the cross.'[1] The centrality of the cross in our salvation is undeniable. Without the resurrection and ascension, however, the work is unfinished.

Along the ceiling of York Minster are several bosses (circular plaques), barely visible from the floor below. Each one depicts a scene from the life of Christ. The ascension—whereby Christ returned to the Father and was glorified—is conveyed with a simple sense of joy and humour. Visible with a pair of binoculars are the bottom of the Saviour's bare feet surrounded by several pair of astonished eyes looking upward.

If ever there was a 'BOO!' moment for the disciples, it was here—in the resurrection and ascension of Christ, as their inner spirits leapt to awake from the slumber of grief. Their Messiah was indeed invincible even over suffering and death—no, even through suffering and death. Paul captures this triumph in his letter to the Philippians: 'Then God gave Christ the highest place and honoured his name above all others. So at the name of Jesus everyone will bow down, those in heaven, on earth, and under the earth. And to the glory of God the Father everyone will openly agree, "Jesus Christ is Lord!"' (Philippians 2:9–11).

Compassionate living in Christ is a life of hopeful expectancy—of empty tombs and bare feet—through our risen Lord. The resurrection established that Jesus was not a martyr for the cause, but the Son of God, Saviour of the world.[2] No martyr, no matter how good, has ever had the power to live again or forgive sins. Paul writes, 'Unless Christ was raised to life, your faith is useless, and you are still living in your sins… If our hope in Christ is good only for this life, we are worse off than anyone else. But Christ has been raised to life! And he makes us certain that others will also be raised to life' (1 Corinthians 15:17, 19–20).

The ascension established that Jesus was not only Saviour of the world, but Lord of the universe.[3] He was exalted to all he had laid aside in his humanity. He was returned to the Father, to the highest place and to authority. The name of Jesus, taunted, ridiculed and slandered on earth, now reflects his rule over all. 'Jesus Christ is Lord' (Philippians 2:11). A time is coming when even unbelievers will confess this, the earliest creed confessed by believers.[4] All of creation will submit, from the hosts of heaven to the demons of hell. Jesus Christ was Lord, is Lord and will be Lord. The dignity of Christ's deity was restored. The dignity of all humanity was raised.

'Body piercing saved my soul.' So says a T-shirt depicting the bloodied hands of Christ. We may not often think of it, but the Father exalted the humanity of Christ with him into the Tri-unity, scars and all. God, who so compassionately lowered the divine into the human, now lifts the human into the divine. As Bruce Milne so aptly puts it, 'God has for ever a human heart'.[5] Out of enduring compassion, Christ is now our royal priest, our advocate.[6] Having paid the sacrifice for our sin himself, he now appears before the

Father on our behalf. Jesus' scars remain not as a sign of physical failure, but as confirmation of his continuing compassion. Nothing can affect or afflict us without his experiencing it too.

When asked about heaven, a little boy replied, 'Heaven is the place your spirit goes but it is also inside us so we don't have to go far to get there.'[7] As we have already noted, the arrival of God's kingdom was a key theme for Jesus—one that he declared at the very outset of his ministry. 'The time has come!' he said. 'God's kingdom will soon be here. Turn back to God and believe the good news!' (Mark 1:15). Jesus professed in word and deed that the kingdom of God is not merely a distant reality, but already here among us as we are transformed in and through him by the power of the Holy Spirit. We do not have to *wait* until we are in heaven for the *hope* of heaven to be realized. The kingdom of God comes to us in the present, wherever and whenever God's will is done. Transformation is achieved—personal, political, economical, institutional, interpersonal and international—as we rediscover who we were created to be and the fullness of community in which we were intended to live. God's kingship is a kingship of the heart, both here and now, now and not yet.

We are to let God so change the way we think that it will have a colossal impact on how we live and serve. Compassion is a primary quality among those seeking to live by heaven's values on earth. Jesus first established his kingdom in the hearts of wounded people. Imprisoned and disillusioned, John asked Jesus, 'Are you the one we should be looking for? Or must we wait for someone else?' Jesus answered, 'Go and tell John what you have heard and seen. The blind are now able to see, and the lame can walk. People with leprosy are being healed, and the deaf can hear. The dead are raised to life, and the poor are hearing the good news' (Matthew 11:3–5). What affirmation and assurance! The kingdom belongs to those who are suffering and to those who show them compassion.

There is a shocking reality at the core of the gospel. Central to the salvation of a weak people by an all-powerful God is his own complete humiliation. God chose to use his power in a way completely contradictory to that of the world. Through the most shameful of human deaths, God chooses to make himself present in what is most detested and diminished in humanity. What hope this gives to those of us who not only feel destitute, but *are* destitute.

Peter Kreeft poignantly describes the ultimate paradox of the cross: 'God removed alienation from the human heart by inserting alienation into the heart of God. God conquered evil by allowing evil to have its supreme triumph—deicide, the introduction of death into the life of God.'[8] The cross introduces new meaning to suffering; it is not now the symbol of a shameful end but the beginning of the hope of eternal life. Out of the devastation and despair of the cross comes the deliverance of the tomb and the ascension. 'God is so good,' says the apostle Peter. 'By raising Jesus from death, he has given us new life and a hope that lives on...You have faith in God, whose power will protect you until the last day. Then he will save you, just as he has always planned to do' (1 Peter 1:3, 5).

A Sunday school teacher once asked her class, 'What does Jesus promise us?' A little girl cheerfully responded, 'Ever-laughing life.'[9] Salvation is not the end, glory is—a glory we are privileged to share. There will be an end to suffering but not to glory. When Jesus rose and ascended, he defeated everything that ever defeated anyone. Christ is dead on the cross and so is our sin. Christ is risen from death and so are we. Christ is gone to heaven and we will follow. The Father raised Jesus by the power of the Holy Spirit. In so doing, he accepted all that Christ did on the cross and made way for the Holy Spirit to continue his compassionate work in us. God promises that those who die with Christ will also live with him. This is our hope, the eager and confident expectation that will sustain us while we wait. We are redefined by this hope, our identity grounded not in the sinners we were but in the saints we become and are becoming on the way.

Hope isn't possibility but expectation. Hope isn't blind but visionary, for it sees the reality of the unseen and future promises of God. 'Other men see only a hopeless end,' says Gilbert Brenken, 'but Christians rejoice in an endless hope.'[10] We are of like mind to Christ when we are like him in hopeful expectancy.

*

In search of a family

Wess Stafford, the president of *Compassion*, tells of a church in Uganda which boasts a lively congregation consisting predominantly of children. Each week new hoards of children make their own way to the small building. These children are the latest victims of the AIDS pandemic that is sweeping the globe. Newly orphaned, they flock to the church because they have no one else to turn to. Despite the material poverty of the church members, when the pastor invites the week's new orphans to congregate at the front of the church, there is never a shortage of families willing to make room for one more in their home.

AIDS has orphaned more than 13 million children since the epidemic began.[11] Besides the emotional trauma of losing a parent, children orphaned by the disease are propelled toward positions of responsibility that should be well beyond their years. As a parent's physical health deteriorates, their capacity to work will also diminish. Expenses will increase, however, as medicines are required to relieve the suffering. In order to compensate for this, children are often taken out of school and sent to work, or left to care for their sick parents.

Without an education, the job opportunities for these youngsters are extremely limited. It is likely that many will end up in hazardous workplaces, unprotected by employment law and prone to exploitation. Many girls may be forced into prostitution, as it is the only type of work they can find.

It is vital that these children are identified as the most needy in their community. *Compassion*'s projects in Africa have been working hard to ensure that children orphaned or struggling to support

HIV/AIDS-afflicted parents are given priority in the projects. *Compassion* and the African church and other relief and development organizations are working together to reach those in greatest need.

✱

Group helps

Worship

At the name of Jesus (SF1 26)
He gave me beauty (SF1 157)
He is Lord (SF1 159)
I am a new creation (SF1 179)
Are we the people (SF2 657)

Word

Isaiah 61
1 Corinthians 15:1–7

Prayer

- Pray that governments will recognize the extent of the HIV/AIDS pandemic and the need to take action.
- Ask for God to guide church leaders as they take a leading role in responding to the HIV/AIDS crisis.
- Pray also for the pharmaceutical companies, that they will relax the patent laws so that cheap medicine can be made available to those who need it most.

Fellowship

Ask each member of the group to bring a backpack containing an object that makes them happy. Talk about these objects and why they were chosen. What hopes do you carry around in your spiritual backpack? Write something you are hoping in God for on a piece of paper. Carry this hope with you until it is realized.

Witness

Discuss the following questions together:

- Who are those oppressed in your community?
- What will it mean for you to bring hope to this specific group of people?
- How will you go about it?

For personal reflection

Refer to one of the photographs of yourself in the front of your journal. Where was God for you at that stage of your life? Use the following poem as a pattern to write your own. You may address your poem to the Father, Son or Holy Spirit or to God in tri-unity.

If you prefer, you may explore this question with a close and trusted friend.

It is the Holy Spirit,
　calling me to rise urgent as daybreak
　spilling over me with kindness
　anointing me with the fresh dews of compassion.

It is the Holy Spirit,
　embracing the child that remains
　expanding my lungs to love
　enlarging my heart to forgive.

It is the Holy Spirit,
  compelling me to heal
  to bring healing
  and the healer
  before night comes
  and there are no more dawns.

© *Renita Boyle*

NOTES

1. S. Briscoe, *Bound for Joy*, Regal, p. 66.
2. Romans 1:4.
3. Philippians 2:9–11.
4. 1 Corinthians 12:3; cf. Romans 10:9.
5. B. Milne, *Know the Truth*, Inter-Varsity Press, p. 174.
6. Hebrews 4:14; 1 John 2:1.
7. E. Marshall, *Kids Talk about Heaven*, Kyle Cathie, p. 21.
8. Summarized from P. Kreeft, *Making Sense out of Suffering*, Servant Books, p.132–133.
9. S. Hughes, *My Favourite Stories about Children*, CWR, p. 16.
10. Castle, *A Treasury*, p. 116.
11. 'AIDS turns back the clock for the world's young', Victoria Brittain, *Guardian*, Saturday 4 May 2002.

IN-DEPTH REFLECTION

Is it our responsibility?

Is the world of poverty really our responsibility? We are not the tyrants who abuse children in sweatshops; we are not the pimps who run brothels; we have no direct power on a governmental level, and yet as Christians we cannot just sit back and watch the death, starvation and exploitation continue.

We have governments and global institutions that are responsible for looking after the organization of our own countries and managing international issues. Such organizations are vital, but over-reliance on them can result in our conviction that anything we do not personally control is someone else's job. We can abdicate responsibility to the point at which we render ourselves useless in changing anything, and in doing so we fail to see the power of Christ within us.

Whether we like to admit it or not, we are all players in the global world. The food we eat, the clothes we wear and the cars we drive are all products from a number of different countries. We are not self-sufficient and cannot exist in isolation. God created us to draw from each other's individual gifts and skills and, through community with each other, find him. This interdependence comes with both reward and responsibility.

Our individual position within this world is often difficult to fathom when poverty is presented to us on such a large scale. The abundance of figures can leave us rather cold—victims of 'compassion fatigue' and voyeurs of a problem that is far too large for us ever to do anything about it.

This is not a healthy way to view our world. When we reduce poverty to purely numbers on a graph, we dehumanise the problem and make those in poverty victims of circumstance rather than agents and change makers. Throughout his ministry, Jesus helps people to see the power they have within themselves. For example, when he heals a paralysed man, he does not carry the man's mat, but enables the man to carry the mat for himself.[1]

When we are challenged with the global problem of poverty, we can be comforted by the fact that God has given us a mentor and a role model to follow—his Son. Although Jesus was fully God, he was also fully human and understands intimately the limitations that go with the human condition. He does not ask that we solve the entirety of the world's problems on our own, but that together we work to do what we can. In fact, one in ten verses in the synoptic Gospels refers directly to the poor. The Bible contains account after account of Jesus showing compassion to individuals on a one-to-one basis. Jesus makes time for the individual, the blind man and the mute,[2] the dead girl and the sick woman.[3] He identifies with those in need, ministering to each one as a unique creation of God and not as a statistic.

It is this uniqueness that is inherent in us all. Janet Root, an employee of *Compassion*, recently spent time with HIV and AIDS sufferers in Ethiopia and Uganda. She noted, 'What I can tell you from each of my encounters is this: I never met one victim or statistic. Instead I met vibrant, flesh-and-blood human beings struggling valiantly to make do with what they have.'[4]

As we come alongside and work with our brothers and sisters, sharing in communion with their lives, then we too can receive. Giving charitably is not a one-way process, and we can expect to be changed and challenged when we seek to do God's will. '"He defended the cause of the poor and the needy, and so all went well. Is that not what it means to know me?" declares the Lord.'[5]

NOTES

1. Matthew 9:1–8.
2. Matthew 9:27–34.
3. Luke 8:40–56.
4. Source article: 'Compassion at Work', Janet Root, Spring 2003.
5. Jeremiah 22:16 (NIV)

CHAPTER THREE

Compassionate prayer

SECTION ONE

Compassionate prayer: abiding in community

A seven-year-old girl was desperate to become a Christian. 'What do you think you need to do?' her leader asked. The girl thought. 'Nothing,' she said. 'Jesus did it all for me.' Then she simply expressed her profound faith. 'Thank you, Jesus,' she prayed, 'for taking me into your heart.'

This girl knew what it meant to abide in Christ, to be so completely at home in Christ and Christ in us that answered prayer is assured. 'Stay joined to me and let my teachings become part of you,' said Jesus. 'Then you can pray for whatever you want, and your prayer will be answered... Then my Father will give you whatever you ask for in my name' (John 15:7, 16).

Prayer is the compassionate provision of God. Having supplied the way of salvation, he now provides the means of relation. Jesus uses a vine, the national symbol of Israel, to illustrate the principle of abiding and the consequences of not abiding. 'I am the vine, and you are the branches. If you stay joined to me, and I stay joined to you, then you will produce lots of fruit. But you cannot do anything without me. If you don't stay joined to me, you will be thrown away. You will be like dry branches that are gathered up and burnt in a fire' (John 15:5–6).

These are harsh words, but logical. Jesus is telling his disciples that he alone is the true vine, not one vine among many. He alone is eternal, not temporal; essential, not optional. Those who embrace Christ share with him in all that he is and does. Those who don't are dead wood, completely lifeless. As Christians, we get our life from Christ, and apart from Christ our lives are meaningless. As Pascal says, 'Not only do we know God through Jesus Christ... but ourselves; we only know life and death through Jesus Christ. Apart from Jesus Christ we cannot know the meaning of our life or our death, of God or of ourselves.'[1] Prayer is an expression of abiding life. It identifies our union and intensifies our communion with God. Theodor Christeleb says, 'The soul is a never-ending sigh after God.'[2] What a beautiful description of abiding prayer! There is an old proverb that says, 'He who has little is not poor, but he who desires more.' We must not be controlled by our earthly desires, but surrender them to our desire for God alone. We can't be sinless, but we can sin less. An abiding life is a surrendered life.

Jesus' prayers resounded with divine abiding, his public life rising from private communion with the Father and the Spirit. Through prayer we are drawn into the unimpeded flow of divine intimacy. We receive every moment from God's abundance. Indeed, abundance-bearing is our purpose. Branches don't produce fruit by generating it; they bear the fruits, more fruit and much more fruit than is generated. The vine's job is to make fruit; ours is to be healthy fruit bearers.

Dead wood is useless, but unpruned branches are not as useful as they should be. As Ronald Dunn says, 'You and I can bear more fruit than we are bearing. We have not reached our potential, and the Vinedresser intends that we should.'[3] Prayer helps us to reach our potential. It reveals God's character and changes ours. Our capacity to love increases, deepens and broadens. Through compassion we affirm others and draw them into communion with Christ. 'We are branches of one vine, members of one body,' says Sergius Bulgakev. 'The life of each enlarges itself infinitely into the life of others. Each one lives the life of all.'[4] Through abiding prayer, we rest in our redeemer, confident that he will use us in redeeming others. Abiding life is an abundant life.

It is our privilege to have not only Jesus' teaching about how to pray, but a record of some of his own prayers. After speaking about upcoming sorrows, Jesus looks up to heaven and prays for all his disciples, including us. Throughout this prayer he repeatedly addresses God as 'Father', describing him as holy and good. He is resolute, even in prayer, that we should have a fitting inner picture of God. 'I have shown them what you are like,' he prays (John 17:6). Our beliefs about God affect our approach and expectations. In his prayers, as in his life, Jesus reveals a compassionate Father who eagerly answers the door and our prayers when we knock, ask and seek. 'As bad as you are,' Jesus says, 'you still know how to give good gifts to your children. But your heavenly Father is even more ready to give good things to people who ask' (Matthew 7:7–11).

Just before the crucifixion, Jesus promised six times to do whatever we asked in his name. Perhaps we don't ask God because we don't believe what God says. Distrust undermines communion. 'If you have faith when you pray,' says Jesus, 'you will be given whatever you ask for' (Matthew 21:22). An abiding life is a believing life.

Jesus' prayer *for* us also reveals his desire for unity *among* us. Praying for his current followers and all those still to come, Jesus says, 'I want them to be one with each other… I also want them to be one with us' (John 17:21). The Holy Spirit brings us to faith and keeps us there. Union with Christ occurs when we come *to* faith, communion as we deepen *in* faith through abiding. The Spirit dwells in each of us and places us all into a single body. 'The church is never a place, always a people,' says John Havlik. 'Never a fold, always a flock; never a sacred building, always a believing assembly. The church is you who pray.'[5] Abiding life is a united life.

A story is told of a child who brought a globe to bed instead of a teddy. When questioned he said, 'If God so loves the world, then I so love the world.' Prayer is vertical in its communication but horizontal in its inclusion. Private prayer affirms that we aren't alone in the universe, public prayer that we aren't alone in God's family. There are times to pray alone and times to pray together. In Jesus' pattern for prayer we address *our* Father, give *our* honour, affirm *our* obedience, request *our* bread, confess *our* sins, *our* debts, *our* lack of forgiveness and *our* desire for protection. We trust in God's nature to meet *our* need. We adopt the golden rule of prayer: pray for others as you would have others pray for you. 'As the day comes,' says Matthew Henry, 'we must pray to our heavenly Father and reckon we could as well go a day without food, as prayer.'[6]

Many of us internalize and spiritualize the Lord's pattern for prayer. We are not physically hungry and are far removed from those who are. We ask for daily bread, but really seek spiritual stamina. We give God honour, but are really commending our own religious activity. We pray for God's kingdom to come, but hope that it's similar to the comfy castle we already possess. The Lord's pattern for prayer doesn't express the same churning expectation for us as it does for those living in abject physical poverty. For these, learning to pray from Jesus includes deep-rooted daily dependence on God for everything, including survival. 'They pray for real food but are also hungry for justice,' says Janet Morley. 'They long for freedom from the intolerable burdens of international debt, and look to that biblical time of jubilee when debts are remitted and justice prevails. And they look, in these times and on this earth, for a kingdom and a power that are God's alone, and not the ones they live under.'[7]

Indeed, Jesus' pattern for prayer reflects God's deep compassion for people. Its communal focus expresses our union with God and others as well as our desire for communion. We must reclaim Jesus' pattern for prayer from the vain repetition so discouraged in his giving of it. The contrast between affluent comfort and abject deprivation is stark but the two are closely connected in today's global economy. The dignity of all human beings is diminished by the destitution of any one. The Lord's pattern for prayer commits us before God to collective responsibility for one another in a world that is unjustly weighted against those who are poor. We must find the connections between us and pray together for physical and spiritual transformation in ourselves and in the world. We are encouraged to corporate ownership of sin as well as personal confession. Jesus concludes his pattern for prayer with a further admonishment to forgive.[8] We can't be 'in Christ' without forgiveness—a forgiveness overflowing from God's abundance in having forgiven us.[9] An abiding life is a forgiven and forgiving life.

Thomas Carlyle says, 'Prayer is and remains always a native and deep impulse of the soul.'[10] Abiding prayer is unceasing prayer. It is the language of God's compassion, the pulse of an abiding life. It flows as freely as sap between vine and branch or as blood pumping through the chambers of a single heart. Prayer is the search for the whole of God with the whole of the soul, one heart opening itself to another.[11] Saint Anthony of Padua once said, 'He prays best who does not know that he is praying.'[12] It is the life that prays, not the lips—a surrendered life.

Two small boys saw their grandmother pacing up and down, reading her prayer book. One boy said to the other, 'What's Grandma doing?' The other replied, 'She's swotting for her finals.' Someone once said, 'Prayer should be our first resource, never be our last resort.' It fits us for God's presence, enables us in God's will and brings sensitivity to God's word. But most of all, says Mother Teresa, 'prayer enlarges the heart, until it is capable of containing God's gift of himself.'[13] This is abiding life.

*

Joining hands to reach out

In the spring of 2002, *Compassion* spearheaded the meeting of 219 representatives from 139 Christian ministry organizations across the Philippines. The country's 1,000 inhabited islands are diverse and yet many share the same challenges and concerns in their fight against child poverty. The organizations took time to listen to the needs and concerns prevalent in each of their communities and make plans to reduce the negative experiences of children there. The churches can find strength by combining their experiences and expertise to confront this challenge.

The accountability and support that each of the organizations offers to the others makes it much easier for the regions to set twelve-month goals toward which they can work. In an area where child abuse is of greatest concern, project workers have begun parent training and workshops to deal with the frequent causes of abuse. Workers are also increasing awareness in the local community through billboard advertising and distributing information throughout the community.[14]

✶

Group helps

Worship

Ask and it shall be given (SF1 20)
Be still and know that I am God (SF1 37)
Father, make us one (SF1 95)
Great is the darkness (SF2 742)
Here I am, waiting (SF3 1271)

Word

Psalm 100
John 15

Prayer

- Thank God for the great relationships that are being developed between churches and their local communities.
- Ask that there will be more opportunities for ministries to share their experiences and expertise with each other.
- Pray that churches will be committed to listening to the needs of their communities.

Fellowship

Arrange a fruit-themed outing—go to an orchard and pick fruit together, or visit a garden centre or coffee shop with fruit-based desserts on the menu—or eat fruit pies together as a group.

Read and reflect on John 15. How is prayer an expression of abiding life both in Christ and in each other? How can we be healthier fruit bearers in prayer for those children growing up in poverty and hunger? Spend some time praying specifically for those who are in greatest global need and those who are working among them.

Witness

How we pray reveals much about the gospel we believe. Contact the Viva Network for information on how your group can get involved in the Worldwide Day of Prayer for Children at Risk. It is held annually on the first Saturday in June. Contact the Viva Network for details: wwdp@viva.org

For personal reflection

Prayer enlarges the heart. Whom do you need to include in God's compassion? Draw a big heart in your journal and write a prayer that begins, 'O God, enlarge my heart…'.

NOTES

1 P. Kreeft, *Making Sense out of Suffering*, Servant Books, p. 129.
2 A.P. Castle, *Quotes and Anecdotes: An Anthology for Preachers and Teachers*, Kevin Mayhew, p. 217.
3 R. Dunn, *Don't Just Stand There… Pray Something!*, Alpha, p. 134.
4 Castle, *Quotes and Anecdotes*, p 130.

5   C. Calver, et al., *'Dancing In the Dark' Seminar Notes*, Spring Harvest, Lynx Communications, p. 28.
6   M. Henry, *Concise Commentary on the Whole Bible*, Moody Press, p. 682.
7   J. Morley, *Bread of Tomorrow: Praying with the World's Poor*, SPCK, p. 2.
8   Matthew 6:14–15.
9   1 Timothy 2:8; 1 John 1:9.
10 T. Castle, *A Treasury of Christian Wisdom*, Hodder and Stoughton, p. 186.
11 Jeremiah 29:12–14.
12 Castle, *Quotes and Anecdotes*, p. 372.
13 Castle, *A Treasury*, p. 188.
14 *Compassion* website, November 2002.

SECTION TWO

Compassionate prayer: abiding in solidarity

'There are no atheists on the battlefield.'

Soldiers use this expression to explain how, in the worst of times, we rely on the best in God. We pray instinctively. Whatever our beliefs, whomever we worship, wherever we are, it's natural to seek solidarity, to cry out when in danger, doubt or despair and hope that someone is listening. Those who abide in Christ can be sure.

As we have seen, God's compassion and solidarity are so great that he didn't reach down but came down. The Son of God became the son of man. Jesus knew the joys and heartaches common to us all. On the cross he knew a depth of sin unique to only one.[1] 'There is no mystery in heaven or earth so great as this,' says Samuel Zwemer, 'a suffering Deity; an almighty Saviour nailed to a cross.'[2] Jesus Christ alone is able to mediate between God and us.[3]

Although Jesus faced specific and exceptional temptations in the wilderness, it is safe to assume that he faced many others that are not recorded for us in scripture. In either case, the author of Hebrews makes it absolutely clear that Jesus was tempted in exactly the same way that we are. His Godhood was not a get-out clause. Jesus could have fallen but did not. This truth is a solid foundation for both his solidarity with us and our salvation. 'Jesus understands every weakness of ours, because he was tempted [as] we are,' says the writer to the Hebrews. 'But he did not sin! So whenever we are in need, we should come bravely before the throne of our merciful God. There we will be treated with undeserved kindness, and we will find help' (Hebrews 4:15–16).

Prayer is proof that God's compassion didn't end on the cross.

During the times when we are most inclined to stop praying, we should start. Whether we are detoured, discouraged or doubtful, faithless or fearful, we can pray. 'Don't worry about anything,' Paul writes from prison, 'but pray about everything' (Philippians 4:6). When we offer prayer with thankfulness, God blesses us with a peace that is beyond comprehension—a peace that changes our perceptions.

Jesus modelled the prayerful peace that comes from abiding. When prayer did not change his circumstances, it gave him the strength to bear up under them and the vision to see beyond them. Jesus prayed and fasted for 40 days before Satan unleashed his fiercest assault on Jesus' integrity. He was prepared but Satan was still no pushover. Jesus overcame but was absolutely exhausted in the overcoming. 'The reason men fail in battle is because they wait until the hour of battle,' says R.A. Torrey. 'Anticipate your battles; fight them on your knees before temptation comes.'[4]

Jesus knew from experience, like we do, that Satan's attacks are always personal and personalized. He knows exactly what is likely to entice us. How much more wonderful to know, then, that through Christ we abide in the triune God and he in us. Satan may know us personally, but God knows us intimately—a fact that turns even failure into an opportunity for intimacy. 'Christ took our sins and the sins of the whole world as well as the Father's wrath on his shoulders,' says Martin Luther. 'He has drowned them both in himself so that we are thereby reconciled to God and become completely righteous.'[5] It should not surprise us that the word 'atonement', as ably described here, includes the words 'at' and 'one'. Through the atonement we are able to abide at one with God unhindered—through prayer. John writes, 'If we confess our sins to God, he can always be trusted to forgive us and take our sins away' (1 John 1:9). Whatever concerns us concerns God. Jesus took more than human memories with him into heaven; he took his humanity.[6] Jesus' scars confirm a solidarity as deep as his compassion.

A woman watched a little girl praying silently in church. Afterwards the woman asked her what she had been praying for. 'Oh, I wasn't asking for anything,' she replied. 'I was just loving Jesus.'[7] Through Christ we gain unrestricted access to the triune God and can approach him from love, not fear. Abiding in Christ gives us confidence that our prayers will be heard. The Holy Spirit abiding in us gives us confidence that we can pray what we mean. The Spirit knows us intimately. He gave us life and is alive in each of us. As has been said, through this incredible act of solidarity, we are no longer our own and we are no longer on our own.[8] In compassion the Holy Spirit prays *for* us from *within* us. 'In certain ways we are weak, but the Spirit is here to help us,' explains Paul. 'When we don't know what to pray for, the Spirit prays for us in ways that cannot be put into words. All our thoughts are known to God. He can understand what is in the mind of the Spirit, as the Spirit prays for God's people' (Romans 8:26–27). Prayer transcends human speech and is no less effective for our faltering words. 'Groanings which cannot be uttered,' says Charles Spurgeon, 'are often prayers which cannot be refused.'[9]

We are intimately known, deeply loved and on God's prayer list. There is no need for fear! Jesus, who prayed for us on earth, continues to pray for us in heaven. 'If God is on our side, can anyone be against us?' asks Paul. 'If God says his chosen ones are acceptable to him, can anyone bring charges against them? Or can anyone condemn them? No indeed! Christ died and was raised to life, and now he is at God's right side, speaking to him for us' (Romans 8:31, 33–34).

What an encouragement to pray! The Father hears us because the Son became one of us and the Spirit lives in us. And as we are praying for others, Jesus and the Holy Spirit are praying for them too. Compassionate prayer comes from abiding love. 'Christ encourages you, and his love comforts you,' says Paul. 'God's Spirit unites you, and you are concerned for others' (Philippians 2:1). Praying for others affirms the concern and solidarity encouraged in us by Christ. Compassion seeks for others in prayer what we seek for ourselves. Make no mistake, those for whom we pray are deeply affected by the power of our presence with them in prayer, and so are we. Abiding prayer increases intimacy. Prevailing prayer increases solidarity. When we abide with others in compassionate prayer, we make them part of ourselves—so much so that we are actually praying with them as well as for them.

Compassion costs. To suffer with others in prayer is more than a mental exercise. 'Comfort draws from the deep,' says Samuel Chadwick. 'It takes heart to comfort.'[10] Praying with those who are most vulnerable will mean being vulnerable ourselves. The Holy Spirit will reveal much of our own selves in the process of prayer, much that we will not like. We will need to repent of our own involvement in the suffering and injustice done to those for whom we pray. We will need to change. If justice, mercy and humble obedience are first among our concerns in prayer, they will also be first on our agenda for action. To pray with compassionate solidarity is to have the sincerest desire for the highest interest of others, the utmost confidence in God's promise and ability to meet the need and the readiness to co-operate with God in the outcome.

In the parable of the unjust judge, a widow—probably without anyone to speak on her behalf—pesters the only one on whom she can depend to deliver justice, until he reluctantly does it.[11] The judge neither fears God nor respects people, least of all the widow standing before him. Nonetheless he does, in the end, uphold the widow's rights.

There are two layers in this lesson on prayerful living. The first is a general encouragement for all who pray, and is stated by Jesus in the text. 'Won't God protect his chosen ones who pray to him day and night?' asks Jesus. 'Won't he be concerned for them? He will hurry and help them' (Luke 18:7–8). The second lesson is more specific. It is inferred in the text but often missed. Here a widow, vulnerable and voiceless, doggedly challenges the abuse of power over her. Her special rights for provision and protection (along with those orphaned, alien or poor) are a fact acknowledged both in Jewish law and by scriptural mandate. She demands deliverance. 'She calls the judge to be the judge that he is meant to be,' says

Leith Fisher, 'and administer the Law in the interest of justice.'[12] Through this parable, Jesus is calling us to persevere in achieving earthly justice for those in greatest need and to pray persistently for the same. We bring those who are wounded in body, mind and spirit; those who are abused, oppressed, tortured, hungry and displaced; those whose inner beauty is hidden by indignity. We bring others and we bring ourselves to the throne of grace.

When those who suffer have nothing left but a cry, God hears. He is not indifferent to those who plead for deliverance. 'Do not ill-treat widows or orphans,' says God. 'If you do, they will beg for my help, and I will come to their rescue. In fact, I will get so angry that I will kill your men and make widows of their wives and orphans of their children' (Exodus 22:22–23). Again God's harshest words and judgment are reserved for those who further wound the wounded. God is not like the corrupt judge and will swiftly act on behalf of those who are determined in prayer.

Prayer is a dynamic of abiding life, not a doctrine of religious life. In Christ, God came so near to us that John said, 'Our ears have heard, our own eyes have seen, and our hands touched this Word. The one who gives life appeared! We saw it happen, and we are witnesses' (1 John 1:1–2). In Christ, God was visible, accessible, approachable and knowable. In Christ, God still is. The battle in intercession is won or lost depending on how far we are willing to go in our solidarity, how much we are willing to sacrifice and for how long. As someone once said, 'The great mystery is not unanswered prayer, it's unfinished prayer.' What prayer remains unfinished in your life? Compassionate prayer is not a single act of charity but a life of patient solidarity.

✶

Price of a girl

The only worth that many girls can command is through their ability to generate an income for their family. Without an education, the only way many can survive is by selling themselves. The abuse of these children is often justified under the shadow of superstition and myth. Some cultures believe that sex with a girl will protect them from HIV and AIDS, or even bring prosperity and fortune. In actual fact, all it does is to breed disease and hopelessness.

Tittaya, a former *Compassion*-sponsored child, has a burden to reach out to the girls who work in the notorious Pat Pong district of Bangkok, many of whom have become addicted to drugs and alcohol in an attempt to dull the pain of their lives.

Tittaya knows that the plight of these girls could so easily have been her own had she not been offered the chance of an education and the opportunity to learn her own self-worth. With this burden she braves the wrath of those who run the brothels, by befriending the girls and offering them an alternative future with vocational training.[13] Tittaya is a living example of God's love in action.

✶

Group helps

Worship

Arise, my soul, arise (SF1 16)
For the healing of the nations (SF3 1235)
How I love you (SF1 174)
Kyrie eleison (SF3 1409)
Praise to Christ, the Lord incarnate (SF3 1503)

Word

Exodus 22:21–25
Luke 18:1–8

Prayer

- Pray that girls involved in the sex trade will be seen as victims and not criminals.
- Pray that girls who want to leave the sex trade can be provided with alternative forms of employment and will not be stigmatized by their past.
- Pray for the safety of girls who have left the sex trade, that they will have protection from their old employers.

Fellowship

Read John 17. God is compassionate and we are on God's prayer list.

- What is God praying for us as individuals?
- What is he praying for us as we meet together as a community?
- How does knowing that God is praying for us change the way we are likely to pray?

Discuss this as a group and pray for one another.

Witness

Read Exodus 22:21–25 and Luke 18:1–8. God promises to hear those who are orphaned or ill-treated, and to deliver justice. Discuss the following questions together:

- Who are the 'orphans' or 'ill-treated' in your area?
- What do you think they are praying for?

- Are you giving God any reason to be angry on their behalf? If so, how?
- How are you co-operating with God to answer the prayers of those in greatest need, locally and globally?

For personal reflection

Read Romans 8:26–34 and compare with Hebrews 4:14–16. What are you finding difficult to express in prayer? What is Jesus praying for you? How is the Holy Spirit helping you pray? Write a prayer for yourself as if Jesus and the Holy Spirit are praying to the Father on your behalf.

If you prefer, you may explore these questions with a close and trusted friend.

NOTES

1. 2 Corinthians 5:21.
2. www.christianquotes.com.
3. 1 Timothy 2:5–6.
4. www.christianquotes.org.
5. www.christianquotes.org.
6. Hebrews 2:14–18.
7. Source unknown.
8. 1 Corinthians 6:19–20.
9. www.christianquotes.com.
10. www.christianquotes.org.
11. Luke 18:1–8.
12. L. Fisher, *The Widening Road: From Bethlehem to Emmaus*, Scottish Christian Press, p. 182.
13. Original source: *Compassion International It Works* trip.

SECTION THREE

Compassionate prayer: abiding in humble servanthood

Carl Jung once said, 'It is no easy matter to live a life that is modelled on Christ's, but it is unspeakably harder to live one's own life as truly as Christ lived his.'[1]

Abiding prayer is quality prayer. Jesus loved to pray, needed to pray and prayed a lot. However, it is the quality of his praying, not the quantity of his prayers that teach us most about abiding. Jesus prayed to the Father in the Spirit at all times for everything. Every subject and kind of prayer, except confession of sin, flowed from his abiding—adoration, thanksgiving, petition, intercession and submission. He prayed in times of decision, crisis and joy. Jesus' life so pulsed with divine abiding that the disciples asked, 'Lord, teach us to pray' (Luke 11:1). His disciples had seen him perform miracles, teach, preach and heal, but it was the power of abiding presence they sought.

Victor Hugo once said, 'There are moments when, whatever be the attitude of the body, the soul is on its knees.'[2] Humility was the essence of Jesus' life and the fragrance of his prayers. As we have seen, Jesus thought so much of the position of others that he surrendered his own to serve them. It is impossible to abide in Christ with pride in ourselves. As Thomas Watson says, 'There are none so empty of grace as those that think they are full.'[3]

In the parable of the Pharisee and the tax collector, Jesus contrasts the prayers of one who perceives himself as humble with one who truly is.[4] The Pharisee is indeed devoutly religious, a well-respected insider, and confirms this in his prayer. He fasts beyond the law's demands, tithes and is not greedy, dishonest or adulterous 'like other people' and, in particular, 'that tax collector over there'. The tax collector, on the other hand, is a much-despised outsider, employed in a system widely regarded to be full of cheats and swindlers. The tax collector's prayer is as heartfelt as it is humble. He stands off at a distance, so full of sorrow over his actions that he pounds his chest as he prays, 'God, have pity on me! I am such a sinner' (Luke 18:13). Needless to say, it was the tax collector and not the Pharisee who pleased God that day.

Comparing ourselves against others is irrelevant to God. As Leith Fisher says, 'There is no hierarchy of piety.'[5] We stand alone before God when we pray, measured only against his holiness, justified only by his love. God doesn't make us humble; we humble ourselves in response to his holiness and compassion. We are not like the hypocrite who prayed from his piety. Rather we are like the tax collector who dared not raise his eyes to heaven but whose heart earnestly sought God, or the son who repented, returned to the father and was restored.

God suffers with us out of supreme love. He continues to serve us, Father, Son and Holy Spirit. What other response can we make? We thankfully renounce ourselves, return his love, submit to his will and serve him. 'God insists that we ask, not because he needs to know our situation,' says Catherine Marshall, 'but because we need the spiritual discipline of asking.'[6] Abiding prayer is a reminder of our need and a reassurance of his presence. 'Be humble in the presence of God's mighty power, and he will honour you when the time comes,' says Peter. 'God cares for you, so turn all your worries over to him' (1 Peter 5:6–7).

Abiding prayer is more about space to pray than a place to pray; more about being than doing, but never about not doing. The compassion that flowed from Christ in healing flowed first from abiding prayer and floods his prayers even now. Christ still washes our feet, serves our interests, esteems our worth, loves with empathy and bridges our divides in prayer. 'If you want to be great,' said Jesus, 'serve others' (Mark 10:43). We must not exclude prayer in this service. We are to be like Christ, who prayed for us from common humanity, and the Holy Spirit whose compassion spills out from within. We are never more like Jesus than when we are interceding. Love sees others as God sees them and compassion responds. In compassionate prayer we present the most pressing of needs to the person who can meet them—Jesus. He is bread to those who are hungry, water to those who thirst, balm to those who are sick. Jesus is life to those who are dying, brother to those who are lonely and the friend of those who sin.[7]

Prayer is not the last only thing we can do for others, but the first best thing—the purest form of unconditional love. We radiantly love God with heart, soul and mind, and others as ourselves, when we lay down our lives in prayer. In the parable of the friend at midnight, one friend asks another friend to give him bread for a third.[8] The hour is late, the request is inconvenient and the sleepy friend is reluctant. Yet the boldness of the approach and the persistence in asking yield more than a favourable result. The friend is not only offered the three loaves he has requested, but all that is needed. How much more will God—who never sleeps and always listens—answer the bold and persistent prayers offered up on behalf of those who are most in need. 'So I tell you to ask and you will receive,' says Jesus, 'search and you will find, knock and the door will be opened for you. Everyone who asks will receive, everyone who searches will find, and the door will be opened for everyone who knocks' (Luke 11:9–10).

'Some people think that God does not like to be troubled with our constant coming and asking,' says D.L. Moody. 'The way to trouble God is not to come at all!'[9] As we have already discovered, humble servanthood isn't thinking less of ourselves but more of Christ. We embrace the concerns of others so that their burdens rest on our hearts too. Like the persistent widow who wouldn't give up until justice was done, or the friend at midnight who boldly begged for bread, we pray for each other for as long as it takes. Jesus promised to be with us until the end. We are part of this promise for others in prayer.

COMPASSIONATE PRAYER: ABIDING IN HUMBLE SERVANTHOOD

Abiding in Christ makes compassionate prayer for others as involuntary as breathing, as selfless as Christ. 'Talking to men for God is a great thing,' says E.M. Bounds, 'but talking to God for men is greater still.'[10] Jesus' whole life was a prayer of compassionate intercession. He stood in the gap between a holy God and a sinful race to provide the very union he prayed that we would know. In humility, the Holy Spirit prays for us and draws us ever deeper into Christ. In servanthood, the Holy Spirit helps us to pray always in love. The Father hears us and answers. He knows our need and is committed to our well-being. 'Jesus Christ carries on intercession for us in heaven; the Holy Spirit carries on intercession for us on earth,' says Oswald Chambers, 'and we the saints have to carry on intercession for all men.'[11]

Prayer means that we never have to say, 'There's nothing I can do' when we hear the cry of afflicted children blaring from the media, screaming behind every statistic or confronting us on every street corner. As long as injustice prevails in the world, God will be looking for intercessors to do something about it—first of all through prayer. Have we ever truly grasped that God will seldom do without prayer what he promises to do through prayer? Billy Sunday says, 'If we are strangers to prayer we are strangers to power.'[12] There are no boundaries to prayer within God's will. God desires justice for every ill-treated child, provision for every child in poverty and inclusion in his kingdom for all children everywhere. We know God's will and it is ours to pray. Imagine what could be achieved just by asking!

Through intercessory prayer we can touch people we don't know in places we've never been. We can affirm God's compassion and know that the Son and the Spirit are weighting our prayers. 'Do something, Lord God, and use your powerful arm to help those in need,' prays the psalmist. 'You see the trouble and the distress, and you will do something. The poor can count on you, and so can orphans... You defend orphans and everyone else in need, so that no one on earth can terrify others again' (Psalm 10:12, 14, 18). Ronald Dunn says, 'Earth waits for heaven to move, but heaven waits for earth to ask.'[13] What will we ask God for today?

Jesus consistently showed God's concern for those who are hurting. 'If you are tired from carrying heavy burdens,' says Jesus, 'come to me and I will give you rest. Take the yoke I give you. Put it on your shoulders and learn from me. I am gentle and humble, and you will find rest' (Matthew 11:28–29). Notice here that Jesus didn't promise immediate release from a burdened life, but rest in the midst of burden. Here he is both our master and our servant. He doesn't remove the yoke from his shoulders and hand it on to us, as most masters would. Instead Jesus invites us to be equally yoked to him so that our burdens rest on him too. We are to do likewise. In learning to bear our burdens patiently alongside Christ, we are able to suffer with and humbly serve those who, in any way, have need. We obey Christ when we bear one another's burdens—especially in prayer.

*

The restavek children

Restavek children are prevalent in cities across Haiti. The word *restavek* literally means 'stay with'. They are children who have been sent away by their families to stay with more prosperous households in the city. Sadly, the new life that parents hope their children will experience in the city is rarely realized. Many children find themselves in an even worse situation of domestic slavery.

Families who have taken in the restavek children see them as cheap servants and are unlikely to allow them to attend school or even a *Compassion* centre. However, there are a few *Compassion*-assisted projects in Port-au-Prince (Haiti's capital city) that are directly targeting this group of vulnerable children. The projects offer a more flexible timetable to fit in with the children's lifestyles and also to encourage the guardians to allow the children out for at least part of the day.

An important element of *Compassion*'s work with these children is building up their self-esteem and sense of self-worth. Where children are at the bottom of the social ladder, they are taught of their true worth in Christ and consequently a number have even become Christians. Through the interaction of project staff with the children's carers, a number of the families have also come to know Christ. These encouraging signs are evidence that, however impossible a situation may appear, there is a way to bring hope to those in need and miraculous changes can take place.

✷

Group helps

Worship

As water to the thirsty (SF2 659)
Love beyond measure (SF1 352)
Lord, I come to you (SF2 895)
To be in your presence (SF2 1067)
You have lifted up the humble (SF2 1137)

Word

Psalm 10
Luke 18:9–14

Prayer

- Pray that God will speak into the hearts of those who see children as cheap labour and show them how unique and precious children are.
- Pray that child slavery will be brought to the attention of authorities who will commit to eradicating it.
- Pray that more *Compassion* projects will be able to directly reach the restavek children in Haiti.

Fellowship

Write the following sentence on a piece of paper. 'God, I thank you that I am not like… or even…' Fill in the blanks with the names of people you know. Read Luke 18:9–14 and discuss the following questions together:

- How did you feel about doing this exercise?
- Where and when do you share the attitude of the Pharisee even on a subconscious level?
- Is there anything you need to alter in your prayer life as a result of Jesus' teaching in this parable?

Ask God to help you set small achievable goals in the direction of change.

Witness

Demonstrate God's compassion by setting aside a special time of group prayer. Approach non-Christian friends, acquaintances, family and neighbours and ask them what they might like prayer for. Perhaps you could even offer to pray with them. Bring those requests that are appropriate for group prayer to the group and pray for more personal requests on your own.

For personal reflection

Read Luke 18:9–14. Think of yourself in a church building and imagine you are one of the characters in the scene—Jesus, Pharisee or tax collector. Explore these questions in your journal:

- What is your physical posture?
- Where are you in the church?
- Who can see you?

- What are you feeling?
- Where are the other characters in relation to you and how are they responding to you as you pray?

If you would prefer, explore these issues with a close and trusted friend.

NOTES

1 Source unknown.
2 A.P. Castle, *Quotes and Anecdotes: an Anthology for Preachers and Teachers*, Kevin Mayhew, p. 373.
3 www.christianquotes.org.
4 Luke 18:9–14.
5 L. Fisher, *The Widening Road: from Bethlehem to Emmaus*, Scottish Christian Press, p.183.
6 T. Castle, *A Treasury of Christian Wisdom*, Hodder & Stoughton, p. 187.
7 Adapted from R. Dunn, *Don't Just Stand There… Pray Something!*, Alpha, p. 81.
8 Luke 11:5–8.
9 www.christianquotes.org.
10 www.christianquotes.org.
11 www.christianquotes.org
12 www.christianquotes.org.
13 Dunn, *Don't Just Stand There*, p. 49.

SECTION FOUR

Compassionate prayer:
abiding in obedient response

Someone once said, 'We are sometimes in the dark as proof that he is light.'[1]

'Jesus walked on a little way before he knelt down and prayed, "Father, if you will, please don't make me suffer by making me drink from this cup. But do what you want, and not what I want." Then an angel from heaven came to help him. Jesus was in great pain and prayed so sincerely that his sweat fell to the ground like drops of blood. Jesus got up from praying and went to his disciples. They were asleep and worn out from being so sad. He said to them, "Why are you asleep? Wake up and pray that you won't be tested"' (Luke 22:41–46). Abiding prayer is obedient prayer.

True obedience (listening) is not an act of unquestioning compliance but communal consensus, an act of intimate trust and ultimate devotion. Those who obey and the one who commands are so intimately entwined that agreement between them is natural. Jesus' prayers reveal the loving and attentive listening so evident among the Tri-unity. He surrendered his own will and did only what the Father told him in the power of the Spirit.[2] This inner abiding unveiled itself in outer obedience even in the agonized questioning of Gethsemane.

The coming cross was not a surprise to Christ; it was his purpose. He had even tried to prepare his disciples for what was to come—both death and resurrection. 'The nation's leaders, the chief priests and the teachers of the Law of Moses will make the Son of Man suffer terribly,' said Jesus. 'He will be rejected and killed, but three days later he will rise to life' (Mark 8:31). The disciples wavered in accepting this plan, especially Peter who flatly refused. However, we have never sensed a shade of doubt in Jesus' devotion to the Father or his mission. In fact, his commitment to the cross is crystal clear in his rebuke to Peter: 'Satan, get away from me! You are thinking like everyone else and not like God' (Mark 8:33).

Obedience was both the focus of Jesus' zeal and the fulfilment of his appetite.[3] In Gethsemane, however, Jesus begs that the cup he was so willing to receive might be rescinded. Although he recommits himself to God's will three times in the night, he doesn't obey unquestioningly.[4] Through the process of abiding prayer, we witness Jesus' progression from compliance to consensus. Jesus stops asking for the cup to pass. Instead he tenderly prays, 'My Father, if there is no other way, and I must suffer, I will still do what you want' (Matthew 26:42). It is vital to understand that Jesus confronts more than human suffering in Gethsemane. He must face his destiny and fight the forces of darkness. In the wilderness, Satan failed to tempt Jesus into sin. Here, in Gethsemane, Satan tries to frighten Jesus out of obedience, for the Son of God will become sin itself to free us from its power and defeat Satan for ever. Jesus resorted to scripture in the desert. In the garden he resorts to prayer.

Prayer itself is an obedient response to God. We may not always understand the answers or the seeming lack of them, but God commands us to pray and promises to respond. It was Jesus who said, 'Everyone who asks will receive' (Matthew 7:8). It was Jesus who taught us to pray, 'Come and set up your kingdom so that everyone on earth will obey you, as you are obeyed in heaven' (Matthew 6:10). It was Jesus who taught us to intercede for others by interceding for us himself: 'I am not praying just for these followers. I am also praying for everyone else who will have faith because of what my followers will say about me' (John 17:20). The span of this prayer is incredible! Every time someone turns to him, the prayer of Jesus is answered again.

Prayer is not an alibi for doing nothing. It is a powerful response in itself and decisive in the conflict between the power of God and the power of evil. Our desperation to help must be shaped by our desire to hear. Through prayer we act rather than react. Prayer is part of our calling to follow Christ in his self-denial. Like Christ, we pay when we pray—sleepless tossing, secret tears and the sacrifice of whatever is necessary to respond obediently. 'As death works in us,' says Ronald Dunn, 'life works in those for whom we pray.'[5] We respond where compassion is most needed and place ourselves in the process of God's promise to answer. Prayer would be worthless if it didn't result in the care of those who are vulnerable.

Like Christ, we too must battle with darkness and doubt. Paul exhorts us to remember this when he commends us to be mighty in the Lord's strength and put on the whole armour of God—every piece of it.[6] This is the only way we can defend ourselves and be found standing firm when the battle is over. 'We are not fighting against humans,' says Paul. 'We are fighting against forces and authorities and against rulers of darkness and powers in the spiritual world' (Ephesians 6:12). Prayer is not to be found among the armour listed by Paul. Instead it is set apart as the power that makes each piece of the armour effective. 'Never stop praying, especially for others,' says Paul. 'Always pray by the power of the Spirit. Stay alert and keep praying for God's people' (Ephesians 6:18).

The power behind the rampant abuse of our children is evil. Make no mistake, we are in the thick of spiritual warfare. Our world is in revolt against its creator and the battle is real. The shredded heart of every wounded child will attest to it. The battle is a spiritual one and so must our armour be—especially supported and unified in prayer. It is not enough to give every child a good home, good food and a good education. It is not enough to burn every pornographic image and put every paedophile behind bars. It is not enough to dismantle crooked businesses and call corrupt employers to justice through the law. It is not enough to release desperate countries and destitute families from their debt. It is not enough to end every war and dismantle every weapon. It is not enough to send every Christian to every part of the globe to reach every child. It is not enough. We may bring hope and help, love and life, freedom and faith, but these will never be enough without prayer—powerful, pleading, persevering, protecting and passionate prayer. Those who commit atrocities should quake at the prayers of God's people against evil deeds, for our prayers are heard by a righteous and just God.

John Henry Jowett says, 'God doesn't comfort us to make us comfortable, but to make us comforters.'[7] Jesus had every right to expect comfort from his friends. He had previously woken from sleep to help them in a storm, but they couldn't do the same. His enemies were awake while his friends slept. Yet even in suffering Jesus had compassion. He wanted his disciples to keep watch with him but Jesus also wanted his disciples to pray for themselves. He knew that they would distrust, disbelieve, deny and desert and that prayer would strengthen their armoury for battle. How different the Gospel accounts might have been had the disciples listened to the inner voice of the Spirit prompting them to stay awake and pray! We can't avoid suffering, but we can be sustained through it. Though our spirits be willing and our flesh weak, though our fallen bodies can't keep pace with our souls, we must not be exhausted by the sorrow that should set us praying.[8]

When others beg our support, we must stay awake to their need and trust our ultimate salvation to the one who never sleeps. 'Jesus begged God with loud crying and tears to save him. He truly worshipped God, and God listened to his prayers,' says the writer to the Hebrews. 'Jesus is God's own Son, but still he had to suffer before he could learn what it really means to obey God... Now he can save for ever all who obey him' (Hebrews 5:7–9).

Matthew Henry says, 'Christ's suffering began with the sorest of all, those in his soul.'[9] In Gethsemane we learn that consensus with God is sometimes reached through the bitterest of agonies. Through prayer we, like Jesus, pursue God's will even when it brings suffering and persecution to ourselves. The inevitability of suffering makes suffering no less painful. However, as Sammy Tippit says, 'We can face the gates of hell if we have been before the throne of grace.'[10]

Jesus rose calmly from conflict to face Calvary. Through abiding prayer we can rise from our Gethsemanes too. Not only this, but we can help others rise also. What Gethsemane are we facing today? How will we rise? How will we help others rise?

✷

Spreading the gospel

A group of former *Compassion*-sponsored children in India are spearheading evangelism in some of East Kerala's most remote tribal groups. These young men spend their weekends preaching and praying with the local people and introducing them to Christ.

Western missionaries have frequently been criticized for bringing westernization rather than addressing the specific needs of a community. However, by drawing on their personal experience and local knowledge, these young men can share the gospel in a culturally appropriate manner.

For this same reason, *Compassion* is working with local churches across the world, equipping them to reach out to their communities. An increasing number of projects are being established with remote tribal groups and indigenous churches that have little contact or support from elsewhere.

In 2003 alone, over 70,000 children gave their lives to Christ through the work of *Compassion*.[11] These children then form their own chain of influence, introducing their parents and families to the Lord.

✷

Group helps

Worship

Father, hear the prayer we offer (SF3 1229)
For this purpose (SF1 110)
Have thine own way, Lord (SF1 153)
Here I am (SF1 161)
With a prayer (SF3 1627)

Word

Matthew 26:36–45
Ephesians 6:10–19

Prayer

- Ask that God will continue to build up dynamic young people to spread the Gospel through their own communities.
- Thank God for the presence of the local church and their commitment to evangelism.
- Ask that we will become enthused with the same vision that the local churches in the developing world have.

Fellowship

Arrange an outing to a country park or some other place where people can sit or wander quietly through natural surroundings. Have each member of the group spend time alone with God, contemplating Matthew 26:36–45. Ask them to identify a time when they felt their own private Gethsemane. Are they facing a Gethsemane moment now? Come together, stand in a circle and each pray for the person on your left.

Witness

Organize a prayer walk around your community. Read Ephesians 6:10–19 and pray together at key locations—schools, churches, libraries, police station, youth hangouts, play parks, banks, supermarkets and so on. Ask God to reveal the needs of your community to you as you pray. Pray for all that is going on (or not going on that should be) and that God would both bless and stir your community for him.

For personal reflection

Find a quiet garden where you can reflect on Matthew 26:36–45 and the following verse from *Amid the Ruins*.

- What is God asking you to be compassionate about?
- How is God calling you to respond?
- What cup do you wish would pass from you?
- To whom is God asking you to remain alert in prayer?
- How will prayer strengthen you to stand fast?
- How does prayer help us to rise from our moments of ruin and broken dreams?

Write your thoughts in your journal or share them with a close and trusted friend.

> *Heavy heart, Gethsemane*
> *'Father take this cup from me!'*
> *Heavy eyes fall fast asleep*
> *Cannot watch nor prayerful keep*
> *A single hour, the hour has come*
> *Son betrayed, disciples run*
> *Nothing is as nothing seems*
> *Nothing now but broken dreams*

COMPASSIONATE PRAYER: ABIDING IN OBEDIENT RESPONSE

Amid the ruins they whisper
'the end of the world will be like this.'
© RENITA BOYLE

NOTES

1 Source unknown.
2 John 5:30.
3 John 2:17; 4:34.
4 Matthew 26:36–45.
5 R. Dunn, *Don't Just Stand There… Pray Something!*, Alpha, p. 85.
6 Ephesians 6:14–17.
7 T. Castle, *A Treasury of Christian Wisdom*, Hodder & Stoughton, p. 42.
8 Mark 14:32–42.
9 M. Henry, *Concise Commentary on the Whole Bible*, Moody Press, p. 737.
10 S. Tippit, *The Prayer Factor*, Scripture Press, p. 32.
11 Dan Brewster, 'A Challenge for our Future', *Compassion International* article.

SECTION FIVE

Compassionate prayer:
abiding in hopeful expectancy

Matthew Henry once said, 'When our prayers make long voyages, they come back with richer cargoes.'[1]

Abiding prayer is hopeful prayer. 'Stay joined to me and let my teachings become part of you,' said Jesus. 'Then you can pray for whatever you want and your prayer will be answered... Then my Father will give you whatever you ask for in my name' (John 15:7, 16).

It is hard to hope when we are suffering, to pray with confidence and expect that God will hear and answer our prayers. We are often as mystified by misery as Job who, though truly righteous, lost everything of value to him with God's permission. Even so, God promises to answer and in our favour—if we are prepared to abide. How hollow this assurance must have felt to those who were heavy-hearted at the foot of the cross, but how glorious when, out of apparent defeat and an empty tomb, Jesus delivered victory in all things, including prayer.

Andrew Murray says, 'The Spirit's breathing, the Son's intercession, the Father's will—these three become one in us.'[2] What a beautiful description of abiding prayer. The Father has made himself known to us through Christ, and in the name of Christ we make ourselves known to the Father. Praying in Jesus' name is to pray with Jesus' authority—to trust in his person and all that his name represents. In Christ we acknowledge the completed work of the triune God in a single saviour on our behalf. We pray as Jesus would if he were in our place, with him and the Holy Spirit as our prayer partners. Through Christ we approach the Father not with a form of speech, but in a frame of mind—an abiding love that seeks the best interests of God and others. Praying in the Spirit places us under his influence.

Jude reminds us to keep building on our faith, walking in step with God's love and relying on the compassion of Christ to bring us into eternal life—tasks that can be achieved only as the Spirit helps us to pray.[3] 'No sincere saint was sent away empty,' says Herbert Lockyear of prayer in Old Testament times.[4] However, partnership in the ultimate prayer triangle is a privilege afforded only to those who abide in Christ and in whom the Holy Spirit abides. What was only partial and, therefore, limited before Christ is now fully realized and unlimited through Christ. In fact, Jesus promised that we would do even greater things than he did. 'Ask me and I will do whatever you ask' (John 14:13). Jesus will accomplish through us everything that is done in his name by prayer in the same. Jesus delivers what he promises—abiding peace, the Paraclete, and answered prayer. There truly are no boundaries to prayer within God's will. As Richard Trench says, 'Prayer isn't overcoming God's reluctance, but laying hold of God's willingness.'[5]

A child once prayed, 'Dear God, thanks for the brother, but what I prayed for was a puppy.'[6] Sometimes our deepest yearnings, however longed for, seem to fall on deaf ears. The raging waters between human suffering and God's silence are no less turbulent today than they were for Job. Says Francis Bacon, 'The pencil of the Holy Ghost hath laboured more in describing the afflictions of Job than the felicities of Solomon.'[7] We know the purpose behind Job's pain, but Job doesn't. God commends him for his faithfulness but never tells him that Satan has been allowed to wreak havoc as proof of it. How often we too feel tested without knowing why. Job's prayers reflect resignation to suffering, pleas for pity, requests for righteousness, innocence against injustice, desire for death, questions about mortality, doubts about prayer and appeals for an answer. When God finally does respond, he answers every question with a few questions of his own. This process returns Job's focus to God's sovereignty and his own servanthood. 'I know that my Saviour lives,' says Job, 'and at the end he will stand on this earth. My flesh may be destroyed, yet from this body I will see God. Yes, I will see him for myself, and I long for that moment' (Job 19:25–27).

Despite all his suffering, Job expects God to rescue him—and God does. Everything Job lost is restored and redoubled. He is scarred by his experience of suffering, but through the process of prayer he gains what is most valuable—a greater vision of God himself. Job is not led to the answer but the Answerer, and so are we. 'God ends his silence and speaks his word,' says Peter Kreeft. 'Christ is the Word of God. The answer is someone, not something, not an idea but a person, not a word but the Word.'[8] The answer to our suffering is always the Sufferer—Jesus Christ. The comfort that is returned to us in prayer is always God's compassionate suffering with us. Although God does not respond to Job until near the end of his story, God has been present with Job throughout it. We are assured of a greater hope than earthly wealth through the kind of suffering that seeks God in prayer.

Jesus tried to prepare his disciples not only for his death but also for his resurrection. How human a response the disciples had. They are so caught up in Jesus' reference to suffering and death that they miss entirely his reference to risen life! 'God would never let this happen to you, Lord!' says Peter. But the Father did allow the suffering of his Son and, out of compassion, suffered with him.

What a long and excruciating pause those three days must have been, especially to those who missed Jesus' promise of risen life. God's pauses are purposeful. Sharing in the triumph of Christ always involves the experience of the cross. A knowing Peter now reminds us that one day for the Lord is as a thousand years. God isn't slow about keeping his promises but is patiently waiting for those who will turn from sin to do so.[9] Abiding in hope takes our focus off earthly time and restores us to a sense of heavenly time. We trust in the fullness of time for an answer to prayer, even though we may never see it ourselves or it may not be the answer we are anticipating. To pray with hope and expectancy is to trust that God is love and is still listening even in silence.

'A man may study because he is hungry for knowledge,' says Leonard Ravenhill. 'But he prays because his soul is hungry for God.'[10] Our primary purpose is to glorify God—to reveal the whole of him in the whole of us. To pray in Jesus' name is to acknowledge that we are also prepared to live in it—to continually abide. 'Whatever you say or do should be done in the name of the Lord Jesus,' says Paul, 'as you give thanks to God the Father because of him' (Colossians 3:17). God's answer will come at the earliest moment consistent with our truest well-being and his truest glory.

A child was once overheard praying the alphabet. When asked why, she said, 'I don't know what to pray for, so I say the alphabet and let God put everything together the way he wants.'[11] 'Now I am deeply troubled, and I don't know what to say,' said Jesus before Gethsemane. 'But I must not ask my Father to keep me from this time of suffering. In fact, I came into the world to suffer. So Father, bring glory to yourself' (John 12:27–28). It is worth asking, with Ronald Dunn, 'What will we pray when we don't know what to say? Father, reveal yourself.'[12] The point of prayer is not getting what we want, but that God may be glorified (revealed) in our getting what he wants. We pray knowing that we will receive when we are not praying *to* God, but *with* him in common will and purpose.

Make no mistake: God's will is accomplished through abiding prayer. Satan is defeated, those who are lost are saved and those who are saved restored. Saints are strengthened, workers sent and those who are sick are healed. The improbable and impossible are achieved. God's will is revealed and his name glorified.

Jesus knew and trusted the Father, and out of this knowledge endured the cross 'for the joys set before him' (Hebrews 12:2, NIV). We are part of this joy. A time is coming when everyone everywhere will confess what we already know: Jesus Christ was Lord, is Lord and will be Lord. Though it's customary to pray with our eyes closed to exclude the world, there are surely times to lift our faces upward, open our eyes and welcome heaven. As the disciples watched Jesus ascend, we may soon see him return—with the ultimate answers to every prayer. The greater the despair, the greater the deliverance.

A woman mourning the death of a loved one was asked, 'What do you miss most?' The woman said, 'I feel deeply the absence of her prayers.' The friend replied, 'How do you know that she is not still praying?' The writer to the Hebrews reminds us that those who have moved on in their journey still play a part in ours. 'Such a great crowd of witnesses is all around us!' says the writer. 'So we must get rid of everything that slows us down, especially the sin that just won't let go. And we must be determined to run the race that is ahead of us. We must keep our eyes on Jesus, who leads us and makes our faith complete' (Hebrews 12:1–2).

Abiding in Christ brings us into union and communion with God and with others. How good it is to know that those children who have been welcomed in Jesus' name are part of this communion, cheering us on in our common Saviour. 'In God and in his Church there is no difference between living and dead,' says Sergius Bulgakov. 'All are one in the love of the Father. Even the generations yet to be born.'[13] Paul reminds us to let our hope make us glad, be patient in suffering and never stop praying.[14] As someone once said, 'You can't tell the exact moment when night becomes day, but you know when it's daytime.'[15] Are we glad in hope? How will we be patient a little longer in our suffering? How will we continue to pray?

*

A nation transformed

When we consider the vast problems of this world and doubt whether or not change can really take place on a large scale, it is worth remembering the country of South Korea.

In 1952 Everett Swanson, the founder of *Compassion*, encountered poverty during the Korean War. At the time, South Korea was one of the poorest countries in the world, and the children were its greatest victims. The need was vast and the future looked bleak, but 50 years on, transformation has truly taken place.

Compassion's work with the children came to an end in 1993 when the country was stable and prosperous enough to care for the children itself. In 2003 South Korea joined *Compassion* as a partner country, sponsoring children in other parts of the world. 'The majority of Koreans believe that now is the time to return all the blessings we have received,' says Justin Suh, Director of *Compassion Korea*. 'Now we need to be able to turn around and do the same for other people.'

The story of South Korea is remarkable. The Christian church is thriving. It is estimated that 49 per cent of the population are Christians and, in the past 15 years, the number of churches has doubled from 30,000 to 60,000.

This nation has truly been transformed, and if we ever wonder whether what we are working toward is an impossible dream, then we should only look to South Korea for inspiration.

∗

Group helps

Worship

At Your feet we fall (SF1 28)
Blessing and honour (SF2 675)
I know not why God's wondrous grace (SF3 1325)
I am trusting thee, Lord Jesus (SF1 183)
Praise God from whom all blessings flow (SF2 980)

Word

Job 19:23–29
1 Peter 3:8–22

Prayer

- Thank God for the way he has transformed the country of South Korea.
- Pray that people in South Korea will use their past experiences of poverty for the benefit of others.
- Ask that we will be encouraged by the change that has taken place there.

Fellowship

Who is cheering you on in the great crowd of witnesses mentioned in Hebrews 12:1–2? As a group, share stories about those who have encouraged you and showed you compassion in your faith in Christ. Who continues to mentor you now? Whom are you mentoring? How will you mentor the children in your local and global faith community?

Witness

Read 1 Peter 3:13–17 together. Explore these questions:

- Can anyone really harm us for being eager to do good deeds?
- Even if we have to suffer, how will God bless us for our compassion?
- How can we help each other not to be anxious or afraid of what people might say, do or think of us because of our witness?
- How can we better honour Christ and reveal God through our witness?
- What answer will we give to those who ask us about our hope?

For personal reflection

Read the following excerpt from *Amid the Ruins*. Describe a time when your life and faith have lain in ruins because of your denial of Christ. How have you 'looked upon the face full of love and crushing grace'? How has the experience of God's compassion motivated you to compassion?

> *Head and heart hung in despair*
> *Peter sobs in courtyard square*
> *For full he looked upon the face*
> *Full of love and crushing grace*
> *In the shadows followed Christ*
> *In the dawn denied him thrice*
> *Oh cursed words Peter knows*
> *And bitter weeps when rooster crows*
>
> *Amid the ruins they whisper*
> *'the end of the world will be like this.'*
>
> © Renita Boyle.

NOTES

1. Source unknown.
2. H. Lockyer, *All the Prayers of the Bible*, Zondervan, p. 180.
3. Jude 20–21.
4. Lockyer, *All the Prayers*, p. 173.
5. R. Dunn, *Don't Just Stand There… Pray Something!*, Alpha, p. 173.
6. S. Hughes, *My Favourite Stories about Children*, CWR, p. 35.
7. S. Ratcliffe, *Oxford Quotations by Subject*, Oxford University Press.
8. P. Kreeft, *Making Sense out of Suffering*, Servant Books, p. 129.
9. 2 Peter 3:8.
10. www.christianquotes.org.
11. Hughes, *My Favourite Stories about Children*, p. 70.

12 Dunn, *Don't Just Stand There*, p. 196.
13 T. Castle, *A Treasury of Christian Wisdom*, Hodder & Stoughton, p. 44.
14 Romans 12:12.
15 R. Backhouse, *1500 Illustrations for Preaching and Teaching*, Marshall Pickering, p. 78.

IN-DEPTH REFLECTION

What is holistic development?

'I came so that everyone would have life, and have it fully' is the promise brought by Jesus (John 10:10). His concern is not only for our spiritual development but also for our entire well-being. As we seek to follow Christ's example, we should mirror his wholehearted concern for others.

Donald Miller points out that development is 'the process of gaining increasing control over one's future'.[1] The future includes every aspect of life, from health to education, to self-esteem; no element of life exists in isolation. The health of a child born into poverty will be influenced by a number of factors such as their home, their diet and the medical facilities available. These factors are determined by their country of residence, their parent's employment, the local crop type, and their family's health and hygiene practices. In turn, the physical health and welfare of a child will impact their capacity to learn and, consequently, their future prospects. On top of all this is the spiritual development of the child and their general outlook on life. The interaction they have with adult care-givers plays a huge role in this aspect of their life. In short, attention needs to be given to holistic development, addressing the physical, economic, social and spiritual needs of a child if they are to live life to the full.

Compassion is committed to developing each of these areas in a child's life. Healthcare is something that we take for granted and yet across the globe hundreds of thousands of children suffer and die from easily preventable diseases. *Compassion* can teach very simple healthcare practices such as cleaning teeth and washing hands, which children are then encouraged to share with their families. The provision of regular medical and dental check-ups will ensure that any serious illnesses can be treated before they become life-threatening. In addition, 1.1 billion people across the world are at risk from infection and disease through a lack of access to clean water and latrines.[2] *Compassion* works to reduce this figure by ensuring that all its projects have clean water and sanitation systems.

A balanced and healthy diet is of paramount importance considering that 27 per cent of children across the world suffer from malnutrition at some point in their life. Not only does *Compassion* provide healthy meals for the children at the project, but parents are also encouraged to learn food preparation methods which they can carry out in their own homes. In addition to the assistance given to children of school age, *Compassion* has developed Early Childhood Development Centres where parents and babies can come and get medical attention and nutritional advice, in the early stages of development.

General life skills enable children to interact with the world around them. The world is a place where the ability to read, write and understand numbers is essential. Without literacy it is easy for those in power to take advantage of the poor. Voting systems, written healthcare instructions and government documents are all unintelligible to those who cannot read. Basic literacy skills will not only open up new employment opportunities but will also allow children full access to society. Perhaps the most obvious cases where people have been exploited through their illiteracy is in some of the world's most remote tribal groups. The native land of these people groups is of prime use for commercial exploits. Without the skills of reading or writing, the tribe leaders can be forced to sign away any right they had to their land without realizing what they are doing. This exploitation takes advantage of the gaps in common knowledge and can be prevented through education.

Many children in the developing world are not in school because they have to work in order to provide financially for their family. Many children are forced into illicit, dangerous or illegal jobs because they do not have the skills to work elsewhere. While in these types of employment, children are not gaining the valuable skills they need to secure safe jobs and a stable future. Literacy and numeracy skills will give children a good grounding but may not necessarily ensure that they can get work. The provision of skills-based non-formal education will ensure that children have a broad range of options available to them.

Children in *Compassion* projects gain knowledge in a specific skill such as carpentry, baking or computing. In Haiti there are some remote regions where the majority of the communities are involved in farming. A few children from this region can expect to go on to further education but the majority will stay in their home village and work with the family business. *Compassion* therefore operates to teach children good farming and business methods so that their family businesses can be the very best that they would hope for.

Opportunities and facilities can be offered to children but, as Steve Wamburg points out, 'an opportunity offered is not always an opportunity realized [and] *Compassion* is in the business of opportunity realized'.[3] The real challenge is to help children make the most of the opportunities they are given and to apply their knowledge to everyday life. Education and the learning process must incorporate not only the fundamental aspects of knowledge but also the empowerment of a person to make good judgments.[4]

Children need self-confidence and self-esteem in order to make good decisions in their lives. The long-term nature of *Compassion*'s projects allows positive role models to support children and invest in their lives over a series of years. It also enables *Compassion* workers to develop lasting relationships with families and encourage them to get actively involved in their children's development.

Compassion believes that every child has the right to know that they are loved and valued by God and for this reason care and attention needs to be placed on the spiritual development of children. When children learn of their identity and their value in Christ, then other aspects of their life blossom. As they learn more about God's will for their lives then they become better decision makers.

Compassion works with needy children regardless of their religion or faith—many children come from families that are not Christian. *Compassion* ensures that their families are made aware of the Christian nature of *Compassion*'s programmes and are encouraged to get involved in church life. Children are encouraged in their faith, but never forced to become Christians.

An opportunity is offered in every aspect of a child's life so children are encouraged to make decisions and steer the course of their own future. The fatalistic attitude that can trap people into a sense of hopelessness is shattered as children are given the resources and self-belief to be all that God intends.

NOTES

1. Donald L. Miller, Director of *The Hunger Corps, The Development Ethic: Hope for a Culture of Poverty*, *Compassion* source.
2. *State of the World's Children 2001*, UNICEF.
3. *A Child's Rights and Opportunities—Warranty Included*, Millstone Devotional by Steve Wamburg, Sept/Oct 2002.
4. *Child's Rights and Opportunities*.

CHAPTER FOUR

Compassionate word

SECTION ONE

Compassionate word: in common unity

Emil Brunner once said, 'The first and most important thing we know about God is that we know nothing about him except what he himself makes known.'[1]

When God speaks, worlds happen—people too. Everything that God creates reflects and reveals him. However, only human beings are created 'in his image'. Only we are to be like him in nature and love him in community. Out of love, God wants us to know him. Out of compassion, he has done everything possible to help us to know him. God is neither distant nor elusive. He is neither an unknowable God, nor, as Paul made clear to the Athenians, an 'unknown God'. God is the creator and sustainer of all life, the Lord of heaven and earth. He doesn't live in hand-built temples but human hearts. He has chosen Jesus to do the judging for him and proved this by raising Jesus from death. Why? 'God has done all this, so that we will look for him and reach out and find him,' says Paul. 'He isn't far from any of us, and he gives us the power to live, to move, and to be who we are' (Acts 17:22–28). God is hopeless at hide-and-seek. He is like the child who shouts, 'I'm here!' before we can even say, 'Ready or not, here I come!'

Peter Forsythe says, 'The word of God is in the Bible as the soul is in the body.'[2] It is an act of deep compassion that the God who authored us, authored the Bible. It is unique in its claim to be the written word of God, to be eternal in content and to offer eternal life through the living Word, Jesus Christ, whom it reveals. As God's written word it lays claim to inerrancy and authority. As testimony to the living Word, Jesus Christ, it lays claim to the human heart. As

Bruce Milne says, 'How much more of God is disclosed by the cross of Jesus than by a star-lit night.'[3] Indeed, the Bible's primary purpose is to bring us to faith in Christ and, consequently, into union with God and community with each other. Paul says to Timothy, 'Since childhood, you have known the Holy Scriptures that are able to make you wise enough to have faith in Christ Jesus and be saved. Everything in the Scriptures is God's word' (2 Timothy 3:15–16). This encouragement ripples through the generations every time scripture is cast into the human heart.

Here Paul's claim about scriptural authority is both retrospective and prophetic. It refers to the collective writings of the Old Testament circulating in his time, and those writings that have since become regarded as the New Testament. *Theopneustos*, the word used to describe God's inspiration or, more accurately, expiration of scripture, literally means 'breathed out by God'. It is no wonder that Martin Luther says, 'The Bible is alive, it speaks to me; it has feet, it runs after me; it has hands, it lays hold on me.'[4] The Bible is much more than a collection of books containing God's word. It is much more than a history of God's ability to save his people. It does much more than inspire us or aid us in self-development. The Bible is and does all of these, of course, but it is much more.

The Bible is holy—not because it deals with holy things—but because the Holy Spirit wrote it. It is God's word, God's witness to himself, the journal of the Almighty laid open to our souls. Our conviction of this grows with every scriptural promise that is fulfilled, every need that is met and every time we allow the Holy Spirit to speak to us and empower us through scripture. The Bible becomes God's word more fully to us as we encounter God in it but it is ultimately God's word even if we choose never to read it at all.

As we have seen, scripture reveals the loving union of God within himself—Father, Son and Holy Spirit—a union that is reflected in our own union with God and each other through Christ. It should not surprise us, then, that the Bible itself remains a remarkable witness to the unity of God. Comprised of 66 books of different types, the Bible was written in three languages, on three continents, over a period of 1600 years and 40 generations. Its 40+ human authors—fishermen, farmers, poets, prophets and kings among them—expressed a variety of experience and emotion. They wrote in different places and times—wilderness and hillside, prison and palace, on the hop and at home, during war and peace—and used several materials and types of instrument.

The Bible spans God's history with humanity from the beginning of earthly time to its end. Although it includes hundreds of controversial subjects written from different perspectives, it is remarkably harmonious. Its overarching theme—the redemption of fallen humanity—reveals the depth of God's compassion. In one continuous disclosure we find everything we need to be reunited with God—Father, Son and Holy Spirit—and each other as originally intended. 'As in Paradise,' says Ambrose, 'God walks in the Holy Scriptures, seeking man.'[5]

A group of children at summer camp were discussing God's purpose for creation with their counsellor. One child said, 'If God has a good reason for everything, why did he make poison ivy?' As the counsellor struggled for an answer, another child said, 'God wanted us to know that there are some things we should just keep our hands off.'[6] It is impossible for us to know God apart from his grace in revealing himself. Originally directed to specific generations, the written word equally addresses all generations. It is a course book in compassion, God's history with humanity, the written record of redemption. Beginning with our creation and fall, it charts our personal and communal history of sin, rebellion, struggle and heartache and demonstrates God's consistent compassion and love for us throughout this history. The written word reveals the living Word, Jesus Christ, and shows us that the only way of salvation is through him. Christ is its central theme and climax. He is set before us in the word, and through the word we are able to receive and embrace him. In Jesus, the living Word, God came among us as one of us. Now, through the Holy Spirit, the God who indwells us instructs us using the word he himself wrote. God has spoken to us. He has supervised the accurate recording of what he wants us to know and given us the means to know it.

The incarnate Word and the written word are inseparable. Jesus is in scripture and scripture is in Jesus. Scripture was always on his lips because it was always in his heart. In the Gospels Jesus mentions 20 Old Testament characters and quotes from 19 different books. Take away his teaching references to events, experiences and exhortations from scripture and there is little left. He spent his whole ministry expounding, fulfilling and pointing others to his fulfilment of scripture. 'In the Old Testament the New lies hidden,' says Augustine of Hippo. 'In the New Testament the Old is laid open.'[7] The Bible presents Jesus as the Messiah like a giant exclamation point in God's timeline that can't be ignored or dismissed. Just before his ascension, Jesus said, 'I told you that everything written about me in the Law of Moses, the Books of the Prophets, and in the Psalms had to happen' (Luke 24:44).

We cannot know Christ without scripture. Nor can we know scripture without Christ. Jesus rebuked those who knew scripture but refused to know him. 'You search the Scriptures, because you think you will find eternal life in them,' he said. 'The Scriptures tell about me, but you refuse to come to me for eternal life' (John 5:39–40). As Bruce Milne says, 'If we are to truly know God, revelation must redeem as well as inform, transform as well as teach.'[8] We are to let the message about Christ so completely fill our lives that our attitudes, words and actions could be mistaken for those of Christ. We are to live in an attitude of constant thankfulness to the Father because of Christ.[9]

God's love for the world is revealed as the motivation behind the sacrifice of Christ for our salvation. God's love for the world is imprinted within us as the Holy Spirit uses scripture to draw us together in compassionate community. There is a sense in which 'we must be saved together or we will not be saved at all,' says Max Warren. 'That would seem to be the deepest truth about the atonement.'[10] Relationship is at the heart of ministry and mission. We are not a collection of individuals but a community of communities, like circles within circles whose beginning is the circle of God himself—Father, Son and Holy Spirit. Indeed, the written word confirms that loving community is at the core of our identity, a community that is not based on rigid rules or constricting structure but on the mutuality of love and compassion so evident within our triune God.

God's written word, both Old and New Testaments, positively thrums with the theme of God's consistent compassion for those who are poor and destitute. The living Word provides an unmistakable portrait of this compassion. Jesus embraced many of the most marginalized people of his time, people for whom the coming of God's kingdom was particularly good news. Some, like those who were tax collectors or prostitutes, were outcasts because of their jobs. Others, like those who were leprous or demon-possessed, were pushed to the edge of the community because of fear and ignorance. Still others, like women and children, remained on the fringes of the community because of their status. However, Jesus offered them all new life in a new kind of community—the kingdom of God where forgiveness, healing, deliverance, dignity and belonging were on offer from the compassionate God himself.

The weight of scripture is unequivocal. God expects us to show this same compassion not only to each other but to anyone in need. Who are the people outcast today? Who have we pushed to the edge of our community because of fear and ignorance? Who remains on the fringe? May the Lord let our lives thrum with his consistent compassion for all.

*

Child labour: a cause of poverty

Child labour is not only a result of poverty but also a major cause. Each second a child spends rolling cigarettes in a factory, shining shoes on a street corner or making bricks is a second in which they are not developing and growing as a person.

Legislation in the form of the Child Labour Deterrent Act[11] has been put in place in an attempt to prevent child exploitation, but it is increasingly difficult to see such legislation implemented. While large multinational companies are under the scrutiny of international media, children desperate for work are forced into more dangerous and unmonitored trades. Hidden from the watchful eye of the world, they are at increased risk.

For many, education is viewed as a pointless activity. In much of the developing world, schooling is extremely expensive and parents do not believe that it will equip their children practically for the world. Evelyn Fernandez, a project director in Davao city in the Philippines, is faced with this attitude on a daily basis. Communities entrapped by poverty have a mindset of fatality, whereby they feel that their situation cannot be changed. Evelyn comments that 'children who want to get an education not only face the challenge of money, but also the challenge of making their parents understand the value of education'.

It is therefore essential that all educational opportunities are free, relevant to the child's situation and able to equip them to survive economically on their own. As children are given choice, they will indeed experience freedom.

*

Group helps

Worship

Breathe on me, breath of God (SF1 47)
In the presence of your people (SF1 244)
Glorious things of thee are spoken (SF1 123)
Tell out, my soul (SF1 498)
You're the Word of God, the Father (SF3 1669)

Word

Psalm 19
Acts 17:16–34

Prayer

- Pray that more appropriate vocational education courses will be established for children in the developing world.
- Pray that parents will learn to understand the importance of education for their children.
- Pray that children will be encouraged in their education by teachers and parents.

Fellowship

Think of the generations yet to be born and, as a group, write an alphabet prayer of what you hope for them—for example, Abundant life, Babies born healthy, Compassion, Deliverance from oppression, and so on. Ask God to help you do your part to make this prayer a reality.

Witness

- How has God gifted us to reveal himself in our local community?
- How can we identify the needs of those around us?
- How have we changed the environment by being a compassionate witness in it? How can we?

Make Jesus' words quoted from Isaiah a manifesto for your ministry (Isaiah 61:1–2; cf. Luke 4:18–19).

For personal reflection

Find a spot by quiet waters to do this exercise. Take a stone and drop it into the water. How many ripples can you count? Think of compassion as a stone thrown into the water.

- What are the rippling effects of compassion?
- How do they start out small and get wider?
- Does the size of the stone matter in how many ripples there are or what they look like?

Explore these questions in your journal. Commit yourself to an act of compassion this week and see if you can detect the beginning of the ripple effect.

If you prefer, you can explore this exercise with a close and trusted friend.

NOTES

1. Source unknown.
2. T. Castle, *A Treasury of Christian Witness*, Hodder & Stoughton, p. 25.
3. B. Milne, *Know the Truth*, IVP, p. 25.
4. Milne, *Know the Truth*, p. 25.
5. Castle, *Treasury of Christian Witness*, p. 211.
6. Source unknown.
7. Castle, *Treasury of Christian Witness*, p. 25.
8. Milne, *Know the Truth*, p. 25.
9. Colossians 3:16.
10. A.P. Castle, *Quotes and Anecdotes*, Kevin Mayhew, p. 165.
11. International Labour Organization, *Strategies for Eliminating Child Labour*, 1997.

SECTION TWO

Compassionate word: in solidarity

Someone once said, 'The God who cares about sparrows cares about our sorrows.'[1]

The abuse of those who are weak by those who are strong is nothing new. Neither is the sense of powerlessness experienced by those who want to help. The Psalms, in particular, are filled with the churning of compassion and the call for justice. 'They murder widows, foreigners, and orphans. Then they say, "The Lord God of Jacob doesn't see or know,"' says the author of Psalm 94. 'Can't you fools see? Won't you ever learn? God gave us ears and eyes! Can't he hear and see? God instructs the nations and gives knowledge to us all' (Psalm 94:6–10).

As Matthew Henry says, 'They are inhuman who take pleasure in wronging those that are least able to help themselves; they not only oppress and impoverish, neglect the fatherless and make a prey of them, but murder them, because they are weak and exposed and sometimes lie at their mercy. Those whom they should protect from injury they are most injurious to. Who would think it possible that any of the children of men should be thus barbarous?'[2]

The Bible is evidence of God's compassionate solidarity with us, especially in suffering. It confirms that God does see and hear and is deeply and personally aware of all that affects or afflicts us. He is not a voyeur of human suffering or an outsider gleaning information from afar as one might do from a television. Instead, God has presenced himself at the hub of human history and is equally affected by it. The Bible is co-written by God and human beings from an insider's point of view. It is, therefore, uniquely useful, says

Paul to Timothy, 'for teaching and helping people and for correcting them and showing them how to live. The Scriptures train God's servants to do all kinds of good deeds' (2 Timothy 3:16–17).

Isn't it just like God to involve his creation in the authorship of his written word? The Holy Spirit, who breathed life into our lifeless clay bodies, breathed out the words of eternal life through human beings. This inspiration was such an intimate act that what we have in the Bible is what God would have written had he chosen to take up a pen himself and not involve human beings at all. He didn't need to involve us, but he chose to do so. God came alongside us in solidarity in the writing of his word even as he so compassionately came alongside us in the person of his Son, Jesus Christ.

Addressing the relationship between the divine author and the human authors of scripture, Peter says, 'But you need to realize that no one alone can understand any of the prophecies in the Scriptures. The prophets did not think these things up on their own, but they were guided by the Spirit of God' (2 Peter 1:20–21). The picture alluded to here is that of a boat being carried along by the wind—the Holy Spirit filling the sails of human authors, directing them as they wrote. In an act of incredible and intimate solidarity, the Holy Spirit became one in spirit with the human authors of God's word. This co-operation is evident in scripture. The personality, perspective and style of each human author shine through, as do the character, purpose and message of its divine author. The Bible is without error in all that it affirms and is the entirely trustworthy word of God. It is the supreme authority in all matters of faith and conduct. It is both the basis of *the* faith and the basis of *our* faith. It reveals what is true about God and is the reason we can trust God.

The Holy Spirit's solidarity goes far beyond even this. Not only did he direct the human authors to reveal the truth about God, but it is he himself who interprets scripture for us. Speaking of the coming Spirit, Jesus said, 'I have much more to say to you, but right now it would be more than you could understand. The Spirit shows what is true and will come and guide you into the full truth. The

Spirit doesn't speak on his own. He will tell you only what he has heard from me... Everything that the Father has is mine. That is why I have said that the Spirit takes my message and tells it to you' (John 16:12–13, 15).

It is because the Holy Spirit knows us so intimately that he can come alongside us so completely. The Holy Spirit who created us recreates us; he who convicts us convinces us, showing us the truth about sin, justice and judgment.[3] The same Spirit who reveals the Saviour brings us to salvation, raising us to life in the same manner as Christ. He who wrote the truth for us reveals the truth to us, replacing human wisdom with God's wisdom as promised. The Holy Spirit who adopts us assures us, settling us into God's family. The Spirit who pleads for us empowers us—his message a sword in our hands and our praying mighty in the Spirit. He who loves us lives within us, filling our lives individually and communally. The Holy Spirit who makes us his home prepares us for heaven. The Holy Spirit does all this using the Bible, which reflects the concerns of both the human and the divine. What compassionate solidarity!

'Faith is not belief without proof,' says Elton Trueblood, 'but trust without reservation.'[4] God's written word clearly displays the triune God as personal and personable, always approaching us in compassionate solidarity. It shows God to be completely moral, punishing injustice and demanding right. It also shows God to be overflowing with love and goodness, standing alongside us and defending those most in need. God is revealed to be the source and sustainer of every living thing—a task that requires his constant presence with his creation. He is shown to be as near to us as our own heartbeat.

The author of Psalm 139 beautifully expresses the constant and compassionate nearness of God. God is all-knowing and ever-present, taking note of our every thought and step. We are never out of reach or out of sight, never beyond his protection or his purposes. He is the daylight in our dark places and has woven us together in our mother's womb. Such is the depth of God's knowledge of us that we are strangers to ourselves by comparison.

God is wholly trustworthy, not just because the Bible declares it to be so but because the broad experiences of its human authors prove it to be so. The author of Psalm 94 not only prays that God would avenge the atrocities of murdered innocents but offers comfort to those who are traumatized. 'Our Lord, you bless everyone whom you instruct and teach by using your Law,' he prays. 'You give them rest from their troubles, until a pit can be dug for the wicked' (Psalms 94:12–13). Here we are assured of God's blessing not because of suffering itself but because of the wisdom God's word can bring to us out of suffering. We are also assured that, as Matthew Henry says, 'the days of adversity, though many and long, shall be numbered and finished'.[5]

We are best prepared for our promised deliverance in the yearning for it. Though we may be cast down, we are never cast off. The psalmist offers himself as evidence of God's compassionate solidarity. 'If you had not helped me, Lord, I would soon have gone to the land of silence,' he says. 'When I felt my feet slipping, you came with your love and kept me steady. And when I was burdened with worries, you comforted me and made me feel secure' (Psalm 94:17–19). Can we offer ourselves as evidence of this same compassionate solidarity?

God's Testament, Old and New, is a testimony to his compassion. Through it he unveils himself in all his eternal power and deity as a God who stands with his creation and stands up for those who are vulnerable and powerless. He is the righteous judge, the loving Father, the king of grace and the living Lord. He is the God who keeps his promises, the God who knows us, the God who searches our hearts and rewards faith. He is a faithful and powerful friend, something we discover more and more as we ourselves befriend scripture.

'The Bible is very like the poor,' says Samuel Butler. 'We have it always with us but we know very little about it.'[6] We face many obstacles in our motivation to study God's word. Perhaps we lack time, energy or confidence. Perhaps we find the Bible lacking in excitement. Whatever our reasons, one thing is sure: to remain unknowing of scripture is to remain unknowing of the God who wrote it, his overwhelming compassion for those who are poor and all that he desires for us as we study it. It is also to remain untouched by the wealth of human experience contained in its pages. The Holy Spirit transforms us through scripture, speaks to us and guides us, deepens us and helps us to discern God's will. We are not the only ones who lose out through our lack of awareness. To remain unenlightened by scripture, especially when God has afforded us with the privilege of having access to it, is to impede all that God would have us become and do through it.

God is not indifferent to the millions of children who are pleading for deliverance but has called us, through his word, to sit down with them and stand up for them. The God who gave us ears and eyes does indeed hear and see. Are we using our ears and eyes to hear and see? The Bible is a testament of God's solidarity. Are we?

*

Family bonds

Saranya misses her sisters. While she and her little brother live with their parents in the city, her two older sisters have a home with their grandparents in the rural region of the Tamil Nadu province in India. The small outhouse that Saranya's family rent from her father's employer is barely large enough for four of them, and the 800 rupees a month that her parents earn barely covers the family's basic needs. 'It is difficult for me,' Saranya's mother reflects. 'I am very sorry that I can't give them what they need very well.' In the face of life's continuous struggle, Saranya's parents are determined that their children should get the education they need and that they should be able to live their lives rather than purely survive from day to day.

But good education costs money in India and if the only way they can pay for their children to be educated is to break the family unit then that is what they feel they must do. One burden off their mind is the education of Saranya. Saranya has been enrolled in a *Compassion* project and the free education, healthcare, food and counselling she receives there means that her parents can channel their earnings into supporting their other children. It also means that Saranya can stay with her parents and her brother rather than having to move back to live with her grandparents.[7]

✶

Group helps

Worship

Let us with a gladsome mind (SF1 324)
Now in reverence and awe (SF3 1468)
O Jesus, I have promised (SF1 400)
Praise, my soul, the King of heaven (SF1 441)
Thy word (SF2 1066)

Word

Psalm 94
Matthew 6:25–34

Prayer

- Ask for God to guide *Compassion* projects as they seek to identify the children who are at greatest risk in the community.
- Pray that families of *Compassion*-sponsored children will take an interest in church life.
- Pray for families who have been separated as the parents go in search of work. Ask that, despite the distance between the family members, relationships and love will remain.

Fellowship

Share with one another a time when you were befriended.

- How can scripture befriend you?
- How can you befriend scripture?
- How can you better befriend one another?

Witness

Think about the following words: salvation, born again, redeemed, repent, gospel, sin, faith, Christian and forgiveness. Break into pairs. Attempt to describe your relationship with God without using any of these words. When you have completed this exercise, reflect on what it has taught you about your own faith and how you explain it to other people.

For personal reflection

Look at the photos of yourself in the front of your journal. Read either Psalm 139 or Matthew 6:25–34 and think about the course your life has taken. Reflect on those times when you especially felt God's presence or care. Write about one of them. *or* personalize Psalm 139 by writing it in your journal, replacing all the personal pronouns with your own name.

NOTES

1 R. Backhouse, *1500 Illustrations for Preaching and Teaching*, Marshall Pickering, p.436.
2 M. Henry, *A Commentary on the Whole Bible, Volume 3*, World Bible Publishers, p. 596.
3 John 16:8–11.

4　Backhouse, *1500 Illustrations*, p. 135.
5　Henry, *Commentary on the Whole Bible*, p. 598.
6　Source unknown.
7　Original source *Compassion International It Works* trip.

SECTION THREE

Compassionate word: in humble servanthood

A story is told of a minister who wore a suit on Sundays only. One Sunday his three-year-old son was watching him change back into his everyday clothes and said, 'Dad, can I help you put your Bible shoes away?'

God's word serves us, like a pair of shoes on the journey of faith. Sometimes we take the Bible for granted, like a pair of comfortable trainers noticed only in their absence. Sometimes the Bible is like a pair of hiking boots that we rely on for especially arduous journeys. Sometimes the Bible is like a pair of rubber boots that protect us from the muck we have to walk through. Never, however, should the Bible be to us like a pair of Sunday shoes tucked away in the cupboard after the 'service' is done.

'Words are the raw material of language,' says Jim Packer. 'They convey meaning, reveal minds, evoke moods and stir thoughts. Their importance lies in the freight they carry and the jobs they do.'[1] In short, words serve us. Nowhere is this more apparent than in the Bible, whose divine author is the definition of servanthood itself.

God's word serves us as the source of all that God wants us to know about him and how he wants us to live. There is enough in scripture to prepare us for whatever is asked or required of us. Our love of scripture may bring us deeper into the love of God and vice versa. It serves us and so equips us. It is our handbook for Christian living, a practical tool in the hands of the Holy Spirit to change our lives. It rebukes us intellectually, corrects us morally and trains us in how to be spiritually upright. Practically it acts as a mirror, a hammer, a fire and a sword. God's word is our nourishment—milk, honey, bread and meat.

God's promises to us individually and as a community cover every area of life. Scripture guides and directs us, gives us courage and encouragement. It helps us to stand firm in trial and temptation, turmoil and trouble. It comforts us when we are despairing and depressed, strengthens us in persecution and transforms our personal and communal relationships. It is as worthy of our complete trust as the God who wrote it.

Perhaps Luther was thinking of the covenant when he described Christianity as 'a matter of personal pronouns'.[2] The covenant is the central promise of God, under which every other promise is embraced: 'I will be your God, [and] you will be my people' (Jeremiah 7:23). This extraordinary relational commitment ignites the pages of scripture in its revelation of the passionate love affair between God and his people. It expresses a love so fathomless, so energizing that everyone who experiences it is utterly transformed by it.

The new covenant, in Christ, is improved but remains essentially the same in its promise. 'Before you knew God,' says Paul, 'you were slaves of gods that are not real. But now you know God, or better still, God knows you' (Galatians 4:8–9). The most compassionate and life-giving promises of scripture are those nearest the covenant. 'Don't be afraid. I have rescued you,' says God through Isaiah. 'I have called you by name; now you belong to me. When you cross deep rivers, I will be with you, and you won't drown. When you walk through fire, you won't be burnt or scorched by the flames. I am the Lord, your God... To me, you are very dear, and I love you' (Isaiah 43:1–4). We are promised God's love and care at all times and his presence even in hard times. We are promised God's compassion.

David Nicholas says, 'God's promises are like stars; the darker the night the brighter they shine.'[3] How often God's word is portrayed as a source of light—the God who is light providing us with a lamp. Through scripture, we can pick out the path before us as we walk through the darkness all around us. The longest psalm in the Bible was written in praise of God's word and reflects the author's own rich experience of God's compassion as found in scripture. 'Don't forget your promise to me, your servant. I depend on it,' says the author. 'When I am suffering, I find comfort in your promise that leads to life... I find true comfort, Lord, because your laws have stood the test of time... No matter where I am, your teachings fill me with songs. Even in the night I think about you, Lord, and I obey your Law' (Psalm 119:49–50, 52, 54–55).

The nature of humility and servanthood permeates God's written word. Ultimately, however, what it truly means to serve with humility becomes tangible only in the living Word—Jesus Christ, the suffering servant himself.

Jesus identified himself with us, with the sins and suffering of individual human beings and of all humanity together. He took his place alongside us and voluntarily served us in humility, even taking our place and our punishment on the cross. He shared in the common life of those he called, exposed himself to criticism and opposition and endured each with humility. As he approached the climax of his ministry, he consciously entered into the anguished suffering that the completion of his mission would entail. Jesus willingly experienced adversity and alienation, ultimately from the Father himself, to overcome the very same for us.

A story is told about a father whose son was killed in World War II. When the minister arrived to offer consolation, the father lashed out at him. 'Where was God when my son was killed?' The pastor replied, 'Just where he was when his own son was killed.'[4] God did not intervene to spare his own Son but allowed the unfolding tragedy in order that a greater evil, the greatest evil, might be defied and defeated. As we have previously seen, the suffering of the Son on the cross fully involved the Father and the Spirit in its anguish. It is impossible, in a world ravaged by violence, to overcome evil without suffering. God does not always spare us grief, but is always compassionately suffering with us in our grief. Alienated as he is by sin, God is not removed from the scene of our suffering. 'In those bitter hours when injustice seems to prevail,' says Merrill Tenney, 'when physical suffering becomes unbearable, or when mental and emotional stress threaten to tear apart the human soul, God is standing in the shadows to meet us.'[5]

The sin that once alienated us from the transforming power of God's love need not alienate us any more. Jesus accepted suffering on our behalf and on behalf of all those who, as yet, haven't accepted or responded to God's love. Through his intimate understanding of our suffering, Jesus helps us to embrace the possibilities of love—even those possibilities that we can't currently comprehend.

Maltbie D. Babcock says, 'Your love has a broken wing if it cannot fly across the sea.'[6] That the children in our global care should suffer alongside the guilty or, worse still, because of the guilty is as definitive an injustice as Christ's death on the cross. Jesus endured the worst that our fallen human nature had to offer on the cross. So too, many of our children are forced to endure every conceivable brutality of body and soul. How deeply our hearts join in the grieving loss of generations as expressed in Lamentations: 'My eyes are red from crying, my stomach is in knots, and I feel sick all over. My people are being wiped out, and children lie helpless in the streets of the city. A child begs its mother for food and drink, then blacks out... lying in the street. The child slowly dies in its mother's arms' (Lamentations 2:11–12).

Through the resurrection, God brought triumph out of tragedy. Oh, how we long for the resurrection of our children out of tragedy. In the meantime, like Jesus, the suffering servant, we ourselves must rise to the challenge of defeating evil with our lives. Compassion is both the willingness to 'suffer with' others and the bond that is formed as we do. Through compassion, we demonstrate that shared suffering can initiate the process of wholeness and healing, even among those who don't currently understand their need of it. The kingdom of God becomes tangible every time others experience the compassion of God in us.

Paul Keenan says, 'The heart is a treasure chest of inner riches.'[7] There is something very sacred about those whose hearts reflect the suffering of Christ in their service of God, who have allowed sorrow to refine them and compassion to define them. Servant power may appear to be weakness but the ultimate paradox is that Jesus utterly crushed and defeated Satan through servanthood. A child once said of heaven, 'You don't have to do your homework in heaven, unless your teacher is there too.'[8] Our teacher is Jesus and Jesus served children. He spoke to them and of them, included them in his healing and in his community, and commended them as role models of discipleship and a focus for care. As William Strange says, 'A church which is faithful to its Lord will show its faithfulness in no clearer way than by its love for children, for whom he cared so deeply.'[9] Jesus is our teacher, and our homework here or in heaven is to serve him. Matthew Henry says, 'God's Word is a treasure worth laying up and there is no laying it up safely but in our hearts.'[10] Here it is always accessible, available to meet our every need and draw us into the service of Christ. The Bible is a testament of God's servanthood. Are we?

*

Living the faith

Compassion's strategic approach to child development seeks to put Christ at the heart of its ministry. As Christians, the Bible is the basis of our faith and children at *Compassion*'s projects are encouraged to make it the foundation of their life as well.

Twenty-three-year-old Leidy from Bolivia has chosen to set her life firmly on the foundations of the Bible. 'My father and I decided to open a small church in our home. We never had formal Bible learning or anything like that. But we read it and we live what we read with a lot of passion.'

Leidy's talent and maturity were noted at a young age when she was involved with outreach programmes to the gang community in her neighbourhood. The unconditional expression of love that she showed to the gang members brought many to the church. Even those who were attacked by fellow members for attending were so impressed by Leidy's care that they kept coming. So far, Leidy has influenced the decision of over 40 gang members to leave their destructive lifestyle.

Leidy has been given the opportunity to go on to further education through *Compassion*'s leadership development programme, and has just graduated with a bachelor's degree in business administration. But her plans are only just beginning. She already hopes to create a botanical garden in her city of Santa Cruz with her sister, which will not only stimulate the local economy but also employ people in need and those with physical disabilities.

Leidy just puts the Bible into practice and lives out her faith with unqualified passion.[11]

∗

Group helps

Worship

O Lord, you're beautiful (SF1 413)
Father, we adore you (SF1 96)
Thank you for saving me (SF2 1015)
All to Jesus I surrender (SF3 1163)
Who is he in yonder stall? (SF1 608)

Word

Psalm 119
Matthew 18:1–10

Prayer

- Ask that God will touch us all with the faith to walk more closely with him and live out his will as given to us in the Bible.

- Thank God for the way he is using individuals to break into some of the most impenetrable gangs in the world.
- Pray for young people like Leidy, that they will encounter people who can support them as they live out their dreams.

Fellowship

Read Psalm 119:49–56. Share together some favourite hymns or songs that are based on particular scriptures and how they have brought you comfort.

Witness

Someone once said, 'Christ is always waiting to be wanted.' Think about your local community.

- Where is Christ waiting to be wanted?
- How can you create a desire for God in your community?

For personal reflection

Reflect on the following poem.

- What do your words and deeds say about the gospel you believe?
- What is the 'Gospel according to you'?

Explore this in your journal or with a close personal friend.

> *You are writing a Gospel,*
> *A chapter a day,*
> *By the deeds that you do,*
> *And the words that you say.*

COMPASSIONATE WORD: IN HUMBLE SERVANTHOOD

Men read what you write,
If it's false or it's true.
Now what is the Gospel
According to you?

ANON. TAKEN FROM A.P. CASTLE, *QUOTES AND ANECDOTES*, P. 147

NOTES

1. J.I. Packer, *God's Words*, IVP, p. 10.
2. Packer, *God's Words*, p. 22.
3. T. Castle, *A Treasury of Christian Wisdom*, Hodder & Stoughton, p. 193.
4. M.C. Tenney, *12 Questions Jesus Asked*, Victor Books, p. 130.
5. Tenney, *12 Questions*, p. 132.
6. Castle, *Treasury of Christian Wisdom*, p. 162.
7. P. Keenan, *Heart Storming*, Contemporary Books, p. 4.
8. M. Hodgin, *1001 Humorous Illustrations for Public Speaking*, Zondervan, p. 101.
9. W.A. Strange, *Children in the Early Church*, Paternoster Press, p.120.
10. Source unknown.
11. Source article by Phoebe Rogers, *Compassion International*, August 2003.

SECTION FOUR

Compassionate word: in obedient response

Robert Louis Stevenson once said, 'All speech, written or spoken, is a dead language, until it finds a willing and prepared listener.'[1]

As we have seen, God's ultimate intention in revealing himself is to give us what we need to have faith in Christ Jesus and be brought back into a relationship with God.[2] 'It is of little avail,' says Matthew Henry, 'if Christ has been revealed *to* us without having been revealed *in* us.'[3] Salvation, the complete restoration of all that we were created to be, is not found in a set of beliefs or doctrines, but in a person—Jesus Christ. Once we have come to Christ, the purpose of scripture is to help us to live in Christ. The Bible may be ancient, but it is not static, not a classic work by a deceased author now silenced. The author is very much alive both in his writings and in us. God doesn't just speak to us *through* scripture; he is also waiting for us to respond *to* scripture through our listening.

A story is told of a child who was posting a Bible to a friend. 'Is there anything breakable in here?' asked the postmaster. 'Just the Ten Commandments,' the child replied. God brought the Israelites out of slavery and into freedom, a freedom shaped by the Ten Commandments. The presentation of these rules was preceded by God's self-testimony of his right to set them—not because he is a cosmic killjoy, like some suppose him to be, but because he is eternally compassionate. 'I am the Lord your God,' he says, 'the one who brought you out of Egypt where you were slaves' (Exodus 20:2). God showed his love through the redemption of Israel and, in Christ, continues to remain loving in his approach to us. The Bible reveals how God wants us to live together in his likeness for the mutual benefit of all. As both our creator and our redeemer, God has the authority to order our lives and we are answerable to him for how we live. 'Whether we live or die,' says Paul, 'it must be for God, rather than for ourselves. Whether we live or die, it must be for the Lord. Alive or dead, we still belong to the Lord. This is because Christ died and rose to life' (Romans 14:7–9).

Someone once said, 'Where did we get the idea that the Bible is some kind of fragile archive that needs our plastic cover protection from pollutants. The Bible is a rapier of steel, to be seized and used against principalities and powers of darkness. It is a weapon not a book.'[4] Indeed, the word of God is described as the sword of the Spirit, and is the only offensive weapon mentioned in the armoury of God.[5] Jesus used scripture to reaffirm, resist and repel. Such was the power of scripture in Jesus' life that Satan failed in his aim to make Christ sin and thereby become an unfit sacrifice for the sin of others.

'Men do not reject the Bible because it contradicts itself,' said E. Paul Hovey, 'but because it contradicts them.'[6] There are striking similarities between the temptation of the first humans and the temptation of Christ. Satan's focus, in either case, was the trustworthiness of God's word. We can hear him sowing the seeds of doubt in Eve's ear: 'Did God tell you?'[7] We can detect him seeking to sow distrust in the heart of Christ: 'If you really are the Son of God…' Failure to believe what God says is fertile soil for sin. The first humans chose to disbelieve what God said, and so failed. Jesus returned again and again to what God said, and prevailed.

Jesus' identity and destiny as God the Son are uniquely his own, but his identity and destiny as a child of God are not. We are now children of God, with a new identity and destiny firmly rooted in Christ. Satan's greatest intention is to cut us off from our Father—our dependence on him, our obedience to him and our communion with him—to destroy the inner trust that would keep us from outer defiance. Satan would delude us into believing either that God is not our Father or that he is a bad parent, purposely vindictive or generally neglectful. This delusion is a form of slander, an attack on the integrity of God's undeniable love and compassion for us. The living Word reaffirmed his identity and remained focused on his destiny through the written word, and so must we.

'We are not to live by bread alone,' says David Hubbard, 'but we were certainly not made to live without bread.'[8] Jesus' response to Satan's temptations tells us much about our own destiny in a world of great need. Jesus did not come simply to feed people—though the whole tenor of his ministry proves his compassion for those who are poor—but to teach us how to share a common life together in him. We too must work to sustain one another spiritually as well as physically in our compassion, bridging the divides of class, race, gender and generation. Jesus did not come to wield power, as is the way of the world—not to conquer in combat but to serve in love and to teach us to do the same. We must recognize the kingdom of God as a present reality wherever there is a pocket of his people practising compassion, listening in obedience to the Holy Spirit.

Jesus loved people more than power, and so must we. Jesus did not come to 'do tricks' but to die on a tree; not to do miracles, but to deliver people. Jesus redeems us through his suffering compassion: whatever the outcome of our ministry, our focus must be the ultimate redemption of others through our own willingness to suffer with them out of compassion.

Jesus spent 40 days in his wilderness experience, symbolic of the 40 years that the Israelites wandered in theirs. Every scripture that Jesus quoted to Satan refers back to this time in Israel's history— the testing after which God would finally deliver them into the promised land. Jesus showed us that God's word is not to be abandoned in our confusion but embraced in conviction; that obedience flows from intimate listening and is an attitude of consensus rather than an act of compliance. Someone once said, 'God's word is just as accurate as his works are. You can set your clock by his sun, and you can chart your course by his word.'[9] We may have scripture in our possession, but without understanding we have no power. We must use scripture to discover God's will and obey it. Jesus himself lived by the scriptures that he consistently applied to himself. In them he found the plan that God had for him. Jesus was not entirely alone in the desert. The same Holy Spirit, who took the word and made it understandable and workable in Christ, makes it understandable and workable in us.

Surely one of the most pointed questions Jesus ever asked was, 'Why do you keep on saying that I am your Lord, when you refuse to do what I say?' (Luke 6:46). Whatever the specifics of God's will for our lives, we are all called to love God with heart, soul, mind and strength and to love others with the same.[10] God's word consistently reveals his special concern for those in greatest need. We are to show justice, compassion and respect to everyone, but especially these. Micah says, 'The Lord God has told us what is right and what he demands: "See that justice is done, let mercy be your first concern, and humbly obey your God"' (Micah 6:8). We can't do what we like as long as it doesn't hurt anyone else, because disobedience—lack of love for God and others—*always* hurts someone else. Scripture reflects God's compassion for us and urges us to express to others the compassion we have experienced ourselves.

There are no short cuts to attaining God's kingdom, no alternative methods of accomplishing the work entrusted to us. Satan will try to deflect us from God's intention for us in ways both subtle and skilled. We must not, however, distrust God's love and compassion that suffered so to restore our identity and destiny as children of God. We must, instead, fulfil our destiny to love. The world's neediest children are depending on it.

✱

Social outcast

Jane lost her husband several years ago to AIDS and now she is alone, struggling to bring up five children on a reduced income while coping with the debilitating effects of the disease herself. Her friends and family want nothing to do with her and she has nowhere to turn.[11] While the physical impact of HIV and AIDS is devastating, perhaps the worst effect is the social rejection that it entails.

The AIDS epidemic carries with it the same social shame that leprosy did in the time of Jesus. Jesus came into regular contact with those suffering from leprosy, and accounts of his attitude toward those who were sick illustrate the love he had. 'Filled with compassion, Jesus reached out his hand and touched the man' who had leprosy (Mark 1:41a, NIV). If Christians seek to mirror Jesus in their lives, then reaching out to those who are suffering from the diseases that alienate them from the world should be an integral part of their actions.

On learning of Jane's plight, the *Compassion* staff in Tanzania immediately registered two of her sons in the project and offered Jane and the rest of the family medical assistance and social care. For a woman unwilling to leave her home for fear of the reception from her neighbours, the *Compassion* project has been a shaft of light, a new hope for Jane and her family. The inclusion of families struck by HIV and AIDS in community projects not only brings help and hope to the affected individuals but it also sends a positive message to the rest of the community, encouraging them to face up to the realities of HIV and AIDS rather than allowing false myths to breed.

*

Group helps

Worship

Father God, we worship you (SF1 90)
From the rising of the sun (SF1 121)
Lord I come to you (SF2 895)
My lips shall praise you (SF2 937)
We bring the sacrifice of praise (SF1 577)

COMPASSIONATE WORD: IN OBEDIENT RESPONSE

Word

Exodus 20:1–17
Matthew 4:1–11

Prayer

- Ask that the Church will be a channel of hope and love to those who have been forgotten by society.
- Ask that communities will be educated about issues of HIV/AIDS and that the myths and stigma attached to those who suffer from the disease will be shattered.
- Pray that God's love will reach and strengthen the children who are coping with the illness of their parents and also with the rejection of society.

Fellowship

Read Exodus 20:1–17. Write the Ten Commandments on a large piece of paper. As a group, restate each commandment in the light of your love for God. For example, 'Do not worship any god except me' might become 'If you love me, you will not want to worship any god except me'; or 'Do not steal' might become 'If you love me, you will not want to steal.' What difference might it make to your obedience if you thought of God's commandments in this way?

Witness

John Wesley said, 'Go not only to those that need you, but those that need you most!' Think about your local community. Who needs you most? Think about your own family and friends. Who needs you most? Make a specific commitment to 'go'.

For personal reflection

'Why do you keep on saying that I am your Lord, when you refuse to do what I say?' (Luke 6:46). In what areas are you refusing to do what God says? Why?

Explore this issue in your journal or with a close personal friend.

NOTES

1 Source unknown.
2 2 Timothy 3:15.
3 M. Henry, *A Commentary on the Whole Bible, Volume 3*, World Bible Publishers, p. 901.
4 R. Backhouse, *1500 Illustrations for Preaching and Teaching*, Marshall Pickering, p. 40.
5 Ephesians 6:17.
6 Source unknown.
7 Genesis 3:1–4
8 D. Hubbard, *The Practice of Prayer*, IVP, p. 22.
9 Source unknown.
10 Mark 12:29–31.
11 Original article by Janet Root, *Compassion—It Works*, December 2002.

SECTION FIVE

Compassionate word: in hopeful expectancy

'Redemption is the great theme of the Bible,' says Jean Fleming, 'and homesickness seeps from the pores of every page.'[1]

As we have seen, the great goal of the Bible is to reveal a God who compassionately draws his people into a loving relationship that enables them to be all that he created them to be. This relationship is covenantal, based on the promise of God to release and transform his people, inspiring them to return love with love. It is a relationship of such intimacy and honesty, such courage and trust, that every aspect of what it means to be human, every layer of human relationships, is transformed in such a way as to reveal the kingdom of God. It may seem contradictory, but even the suffering brought to bear on humanity because of sin is embraced in God's grace and can reveal him. Indeed, it is only through suffering and death that God's kingdom will ultimately be revealed.

A little girl asked God, 'How did you know you were God?'[2] We smile, not necessarily at the question being asked here but at the fact that God often answers our 'want-to-know' questions on a 'need-to-know basis'. Although it is true that God has already communicated all that we need to know in his written word, it is also true that God's fullest revelation is yet to come. The second coming of Christ will surpass it all. Every eye will see him and every tongue, happily or not, will confess him for who he is. He will deliver us to an eternity that we have been able only to hope for. 'Your faith,' says Peter, 'will be like gold that has been tested in a fire. And these trials will prove that your faith is worth much more than gold that can be destroyed. They will show that you will be given praise and honour and glory when Jesus Christ returns. You have never seen Jesus, and you don't see him now. But still you love him and have faith in him, and no words can tell how glad and happy you are to be saved. That's why you have faith' (1 Peter 1:7–9). Have we truly grasped this? We will be face to face with the one we have loved without seeing, and we will see him as he really is.

Transformation, whether partial, as is now the case, or complete, as will be the case, is possible only if we remain loving in our relationship with God. As Charles Elliott says, 'We must not replace a real marriage with a comfortable living arrangement.'[3] This, of course, is what human beings have always been wont to do.

The love between God and his people has been under constant pressure from the threats of idolatry and institution as his people have looked for something more tangible to hold on to than a God who simply cannot be contained or fully comprehended. The Old Testament law, far from being a restricting set of rules, was an acknowledgment of God's love and an affirmation of the compassion to be shown to one another. 'At its best,' says Charles Elliott, 'the law was a working out of what loving kindness means in everyday relationships.'[4]

When God guided his people into the promised land, he also guided them in how to distribute their resources justly. The land was divided equally among the people and, should anyone fall into such poverty that their land might need to be sold, a kinsman 'redeemer' was given the right to buy it and keep it within the family. To avoid further the selfish accumulation of resources at the expense of those who were poor, Jubilee was established. Every fiftieth year, on the great Day of Atonement, trumpets were to be blown everywhere in the land, heralding a sacred year-long celebration of freedom in which everyone was to be given back their original property and indebted people returned to their families. Nothing was to be planted or harvested and only what grew on its own could be eaten.[5] Further to this, no land—Jubilee year or not—could be permanently bought or sold. God says, 'It all belongs to me—it isn't your land, and you only live there for a little while' (Leviticus 25:23).

The law was a reflection of God's compassion, particularly for those who were vulnerable with no claim on anything in their own right—those who were widowed, orphans, or aliens named among them. It was also a constantly outworking reminder to God's people of where they came from. Having been slaves in Egypt—aliens and sojourners—until God rescued them, they too could expect nothing by right and everything by grace.

As the spiritual ancestors of God's chosen people, the Israelites, we continue as a dynamic community of people, experiencing the dramatic and compassionate intervention of God. We move forward together in him and with him. We too have no right or claim on anything, although God demonstrates his grace by giving it to us. We too are, as John Perkins says, 'God's guests and stewards of God's resources'.[6] We too are called to celebrate our own individual and communal liberation by lavishing God's compassionate generosity on others—even those who, we may feel, have no right to it. Here is the 'love ethic of the kingdom', as Charles Elliott calls it. 'We give out of the lived experience of being loved. We give lovingly because we are loved.'[7]

Satan would paralyse us in the face of global suffering, turning the guilt we feel into a nagging internal gnawing, the overwhelming responsibility we feel into an overbearing powerlessness to do anything about it. It is, however, our sorrow and acknowledgment of sin that brings forgiveness from God and the transforming power to act as he wants us to in the world. The first day of Jubilee was, quite significantly, the great Day of Atonement when God's people could confront their wrong, ask for forgiveness and take steps to put things right. Through Christ, we are set free from guilt to serve freely and better to confront the injustices to which we have contributed. We do not have to live below the dignity with which we were created. In Christ we are able to live a life elevated by forgiveness, not eclipsed by failure. 'We have everything we need to live a life that pleases God,' says Peter. 'It was all given to us by God's own power, when we learnt that he had invited us to share in his wonderful goodness. God made great and marvellous promises, so that his nature would become part of us. Then we could escape our evil desires and the corrupt influences of this world' (2 Peter 1:3–4). In Christ we can be who we are—on our way to becoming, a little at a time, who we are meant to be. The year of Jubilee was a sacred time, a holy time, a time of remembrance and return and of reaching out.

'I have found that there are three stages in every great work of God,' said Hudson Taylor. 'First it is impossible, then it is difficult, then it is done.'[8] If we truly want to see God's kingdom reflected on earth and experience God's values in practice, we must be prepared for the love of God to transform us. The rich young ruler who came to Jesus to ask about eternal life is often as misunderstood in his response to Jesus as Jesus is in the demand he made of him. It is clear that this life-seeking and commandment-keeping man had a problem with wealth, but it was not merely his trust in wealth that kept him from the kingdom. Jesus did not ask him to sell everything and give to those who are poor in order to gain the riches of heaven. No, Jesus asked him for much more than that. 'Then come,' Jesus said, 'and be my follower' (Matthew 19:21). Jesus was inviting this young man to abandon his earthly kingdom with its attendant security, position and power, and embrace the kingdom of God among a community whose members find security in faith, position in service, and power in mutual compassion for each other. The rich young ruler was not yet ready for the love of God to transform him. Are we? There is a radical demand for our hearts at the heart of God's kingdom. There is also a radical expectancy.

A story is told of a boy who was reprimanded for laughing out loud in class. 'I can't help it,' he said. 'I was smiling and the smile busted.'[9] The Bible is a testament of hope. It places sin and suffering in the broad scope of history and assures us that everything that currently inhibits us from living in dignity is a temporary intrusion in the purposes of God. We were not created for sin and suffering and, because of Christ's atonement, sin and suffering will not be an enduring characteristic of our experience. The God who so compassionately presenced himself with us in the garden, wilderness, tabernacle and temple, in the incarnate Christ and the indwelling Holy Spirit, will, in glory, make his home among us for ever. 'God's home is now with his people,' says John. 'He will live with them, and they will be his own. Yes, God will make his home among his people. He will wipe all tears from their eyes, and there will be no more death, suffering, crying, or pain. These things of the past are gone for ever' (Revelation 21:3–4).

Someone once said, 'When we read the Bible, it reads us. It repairs our spiritual clock, winds it, corrects it, and sets it going.'[10] Waiting for all that will be delivered to us in God's time does not excuse us from delivering others in our own time. Time is running out for many millions of children with every tick and tock of our earthly clock. The present order may not be the final reality, but it is real enough for those who are suffering. We must be a community in the here and now that makes the coming kingdom evident. The resurrection assures us of God's triumph over all the forces of evil and darkness. Through his compassionate word, God has given us a vision of what is yet to come. We must own this vision and allow this vision to own us. Through our compassion, we can bring to the experience of those who are suffering some measure of the coming age in which all the forces of destruction will be destroyed, and these things will be past and gone for ever.

*

More than just the reading and writing

Formal education is rarely enough to secure a stable job for children in the world's poorest communities. In Western cultures, academic education is highly esteemed and the promise of higher wages for university graduates pulls many into further study. However, jobs for those with academic qualifications just don't exist in much of the developing world. In Kenya, 400,000 young people hit the formal education market each year and, with only 50,000 jobs available, competition is high—as is unemployment.[11]

For the very poorest children, academic qualifications alone will not equip them sufficiently to find work. Those who have expertise in a specific field will find it much easier to gain employment. Knowledge of a trade such as metalwork, tailoring or baking will open a new world of opportunities to children and will prevent them from falling into hazardous workplaces where they may be exploited.

One of five children, Wilmer lived with his family on the poverty line in Lima, Peru. When his father lost his job, Wilmer feared that he would have to seek work and become the chief breadwinner in the family while he was still in his teenage years.

Wilmer was encouraged to continue his studies at the Maranatha student centre where he was given the opportunity to learn management and financial skills. The time he spent here rather than out at work has proved to be invaluable for Wilmer and his family. Wilmer used his knowledge and expertise to set up a snack stall selling nutritious foods. The vending stall provides a profitable service which has afforded his family opportunities to which they would never have had access if Wilmer had not been able to finish his education.[12]

*

Group helps

Worship

O the valleys shall ring (SF1 423)
Seek ye first (SF1 471)
The steadfast love of the Lord (SF1 541)
Over the mountains and the sea (SF2 975)
Thou, whose almighty word (SF1 554)

Word

Leviticus 25:8–54
Revelation 21:1–7

Prayer

- Thank God for those formerly sponsored children who are now sharing their knowledge with future generations.
- Ask that God will enthuse children who have been given hope through sponsorship with a passion to pass on what they have learnt to those around them.
- Pray that whole communities will be transformed through the *Compassion* projects.

Fellowship

Have a book-swap night. Everyone should bring a copy of one of their favourite books—classic, modern, mystery, romance, self-help, biography, and so on. Talk about these books and exchange them with each other so that every person goes home with a different book. Discuss together how the Bible is similar to and different from these books.

Witness

- What vision do you have for the children in your home, church, local, national and global community?
- What are the common needs of all children? What are the specific needs of each group of children?
- How does your vision reflect God's vision?

Take some concrete steps to act on this vision.

For personal reflection

'The Lord your God... is always with you. He celebrates and sings because of you, and he will refresh your life with his love' (Zephaniah 3:17).

- How does God refresh your life with love?
- How does God celebrate you and sing because of you?
- If God were to write a love song to you, what would the lyrics be?

Explore these questions in your journal or with a close and trusted friend.

NOTES

1. Source unknown.
2. S. Hample and E. Marshall, *Children's Letters to God*, Workman Publishing.
3. C. Elliott, *Praying the Kingdom*, Darton, Longman & Todd, 1985, p. 68.
4. Elliott, *Praying the Kingdom*, p. 60.
5. A full description of Jubilee can be found in Leviticus 25:8–54.
6. J. Perkins, *With Justice for All*, Regal Books, p. 153.
7. Elliott, *Praying the Kingdom*, p. 63.
8. Source unknown.
9. M. Hodgin, *1001 Humorous Illustrations for Public Speaking*, Zondervan, p. 319.
10. R. Backhouse, *1500 Illustrations for Preaching and Teaching*, Marshall Pickering p. 40.
11. George Mullenix, *Compassion*'s senior research specialist, *Compassion at Work*, Summer 2000.
12. Bradd Hafer, for article entitled 'Peru's Merchant of Grace' in *Compassion at Work*, Summer 2000.

IN-DEPTH REFLECTION

Why children?

Children remain at the heart of *Compassion*'s ministry. They do not cause war, they do not build sweatshops and they do not run brothels, but they fall victims to them. Often raised with distorted views of the world, they become trapped by the limitations of their situation. This is not the way it should be. Child sponsorship is not a cute gimmick to raise funds, it is a strategic means by which to give children the value that they have lost, and equip them to fulfil their potential.

It has become a cliché to refer to the future being in the hands of our children. Whether we like it or not, it is these youngsters who will go on to shape the world of tomorrow. They will either grow up as caring parents, leaders, teachers, pastors and positive change makers, or they will grow up to become alcoholics, terrorists, abusers and drug addicts. The responsibility to determine which of the above our children grow up to be lies solely with us. Children's perceptions and attitudes to life are formed at an early age, so if we wait until tomorrow then it will be too late.

If we still need to be convinced of the importance of childhood, then we should turn to the Bible. It is worth remembering that our Lord himself came to us as a child. He did not bypass childhood but experienced the innocence and freedom that it offers. The Bible is littered with references to the importance of children, confirming the vision of the future that Jesus sees in the little ones. Proverbs 22:6,[1] Matthew 18:6[2] and Matthew19:14[3] are just three examples of places in the Bible where Jesus shows his identification with children and the heart he has for them.

Poverty is perpetuated when children are denied the opportunities to change the future for themselves. Children have to depend on those around them to teach them right from wrong. The vulnerability of children means that they are more easily exploited, and when the exploitation of children becomes normality then the cycle of depravity is perpetuated. UNICEF have concluded, 'When children are excluded or ignored by adults their potential to contribute to their communities is compromised. Such children are likely to act as they have been treated, i.e. as social outcasts with their energies and creativity directed in subcultures away from creating cohesive societies.'[4]

The clearest evidence of this is in the growth of the gang culture. Young people who struggle to find acceptance and identity in society search for a sense of belonging in alternative forms of community, which frequently take the form of gangs.

While children are most susceptible to adverse situations, they are also more receptive to positive input. Children take a more progressive approach to literacy, hygiene and nutrition, which they will then go on to share with their family. In this way they also share the gospel with those around them. Over 85 per cent of all those who have come to know and love Jesus Christ did so between the ages of four and 14.[5] Therefore, taking the gospel directly to the children is a powerful outreach exercise.

As with any area of development, change cannot happen overnight. *Compassion* wants to be more than an ephemeral glimpse of hope in the life of a child, which is why a long-term development strategy has to be implemented. Life for the poorest of the poor often revolves around where the next meal is coming from and whether there will be a safe place to sleep at night. In order to encourage children to have long-term dreams and plans for their lives, *Compassion* needs to be committed to children for a significant period of time. Where change and uncertainty are common, it is especially important that children understand the unchanging God who loves them unconditionally. The constant love of God can be shown through an organization that is committed to being there for the children for the long run.

IN-DEPTH REFLECTION: WHY CHILDREN?

It is the responsibility of the adult community to care for children and direct them on the right course, but it is also of vital importance to listen to what children have to say. No one knows what it feels like to be a child on the streets of São Paulo except a child on the streets; no one knows what it is like to scavenge a living from a rubbish dump except those who must do that on a daily basis. In 2002, UNICEF held its first ever conference for children, in order to give a voice to those who are so often voiceless.

Children are close to the heart of God and often speak more wisdom and with greater faith than we give them credit for. It can be a blessing to listen and learn from a child in poverty and a privilege to walk the journey with them.

NOTES

1 Proverbs 22:6: Teach your children right from wrong, and when they are grown they will still do right.
2 Matthew 18:6: 'It will be terrible for people who cause even one of my little followers to sin. These people would be better off thrown into the deepest part of the sea with a heavy stone tied around their necks!'
3 Matthew 19:14: 'Let the children come to me, and don't try to stop them! People who are like these children belong to God's kingdom.'
4 *State of the World's Children* 2003, UNICEF.
5 *Compassion's Role in Furthering the Kingdom*, Dan Brewster, March 2003.

CHAPTER FIVE

Compassionate community

SECTION ONE

Compassionate community: in common unity

Let us love one another, so that we may with one mind confess Father, Son and Holy Spirit—the Trinity—one in essence and undivided.[1]

As we have previously discussed, the deepest truth about God is not that he is personal but that he is communal—a loving, unbroken community of equal persons— Father, Son and Holy Spirit. John simply states, 'God is love' (1 John 4:8). The deepest truth about us is that we're also communal, created in God's image to belong together in love. This is the bottom line. Christian faith begins with a personal response to God's compassion but can be fully expressed only in compassionate community.

There are few words that turn people off more than the word 'church'. Even those in regular attendance are apt to use words like 'boring', 'stuffy', 'hypocritical' and 'irrelevant' when asked about it. In fact, George Carey once described the church as 'an old lady who mutters away to herself in a corner, ignored most of the time'.[2] If anything was ever in need of some good PR, it's church.

The Greek word commonly translated 'church', *ekklesia*, literally means 'called out'. It was taken from daily life and refers to a body of people called out in participation together. Early Christians met to worship, learn and celebrate communion. They shared encouragement, fellowship and prayer and cared for each other's practical needs. The Christian faith was not, for them, an alternative to other religions, but a new society, a new kingdom, a different kind of government and way of being, based entirely on inner transformation. There was no gathering up of troops, no taking up of arms, no defeating power with power—not, at least, in the sense that the world might expect. Instead, Jesus gathered around him a community armed with compassion and the power of the Holy Spirit.

Indeed, the kingdom of God always remains not a place where he rules but a community in which he lives—a community that includes those who have been excluded elsewhere and offers security to those who are most insecure. A bloody revolution is occurring, but the blood has already been spilled on the cross.

'Love does not dominate, it cultivates,' says Johann Goethe. Love is both the core value and the principal aim of compassionate community. As we *suffer with* one another, we cultivate a radical shift in all levels of human relationship, personal or interpersonal, political or economic, institutional or international. God's kingdom is not yet imposed on this world, though it one day will be when Christ returns to the recognition of all people. Neither is embracing the kingdom an internal personal process that makes little or no impact on the way we live externally. 'It is,' says Charles Elliott, 'the liberation of the world we live in… from all that corrupts and destroys it.'[3] As we rediscover and recover our own potential as God's image bearers, we also rediscover and recover the full potential of all creation.

A little girl once asked God, 'Who draws the lines around countries?'[4] As we have previously noted, sin causes division and enmity in every direction. The word 'reconcile' is derived from the Greek word *katallasso*, which means to 'change' or 'exchange'.[5] Through Christ we are able to change from enmity to friendship, to exchange hostility for peace. As a compassionate community our calling is relational rather than institutional. The 'good news' that we are bound to share is the same reconciliation that is demonstrated among us. In Christ, sin has been accepted and atoned for, fallen humanity reconciled and returned to intimacy and dignity restored. We are at peace with God, Jesus having become human and died to make it so. We are at peace with ourselves, trusting in Christ to rescue us in the daily battle against our own selfishness. We are at peace with each other, able to embrace complete strangers and former enemies in love, and we are at peace with other cultures, transcending earthly boundaries and differences in the Holy Spirit who unites us.

John Stott says, 'Before we see the cross as something done for us, we have to see it as something done by us.'[6] We are truly a reconciled people expressing and ministering the peace we have experienced. 'God... sent Christ to make peace between himself and us,' says Paul, 'and he has given us the work of making peace between himself and others' (2 Corinthians 5:18). Church happens organically wherever and whenever we express compassion and love together.

William Temple says, 'The reality of our communion with Christ and in him with one another is the increase of love in our hearts.'[7] Love characterizes the deepest essence of God. Early Christians were known for compassionate community as, in Christ, they met the yearnings of the human spirit for love and belonging. They didn't express their faith so much in the joining of a community as by living in community.[8] Theirs was a radical alternative to secular society. 'The group of followers all felt the same way about everything,' recalls Luke. 'None of them claimed that their possessions were their own, and they shared everything they had with each other. In a powerful way the apostles told everyone that the Lord Jesus was now alive' (Acts 4:32–33).

This demonstration of compassionate community—and the fruit of Christ' prayer for unity among his followers—is striking. The early believers loved one another, truly and compassionately suffered with one another. Having been shattered by Christ's death and scattered by their doubt, they were resurrected in hope, reunited in purpose and empowered by the promised Spirit of God. The communal spirit exercised among them was evidence of the Holy Spirit within them. These early followers were indifferent to every possession, apart from Christ. 'No marvel that they were of one heart and soul,' says Matthew Henry, 'when they sat so loose to the wealth of the world.'[9]

The common unity encouraged and experienced between us—

locally, nationally and globally—comes from our union with one God. We're brought into this union through Christ and remain there in the Holy Spirit. We are one body. We are of one parentage, one Spirit, one Lord, one faith, one hope and one baptism. We are one. We show ourselves worthy of God when we live as one.[10] As we are transformed by God's love and filled with compassion, we reveal God among us. As we respond to God's love with love, we live the life of the Tri-unity as a community of love on earth. 'No one has ever seen God,' says John. 'But if we love each other, God lives in us, and his love is truly in our hearts' (1 John 4:12).

We also possess the promise of Pentecost. 'At Pentecost, the church celebrates the coming of the Spirit,' says Janet Morley, 'the outpouring of the sudden power of God to transform a wounded and disillusioned band of stragglers into a community that changed the world.'[11] The gospel changes the way we relate to everyone and everything and proves that love is stronger than hatred. We are able to reject bitterness and revenge, serve others (even our enemies) and win others with the same love that won us. A gospel that doesn't change us or challenge the vandalism of sin—including poverty and injustice—and affirm human dignity is completely irrelevant. 'Faith in Christ Jesus is what makes each of you equal [one] with each other,' writes Paul. 'Whether you are a Jew or a Greek, a slave or a free person, a man or a woman' (Galatians 3:28). Do we really believe that the gospel has the power to dismantle evil traditions and institutions? Do we really believe that our common faith is stronger than our different cultures? Do we really believe that God has given us the power to burn through all that divides—racial, cultural, economic and social—and live as community?[12]

We are not only God's partners but also the garden where he chooses to walk and the building where he chooses to live. We are not an institution, not a hierarchy, but a community in which he dwells. We are a body of people, not a building full of people, called out together from 'every tribe, language, nation, and race' (Revelation 5:9). We share the fundamental oneness of God despite our differences and denominational divides. We exhibit one fruit of the Spirit multiplied among us—love, joy, peace, patience, kindness, goodness, faithfulness, gentleness and self-control (Galatians 5:22–23). All these qualities are present in each and abundantly evident in compassion.

Someone once said, 'We come to church to share God, not to find God.'[13] The observance of communion—the Lord's Supper—is a deeply significant affirmation of our coming and sharing together with God and each other. We commemorate a greater and deeper deliverance than that of the Israelites out of Egypt. We accept what Christ offers and receive it, all of it, including the responsibility to demonstrate Christ's compassion in the world. 'Are we aware,' asks Leith Fisher, 'what a challenge this table presents to the way things are, in ourselves and in our world?'[14] 'Anyone who belongs to Christ is a new person,' says Paul. 'The past is forgotten, and everything is new' (2 Corinthians 5:17). In Christ there is a new world and a new way of being in the world. Sharing in the bread and body of Christ should not only remind us of our need for spiritual sustenance but also compel us to share our food and ourselves with those in great need of physical sustenance.

Our union in Christ will express itself in our union together, in the tone of our relationships one with another, our compassion and character. The early Christians didn't always get it right, and neither do we. Paul was alarmed by the mistreatment of Corinthian believers who were poor. During communion, the 'haves' had more while the 'have nots' went hungry! 'But if you eat the bread and drink the wine in a way that isn't worthy of the Lord,' says Paul, 'you sin against his body and blood' (1 Corinthians 11:27).

We must stop sinning against Christ's body and blood and challenge our most hidden prejudices. We must allow the Spirit to transform us from a lump of helpless persons into one people of God prepared to use his gifts with his power among those who are most in need. 'When we drink from the cup that we ask God to bless, isn't that sharing in the blood of Christ?' asks Paul. 'When we eat the bread that we break, isn't that sharing in the body of Christ? By sharing in the same loaf of bread, we become one body, even though there are many of us' (1 Corinthians 10:16–17). Who among us is without bread today, physically or spiritually? How will we be sharing our loaf today?

*

The weakening of a nation

HIV/AIDS is a disease that affects the individual, but it also has a devastating impact on communities and in turn nations, creating disasters from already difficult circumstances.

In 2003, sub-Saharan Africa experienced the most severe drought and famine since 1985. Already 14 million people in six countries across the south were in desperate need of food aid and another 14 million in Ethiopia were struggling to get the correct nutrition.[15] The adverse weather conditions alone put immense pressure on communities, but coupled with the AIDS crisis in the region, nations are struggling to an even greater extent. A generation of once-healthy adults became a generation weakened, unable to till the earth and produce the fundamental resources that a nation needs to survive.

With a reduced workforce, the demand for food is made on an increasingly reduced number who simply cannot meet the new need. Many of those who now have responsibility as farmers are children, unskilled and weaker than the regular workers. Many nations are forced to become reliant on overseas aid. While aid is important in getting countries in dire circumstances back on track, it will not provide a long-term solution to the problem. The immediate meeting of needs must be accompanied by a long-term strategy of self-sufficiency.

*

Group helps

Worship

For I'm building a people of power (SF1 109)
Gracious Father (SF1 138)
Let there be love (SF1 318)
Lord of the Church (SF3 v)
Love is patient (SF3 1442)

Word

Psalm 15
1 Corinthians 11:23–29

Prayer

- Pray for governments who face economic crises in their countries due to the AIDS pandemic.
- Ask that governments will not shy away from the problem but will face up to the issue and address it effectively.
- Pray that governments of more prosperous countries will cancel world debt and ease the burden on the developing world.

Fellowship

Have a simple meal together. At the end of the meal share in an informal communion together. Ask a volunteer to read 1 Corinthians 11:23–29. Have a time of open prayer that includes prayers for those that are trapped in global poverty. Have a time of open singing that includes well-loved children's songs. Make sure the children among you are welcomed and encouraged to participate in the taking of the elements.

Witness

Think of some of the ways that the 'church' has been described in scripture—temple, bride, family, body and so on.

- Is there a better word than 'church' to describe who we are together and what we do together?
- What image would you use to correct a negative picture someone might hold of 'church', or to describe 'church' to someone who has no experience of it? Aim to make the thought of 'church' seem less threatening to others.

For personal reflection

Create a sacred space for yourself in which to share communion—bread and drink—with God alone. Reflect on the lyrics of one of the songs under 'Worship' above. Choose one of the lines to explore more fully and personally in your journal.

If you prefer, you may explore this exercise with a close and trusted friend.

NOTES

1 Russian Orthodox prayer
2 S. Ratcliffe, *Oxford Quotations by Subject*, Oxford University Press.
3 C. Elliott, *Praying the Kingdom*, Darton, Longman & Todd, p. 1.
4 Source unknown.
5 W.E. Vine, *Vine's Concise Dictionary of Bible Words*, Thomas Nelson, p. 303. (2644 Strong's Concordance).
6 www.christianquotes.org.
7 T. Castle, *A Treasury of Christian Wisdom*, Hodder & Stoughton, p. 43.
8 Acts 2:44–47.
9 M. Henry, *Concise Commentary on the Whole Bible*, Moody Press, p. 812.
10 Ephesians 4:1–6.

11 J. Morley, *Bread of Tomorrow*, SPCK/Christian Aid, p. 143.
12 Adapted from J. Perkins, *With Justice for All*, Regal Books, p. 52.
13 Source unknown.
14 L. Fisher, *Will You Follow Me?*, Scottish Christian Press, p. 94.
15 UNICEF website.

SECTION TWO

Compassionate community: in solidarity

Eugene Peterson says, 'The single most important thing about the people of God is that they are there.'[1]

The early Christian community was a great advert for the 'good news'. Their compassionate presence in society changed it just by being. Tertullian quoted pagans of the day saying, 'See how these Christians love one another.'

The Greek word commonly translated 'fellowship', *koinonia*, was used to describe friendship, co-operation and brotherly love. *Koinonia*, however, extends beyond a simple connection between people to an absolute connectedness or solidarity. It expresses the rich, intimate and committed quality of relationships within the compassionate community of Christ. These partnerships are based in the sharing of a common life of love and service to Jesus Christ. Compassionate solidarity among Christians is not essentially what we do together, but in whom we share together.[2] We are in solidarity with God—Father, Son and Holy Spirit—three in one, and everyone else who is also in him.

'The essence of a perfect friendship,' says Robert H. Benson, 'is that each friend reveals himself utterly to the other, flings aside his reserves, and shows himself for what he truly is.'[3] Christ calls us his friends. He has revealed himself utterly to us through arms flung wide on the cross; he has shown us who God truly is and who we were created to be in him. 'Now I tell you to love each other, as I have loved you,' Jesus said before his death. 'The greatest way to show love for friends is to die for them. And you are my friends, if you obey me. Servants don't know what their master is doing, and so I don't speak to you as my servants. I speak to you as my friends, and I have told you everything that my Father told me' (John 15:12–15). It is hard to believe that we could ever return such devotion, yet that is what we do when we abandon ourselves utterly to God and serve him without reserve. In so doing, we demonstrate who God really is, both among ourselves and in the world.

Our compassion with each other directly reflects our partnership with Christ. *Koinonia* is a solidarity of sincere giving and receiving, unforced and unconstrained. It is to accept and honour one another and live in harmony, to express concern in such a way as to carry one another's burdens. It is not only to *suffer with* each other but to do so patiently and kindly for as long as it takes. *Koinonia* is a true fellowship of forgiveness and service based in love. If the church is to be a compassionate community, it must first be a transparent community, committed to a free flow of counsel and encouragement between each other, prayer for one another and confession of our sins to each other. It will require the nurture of mutual trust and accountability, honesty and humility, dignity and equality.

Everything we need to live in compassionate community is ours through God himself. The Holy Spirit continually gives himself to us from within us: hence, we are stockpiled with the gifts and fruit of the Spirit. These not only conform us to the character of Christ but are used by the Spirit to nurture others from the infant steps of salvation to the strides of maturity. 'If Christ lives in us, controlling our personalities,' says Eugenia Price, 'we will leave glorious marks on the lives we touch. Not because of our lovely characters, but because of his.'[4]

Just think of it! Some in our community can speak with wisdom or knowledge; others have great faith or the power to heal or perform miracles. Some in our community can prophesy or especially recognize the Holy Spirit's presence. Others can speak in tongues or interpret them. Some in our community can especially serve, teach, lead or encourage; others are especially generous or helpful.[5] All of us, however, possess the fruit of love, joy, peace, patience, kindness, goodness, gentleness, faithfulness and self-control. If we are to exercise the true solidarity that is *koinonia*, we must cherish and cultivate these gifts and this fruit in our compassionate commitment to one another. God himself is our model and he never leaves us without the means to live as we were created to.

'Friendship is in loving rather than being loved,' says Robert Bridges.[6] Jesus came alongside others in their need and fully identified with their concerns. He practised genuine partnership, a solidarity that received as well as gave. He not only depended on his heavenly Father and the Holy Spirit, but on his earthly parents and his cousin John. He benefited from the ministry of angels and the kindness of those who offered him hospitality. He valued others, including children, making many friends from among those he helped and close companions of those he called—especially Peter, James and John. He attended worship, weddings and funerals and accepted gifts. He asked others to pray for him and with him. Such was his solidarity and partnership that he died for his enemies and trusted his friends, even when betrayed and wounded. He not only forgave Peter but entrusted him with the fledgling church.

We too must seek a genuine partnership, to allow others to expand our own experience of life and thought. To stand in solidarity with Christians who are in poverty is not only to give materially but to receive spiritually. We must recognize the difference between patronizing charity and compassionate generosity, relinquish any condescension and reassess the cost of our own discipleship in light of the cost of theirs. Those in the early Church not only gave to those who were poor, but those who were poor gave too. Paul testifies to the physical and spiritual generosity of the Macedonian believers in his own life, who 'have shown others how kind God is... they were glad to give generously. They gave as much as they could afford and even more, simply because they wanted to' (2 Corinthians 8:1–3). Some in our community hunger for all the human rights denied them but have an abundance of wisdom. It is truly ironic that we who have an abundance of human rights hunger from spiritual deprivation. Janet Morley says, 'There is much wisdom we desperately need to receive from those who are in a better position than we are to see the world accurately—if only we could acknowledge our lack.'[7]

Someone once said, 'Bees fly thousands of miles to gather enough nectar to make a pound of honey. Then someone comes along and steals it from them. Maybe this is why they get so angry.' Ordinary people were attracted to Jesus and he to them. He himself understood the pressures and injustices of poverty. His first resting place was a feed-bin, his last another man's grave, and in between he had nowhere to lay his head. He had to borrow a coin for an illustration and when he did have money he was inclined to give it away. Jesus' sermons were quite unsettling. He pronounced blessings on those who were poor, hungry, rejected and persecuted—those who were generally despised and deprived. He made radical statements about loving enemies and not storing up wealth on earth.[8] If God is so concerned about issues of justice, so should we be. We are not only to show compassion for those at a distance, but also those who are marginalized in our own community. We must open our inner selves, not just our outer shells, to the presence of those in need.

'God evidently does not intend for us all to be rich or powerful or great,' says Ralph Waldo Emerson, 'but he does intend for us all to be friends.'[9] A story is told of a little girl who, on her first day at a newly desegregated school, sat next to a little white girl. When her mother asked the girl what happened, she responded, 'We were both so scared, we held hands all day.'[10] As the compassionate community of Christ we must practise true *koinonia*, not as a cup of tea after the morning service but as the flowing cup of fellowship that is daily service. We must stand with the stricken wherever they are found, locally, nationally and globally, loving together with honesty and commitment, exploring our connectedness and working together for change. We are called not only to give out of our abundance, but to be transformed in the giving of it— something that is always frightening. We must acknowledge our own participation in global woundedness and change the way we live to lessen it. Compassionate community will demonstrate the *koinonia* of Christ only as we share his needs, sorrows and compassion for the vulnerable.

True *koinonia* is possible only through God's compassion, an overwhelming love that is compelled to express itself in excessive generosity. The supreme expression of this generosity is found in Christ who, though rich with the glories of heaven, became poor that we might become rich.[11] 'We know what love is because Jesus gave his life for us,' says Paul. 'That's why we must give our lives for each other. If we have all we need, we must have pity [compassion]... or else we cannot say we love God. Children, you show love for others by truly helping them, and not merely by talking about it' (1 John 3:16–18).

*

Search for escapism

At the age of 14, Gualberto Gabriel Gonzales Franco decided he had no future. Living as he did in the slum area of Esmereldas in Ecuador, opportunities for employment were limited. With no visible way to overcome his situation, the next best option was to run away from it.

The gang culture of Esmereldas looked attractive to Gualberto and appeared to offer the antidote for life that he had been searching for. One Sunday, Gualberto saw three Bibles on the desk of the director of the *Compassion* project that he had been attending. Gualberto thought he could sell one of these Bibles to raise the cash to buy drugs and alcohol for a party he was attending that evening. After he had made an unsuccessful attempt to persuade his project director to give him one of the Bibles, she actually gave him her own personal copy on the understanding that he attended church with her that evening.

Keeping his word, Gualberto found himself at the church that evening, although he was intending to leave for the party during the pastor's address. When the pastor called anyone wishing to make a commit-ment to Christ to the front, he was shocked that the lady next to him suggested he might like to go. Gualberto felt a strong pull on his heart that he should act upon what he'd heard but, fearful of the experience, he fled home. Once at home, Gualberto forgot about the party and fell asleep. In the morning he learnt that a friend of his who had attended the party had been killed. It was on hearing this news that Gualberto understood that God had been protecting him.

Gualberto now works in Ecuador's Mizpa Student Centre where he can draw upon his own experiences to reach out to children who, like him, are looking for meaning and direction in their young lives.[12]

*

Group helps

Worship

An army of ordinary people (SF1 11)
Praise him! Praise him! (SF1 441)
Soften my heart (SF2 1004)
We are never alone (SF1 575)
We rest on thee, our shield and our defender (SF1 588)

Word

Proverbs 9:1–17
1 John 3:11–24

Prayer

- Pray that more *Compassion* projects can be established in communities where gang violence in rife.
- Pray for gang members who have turned their back on the violent lifestyle, that they will find love and support as they seek to walk a new path.
- Pray for the children of gang members who are in *Compassion* projects. Ask that they will be protected from the violent lifestyles of their parents.

Fellowship

How child-friendly is your sanctuary—the central space in which your faith community meets? Imagine you are a child walking into the sanctuary.

- What do you see at eye level?
- What do you see when you sit down?
- What do the decorations, if there are any (for example, banners, stained-glass windows, posters and so on) communicate to you?
- Are you encouraged to touch the things in this space?
- What do you hear?
- How do the physical surroundings of the sanctuary engage you to explore your faith or make you feel welcome?

Now, as a group, begin to address this issue. Involve a group of children in helping you to create a more child-friendly sanctuary in which children will feel more welcome and included.

Witness

Do a group role-play. One of you has accepted an invitation to go to church with a friend. Nothing looks, sounds or feels familiar and the people speak a language unknown to you. Several people greet you warmly. Someone other than your friend approaches you and you would like to respond but feel that you will not be understood or that you will feel stupid. What do you do?

What happens next and how do things unfold? How devoted are you to what we are destined to become in Christ?

For personal reflection

Reflect on the following excerpt from *Amid the Ruins*. How is remorse different from repentance? How might Judas' history have been altered if, after betraying Christ, he had understood God's compassion, sought and experienced the forgiveness of Christ?

Choose one of the pictures of yourself from which to write. Describe a time when you betrayed someone or they betrayed you. Which response brought healing, remorse or repentance, and how?

Judas hangs himself

Twisted in torment remorse regret
One fatal kiss could not forget
Thirty coins could not repay
The debt of guilt nor take away
Judas swinging from a rope
Dangled feet the death of hope
Buried in the Field of Blood
Purchase price the Son of God

Amid the ruins they whisper
'the end of the world will be like this.'

© RENITA BOYLE

NOTES

1 Source unknown.
2 C. Calver, et al., *Dancing in the Dark*, Spring Harvest seminar notes, Lynx Communications, p. 34.
3 T. Castle, *A Treasury of Christian Wisdom*, Hodder & Stoughton, p. 93.
4 Castle, *Treasury of Christian Wisdom*, p. 250.
5 1 Corinthians 12:7–11; Romans 12:6.
6 Castle, *Treasury of Christian Wisdom*, p. 92.
7 J. Morley, *Bread of Tomorrow*, SPCK/Christian Aid, p. 62.
8 Matthew 5:44; 6:19.
9 Castle, *Treasury of Christian Wisdom*, p. 93.
10 M. Hodgin, *1001 Humorous Illustrations for Public Speaking*, Zondervan, p. 55.
11 2 Corinthians 8:9.
12 Source article: *Compassion International* website, July 2002.

SECTION THREE

Compassionate community:
in humble servanthood

Someone once said, 'The church is not made up of people who are better than the rest, but of people who want to become better than they are.'[1]

Apart from himself, the greatest gift that God has given us is each other. God intends us to serve one another humbly, to thrive in compassionate community rather than survive in isolation. We may quest for personal growth but discipleship is a group dynamic. 'Whenever two or three of you come together in my name,' says Jesus, 'I am there with you' (Matthew 18:20). Only three of the New Testament letters are addressed to individuals. In the main, scriptural teaching about discipleship is directed to groups of Christians together. 'Together you are the body of Christ,' says Paul. 'Each one of you is part of his body' (1 Corinthians 12:27). This description yields deep insights into compassionate community as a community of humble servanthood.

'Dear God,' said a little boy in prayer, 'we had a great time in church today but I wish you'd been there.'[2] How easy it is to forget that we are Christ's body and he is our head. The body of Christ belongs to Christ and he is not only present with us but in charge. What does he do with his authority? How does he display his greatness? He humbly serves others and teaches us to do the same. Jesus says, 'Whoever is the greatest should be the servant of the others... if you humble yourself, you will be honoured' (Matthew 23:11–12). In word, deed and death, Jesus demonstrated servanthood not as the way to greatness but as greatness itself, not as the way to achieve excellence but to show it. We are now his body, his servants and the servants of others. 'A body is made up of many parts,' said Paul, 'and each of them has its own use. That's how it is with us... we are each part of the body of Christ, as well as part of one another' (Romans 12:4–5).

Each of us is to be a temple fit for God's presence. Together, however, we are the body of Christ—an organism, not an organization—under his headship. 'One hundred religious persons knit into unity by careful organisation do not constitute a church any more than eleven dead men make a football team,' says A.W. Tozer. 'The first requisite is life, always!'[3] We depend on Christ for life, growth and direction. He strengthens us as his body, using our parts to hold us together and help us to function. We are a growing body, maturing in God's power and love.[4] As the body of Christ, we have not been left alone in person or in purpose. Jesus continues his ministry through us by the power of the Holy Spirit as we reveal God among ourselves and in the world.

We are to imitate Christ, living always in a way that becomes his kingdom. Faith in Christ, however, comes not by imitation but through initiation—new birth. Jesus made this clear to Nicodemus when he said, 'I tell you for certain that you must be born from above before you can see God's kingdom!' (John 3:3). It is hard to think of any picture so expressive as childbirth of both God's compassion and the changed character experienced by those who accept his love in Christ. This is a deeply humbling and maternal image. God bears us and brings us to birth, a personally painful process—all of his own grace and love. There is no scope for arrogance. Something is accomplished in us and for us that cannot be achieved by us. Speaking of motherhood, Erich Fromm says, 'The child in the decisive first years of his life has the experience of his mother as an all-enveloping, protective, nourishing power. Mother is food; she is love; she is warmth; she is earth. To be loved by her means to be alive, to be rooted, to be at home.'[5] So it is with God. He is always compassionately suffering with us with all of himself.

Through spiritual birth we are shaped by Christ and receive a new nature, life and community. We are baptized by the Holy Spirit into one body, whatever our differences or divisions.[6] We are not in uniformity but are possessed of a spiritual unity. Each of us contributes uniquely to the whole. We are not to be like a slapstick boxer who beats, bloodies and bruises himself instead of his opponent. There can be no anarchy in the body of Christ. We are all necessary and useful to each other, the good of the whole being the goal of all (1 Corinthians 12:21–22, 24, 26).

Someone once said, 'The body becomes stronger as its members become healthier.'[7] Living as a compassionate community runs counter to our cultural norm. Individualism, independence and self-sufficiency are held in contempt. Pride and envy, bitterness and élitism have no place.

It is not surprising that, of all the parts of the body, the tongue is singled out as a stumbling block to compassionate living. 'With our tongues we speak both praises and curses,' says James. 'We praise our Lord and Father, and we curse people who were created to be like God, and this isn't right' (James 3:9–10). Gossip, criticism and backbiting are destructive to compassionate community. We cannot stab one another in the back without mortally wounding the body of Christ.[8] We must affirm each other's worth, not wither it.

Encouragement has the word 'courage' at its heart. The tongue that can so sap courage can also be the source of courage to live in Christ. The tongue that is powerful enough to set a forest ablaze can equally set our lives alight with compassion. As the body of Christ, we must use our tongue to reinforce and refresh community, strengthen and build one another up in compassion. We are to nurture, counsel, encourage and confess our sins to one another. We are to speak up and out for those who cannot speak for themselves. Ours is an alternative society rooted in the love and compassion of God himself. It is little wonder that we cannot experience God's kingdom until we experience new birth in Christ.

The call to self-sacrifice is a strong message in a self-obsessed world. We are increasingly distanced from this world as we adopt an entirely different framework of values. We are a community with compassion at its core. Just as a healthy body works together for the good of the whole, we serve one another for the love of the whole. Jesus was born bodily into the world because of God's love and used his own body to serve, sacrifice and suffer, culminating in his death on the cross. The physical body of Christ was also raised to life. As the body of Christ, we too are born into the world to demonstrate love. We are to use our body to serve others sacrificially. We must either give up the pretence *of* compassion or back up the profession *with* compassion, even when it requires suffering. As the body of Christ, we wait for our own ultimate resurrection. Meanwhile, we are a living sign of the new life on offer through Christ right now. We not only proclaim this new life but experience it for ourselves and demonstrate it through compassionate community.[9]

A compassionate community cannot be other than a serving community. Servanthood is a quality to be expressed by every Christian, but it is also a gift. 'If we can serve others,' says Paul, 'we should serve' (Romans 12:7). We are not to flaunt our gifts as if we have somehow earned them. Neither, however, are we to allow any pretence of humility to stop us from using our gifts to serve one another. As Matthew Henry says, 'We must not say, "I am nothing, therefore I will sit still and do nothing"; but, "I am nothing in myself, and therefore I will lay out myself to the utmost, in the strength and grace of Christ."'[10]

We are created in the image of God to depend on one another and all together in Christ. The church is a universal body of people, encompassing all believers everywhere, living and dead. In humility we recognize this interdependence; through servanthood we respond to it. We suffer and rejoice together and become better than we are as we reclaim our identity in Christ and reveal God's greatness in how we serve. 'If you love each other,' said Jesus, 'everyone will know that you are my disciples' (John 13:35).

A story is told of a boy who went on a road trip with his father. Every so often the boy would ask, 'Are we there yet?' His father would reply, 'Not long now, son.' After a few hours the boy asked, 'Dad, how old am I going to be when I get there?' Jesus taught that the kingdom of God belongs to children. He did not, however, impose upon children an adult standard of discipleship. Jesus affirmed children for who they are and as an example of what we, as adults, can become. However, children are still children in the kingdom of God and in the body of Christ. We must serve them in a way that affirms childhood and find ways of encouraging their service in a way appropriate to them as children.

Dietrich Bonhoeffer once said, 'The church is the church only when it exists for others.'[11] Christ is the head of the body and we are accountable to him for the care of our most vulnerable parts. God has consistently shown his compassion for all and others, especially those in most need. We can't be converted to Christ without also being converted to those who are in need. When did we last promote others with honour? How transparent are we with one another? How selfless are we in our motivation to serve? Are we really interested in each other? Are we resisting the temptations to flaunt or hide our gifts? How will we bridge our divides and differences to demonstrate that we are one body, the compassionate community of Christ? How will we serve our children?

*

Girls and education

Santi's father believed that she was just one more mouth to feed, another drain on the family's precious resources, who would do better to get married at 15 than finish her education.

In many countries, to be born a woman means to be born a second-class citizen. Poverty and cultural customs breed a notion of female inferiority which is passed from one generation to another, resigning girls like Santi to positions of submission where they are denied the opportunity to be all that God intended.

Attending school can offer children, and specifically girls, the chance to gain practical skills, self-confidence and a greater understanding of the world around them. It also gives them the chance just to play and be children.

Schooling is expensive in many developing countries and, where it must be paid for, preference is always given to the boys in a family.

Staff at the project that Santi attended saw her capability and encouraged her to pursue her dream of being a teacher. After intervention with her family, the project workers persuaded her father to allow Santi to complete her education, and as a result Santi is now both a blessing to her family and to the children with whom she works.[12]

*

Group helps

Worship

O Breath of Life, come sweeping through us (SF1 388)
O for a heart to praise my God (SF1 393)
Spirit of holiness (SF2 1010)
What kind of love is this? (SF2 1111)
Within the veil (SF2 1121)

Word

Micah 6:6–8
1 Corinthians 12

Prayer

- Pray for strength for project workers who face opposition as they seek to build relationships with children and their families.
- Ask that parents will be greatly impacted by the love and support their children are receiving and be encouraged to take a leading role in their children's development.
- Pray for more educational opportunities for girls and women.

Fellowship

Arrange a family games night. Play games that require teamwork, such as Trivial Pursuit in teams, Operation, Pictionary, Happy Families, Charades and so on. Choose games appropriate to all ages.

Read 1 Corinthians 12 as an epilogue.

Witness

Explore these questions together as a group.

- How has the ministry of your faith community grown up from the needs of your physical community?
- Does your ministry reflect the current needs of your physical community, particularly those who are young?
- How can your ministry truly reflect the compassion of Christ in the wider community?

For personal reflection

Cut out different body parts from pictures in magazines and make a collage of a single human being in your journal. How is this a reflection or not a reflection of what Paul is trying to convey in 1 Corinthians 12?

- What part of the body are you?
- When are you most likely to 'beat yourself up'?
- In what ways do you need healing?
- How can you contribute to the body?
- How will you help develop compassion in those around you?

If you prefer, you may explore these questions with a close and trusted friend.

NOTES

1. A.P. Castle, *Quotes and Anecdotes: An Anthology for Preachers and Teachers*, Kevin Mayhew, p. 42.
2. M. Hodgin, *1001 Humorous Illustrations for Public Speaking*, Zondervan, p. 163.
3. www.christianquotes.org.
4. Colossians 2:19; Ephesians 4:15, 16.
5. T. Castle, *A Treasury of Christian Wisdom*, Hodder & Stoughton, p. 165.
6. 1 Corinthians 12:13.
7. www.christianquotes.com.
8. C. Calver, *Dancing in the Dark*, Spring Harvest seminar notes, Lynx Communications, p. 41.
9. Adapted from Calver, *Dancing in the Dark*, p. 37.
10. M. Henry, *A Commentary on the Whole Bible, Volume 3*, World Bible Publishers, p. 863.
11. Source unknown.
12. *Childlink Magazine*, Winter 2001/2.

SECTION FOUR

Compassionate community: in obedient response

Here is a well-known saying: 'You can pick your friends, but you're stuck with your relatives.'

Love them or loathe them, we all have families—delightful or dysfunctional, connected or constructed, well-known or never known, no one has a more significant impact on the people we become. We were created by the triune God to reflect him together in a community of love, beginning with our families. There is no greater expression of community than family and no greater betrayal than when they fail us. Thankfully, the wry insight above can take on a whole new meaning when applied to the family of God. God has picked us as his friends and placed us in his family. The glue that sticks us together is forgiveness; the blood that runs thicker than water between us is the blood of Christ, God incarnate. The Christian community is a compassionate community because we are the family of God.

Our adoption into God's family is an act of astonishing compassion. Though we have done nothing to deserve his love and everything to undermine it, we were chosen in Christ before we were even created, destined in God's love and compassion to be his children. Through the Holy Spirit we are born again and adopted into God's family. We receive a new nature—a growing family resemblance to Christ—and a new position as co-heirs with Christ. We also receive each other—siblings in the Saviour—and an opportunity to experience and express compassionate community. God the Father is our Father, Jesus our brother and the Holy Spirit the guarantee and guardian of our rich inheritance.[1] In God's family, our God-given need to belong, be loved and be loving is fulfilled.

'We are all like hurt children who need reassurance,' says Peter Kreeft. 'We get the reassurance of the Father in the person of the Son.'[2] In Christ we experience the fierce, intimate and universal love of the Father. His holiness is never diminished but his love is exalted, his compassion inspiring obedience that seeks to please rather than appease. This kind of obedience was a prominent characteristic of Jesus' life. It surged from the depth of divine abiding—Father, Son and Holy Spirit—and was the secret of his authority over fleeing demons and the forces of nature. Jesus' free-flowing surrender coursed through his life and culminated in his death.[3] His was not an obedience of unwilling compliance and blind faith, but of communal consensus and measured trust. 'Being a disciple always means staying close to Jesus, knowing his living voice and trusting his risen presence,' says Leith Fisher. 'The discipleship journey is not a solitary assault course of the spirit; it's a way we take knowing there is a hand to bear us up.'[4]

Jesus offers the parent–child relationship as a mental and emotional picture of discipleship. His own prayers are phrased in familial terms and reflect the intimacy of family living. As we have seen, Jesus prays to God affectionately as Dad (Abba) and teaches us to do the same. We are God's children and we are to pray together as brothers and sisters in his family.[5] He is not only 'my Father' but 'our Father'. Together we acknowledge that we are not in possession of God but being possessed by him; we are not governing but being governed; we are not holding on but being held. We ask *our* Father to help us honour and obey him. We ask for each other what we long for ourselves—daily food from God's abundance, protection from temptation and evil, and forgiveness in the same measure as we have forgiven.

George Herbert says, 'He who cannot forgive others breaks the bridge over which he must pass himself.'[6] The cross of Christ is the bridge over which each of us must pass—its whole purpose reconciliation, forgiveness the first step. From it Jesus asked his Father to forgive the very enemies he was dying for.[7] Is it any wonder, then, that our own unforgiveness of others is near unpardonable? 'If you forgive others for the wrongs they do to you, your Father in heaven will forgive you,' said Jesus. 'But if you don't forgive others, your Father will not forgive your sins' (Matthew 6:14–15). If we are to find mercy, we must offer mercy. Jesus died to make peace not only between God and us but between us and others. To forgive one another is to fulfil God's greatest commandment to love one another and so love God.

Robert Frost says, 'Home is the place where, when you have to go there, they have to take you in.'[8] Forgiveness is fundamental in the family of God, proof that we are his children and bear his likeness. A well-functioning family is a place where we learn about how to live and can make mistakes without condemnation. This does not, however, mean that we condone evil. Forgiveness does not validate the actions of those who offend, and does not diminish the responsibility they must take or the restitution they must make to the one offended. Peter says, 'You are free, but still you are God's servants, and you must not use your freedom as an excuse for doing wrong. Respect everyone and show special love for God's people' (1 Peter 2:16–17).

We must be mindful of those among us who have suffered most. Jesus announces God's special blessings on those who endure what we'd most like to avoid—poverty, hunger and mourning, hatred, rejection and insult. What a constant challenge Jesus presents to our own values as he invites us to live differently in our world and among ourselves. 'Love your enemies, and be good to everyone who hates you. Ask God to bless anyone who curses you, and pray for everyone who is cruel to you... Then you will get a great reward, and you will be the true children of God in heaven. He is good even to people who are unthankful and cruel. Have pity on others, just as your Father has pity on you' (Luke 6:27–28, 35–36). The kind of love (*agape*) being spoken of here is not that of passionate devotion (*eros*) or warm affection (*philia*). It is a determined, undeterred graciousness that is based completely on God's own love and compassion—*suffering with*. It doesn't seek retaliation or reward and isn't reproachful. Neither is it passive. It is a love that wrong-foots the enemy by returning good for evil, replacing curses with blessings and prayerful kindness in the face of cruelty.

Forgiveness is surely the hardest test of obedience, the hardest quest in obedience, for any child of God. That God's love should extend not only to those who are abused but to those who do the abusing, that God's forgiveness is equally available to those who are victimizers as to those who are victims, is surely the hardest cross for any to bear. Perhaps God is most compassionate about those in greatest need because they have most to forgive. God himself knows the cost of true forgiveness, what it is to have compassion enough to *suffer with* despite the agony to himself.

Someone once said, 'Whenever a man is ready to uncover sins, God is always ready to cover them.' We can't be 'in Christ' without forgiveness—a forgiveness overflowing from God's abundance in having forgiven us.[9] When we forgive, we make visible in the world what has already been accomplished in us. If we would exercise Jesus' authority, we must surrender to God's, not because we fear him but because we know him. We may not always understand but we must always undertake what is asked of us—beginning with forgiveness. Redemption commits us irrevocably to the abandonment of revenge and the pursuit of peace. Forgiveness may be gradual, but it is never optional.

Ultimately, we know that only God can forgive sin. How extraordinary it is, then, that we are called by God to forgiveness, and even more extraordinary that we are capable of it. To forgive one another and ourselves as the Lord forgives us is nothing short of divine—a positive proof that the triune God is indeed dwelling in us as a family.

We forgive to the degree that we love. Faith in Christ unites us more closely than any relationship offered by the world. Commitment to Christ is divisive in the sense that it will result in wrenching distance—spiritually if not physically—from everything and everyone who is not also committed to Christ.

As followers of Christ, we must be willing to count the cost, to replace the comforts of our strongest earthly networks with those of God's. We ourselves become the fulfilment of Jesus' promise to provide a new family as we become family to one another in him.

A little boy was praying. 'Dear God,' he said, 'did you really mean "do unto others as they do unto you"? Because if you did, then I'm really going to do unto my brother!'[10] It is grievous but true that our worst enemies are often our nearest of kin. As the family of God we have a special responsibility to show compassion for those who have known least of it in their lives. What does 'turning the other cheek' mean for those, children among them, whose cheeks are crimson from physical abuse? What does 'giving your shirt too' mean for those living rough on the streets? What does 'giving without asking anything in return' mean for those in forced or bonded labour? How do we help one another to 'treat others just as you want to be treated' (Luke 6:31)?

It is impossible to answer these questions for anyone else. Through compassion, however, it is possible to stand with those who are asking the questions and be a new kind of family, a family that provides support and solace, protection and presence. Commitment to Christ is all-consuming and, in him, so must our compassion be. How all-consuming and all-encompassing is our compassion? Who needs to be included and how can we include them?

*

Child labour

Childhood should be a period of utter freedom—freedom from responsibility and pain—and yet, for millions of children across the world, childhood is merely a stepping stone in the struggle of life. Situations such as war, natural disasters or epidemics take parents away, leaving children to fend for themselves or to survive on an extremely reduced income. Many have no choice in their quest to survive other than work.

Uneducated, unskilled and unaware of their rights as workers, children are often subjected to the most hazardous types of work. Chained to benches, some must wash car parts in dangerous toxic chemicals. Others carry building materials that physically deform their fragile bodies, and others have no choice but to put themselves at risk as child prostitutes.

Martin is one such child living in Kabale, Uganda. After the death of their mother, Martin and his brother were left in the care of their uncle, a boy of just 15 years. As a child himself, Martin's uncle was forced to walk the streets daily in search of whatever work he could find. This hopelessness and subsistence lifestyle would have been all Martin and his brother could look forward to had Martin not been offered healthcare, education, food and clothing at the *Compassion* project he attends. Martin can now look to his future with options for his life. The assistance that is provided for both him and his family offer them the chance to think beyond the next meal.[11]

*

Group helps

Worship

At this table we remember (SF3 1181)
Father God we worship You (SF1 93)
Father I place into your hands (SF1 97)
Restore, O Lord (SF1 464)
When we walk with the Lord (SF1 605)

Word

Psalm 51
Luke 6:27–36

Prayer

- Pray for more safe havens where children can play away from harm.
- Pray that parents will understand the importance of the freedom of childhood and won't place too great a responsibility on children at a young age.
- Pray that companies will stop employing children and start offering education for them instead.

Fellowship

Have each person in your group create a 'family tree by bond'. This works much like a family tree, except that the relationships are based on spiritual rather than physical birth. It can include members of your birth family if appropriate, but the focus is on those regarded to be spiritual parents, grandparents, brothers, sisters, aunts, uncles and cousins. The tree can include those who are dead as well as living, young as well as old.

Use this exercise to explore Mark 10:29–31 together. Close with the Lord's Prayer.

Witness

Read Luke 6:27–36. Imagine you are living in a situation of abuse.

- What messages is the church sending to you about forgiveness?
- Are these messages appropriate and what Christ intended for us to communicate? Do they communicate compassion?
- How do we help one another to 'treat others just as you want to be treated' (v. 31)?

For personal reflection

Read Psalm 51. Choose one of the pictures of yourself in the front of your journal from which to write. Think about yourself at that age. Write this statement in your journal and fill in the blanks. Do not elaborate.

I will never forgive.......... for..........

Now take the first steps in committing yourself to forgive this person. Write a letter to yourself about why you want to forgive and what the result of this forgiveness might be, or write a letter (which you will not send) to the person who has hurt you. Explore the feelings surrounding the incident, why you are finding it difficult to forgive and why you want to be able to forgive.

NOTES

1   Romans 8:15–16.
2   P. Kreeft, *Making Sense Out of Suffering*, Servant Books, p. 131.
3   Matthew 26:39; 1 Corinthians 15:28.
4   L. Fisher, *The Widening Road*, Scottish Christian Press, p. 67.
5   Matthew 6:9–13.
6   A.P. Castle, Quotes and Anecdotes: *An Anthology for Preachers and Teachers*, Kevin Mayhew, p. 323.
7   Luke 23:34–35.
8   J. Green, *Cassell Dictionary of Cynical Quotations*, Cassell, p. 90.
9   1 Timothy 2:8; 1 John 1:9.
10 Source unknown.
11 *Compassion Childlink Magazine* 2003, Number 3.

SECTION FIVE

Compassionate community: in hopeful expectancy

'Redemption is a process with a climax,' says Jean Fleming, 'a longing with a consummation, a divine romance that proceeds to marriage.'[1]

Surely the most striking and stunning portrait of Christian community is framed in its description as 'the Bride of Christ'.[2] No other image is so expectant, so joyful, and so hopeful of the heaven yet unseen. Christ loves his bride purely and sincerely with an unequalled constancy of devotion. She is set apart for him in this world and he will glorify her in the next. Although the lovers of Christ who have gone before us are now sharing a richer communion with God, we are all eagerly anticipating our wedding day. We will no longer be *being* perfected but will *be* perfect and glorified in love. The bridegroom will return for his bride, the betrothed, beloved for ever.

This imagery is foreshadowed in God's compassionate husbandry of Israel. However, as the new people of God established in Christ it is equally applicable to us. No longer called 'Deserted and Desolate', God rejoices in us as a bridegroom rejoices over his bride.[3] As the creator of all people and the spouse of a specific people, God's knowledge of his bride is unfathomable. God rejoices in us as his intended bride despite knowing that he will also have to redeem us from constant infidelity. Matthew Henry says, 'As God is slow to anger, so he is swift to mercy.'[4] Our maker, the Lord Almighty and holy God of all the earth himself, is our husband and redeemer. Though God is angry for a moment, his long-suffering compassion is for ever. He brings us back with love and tenderness to his embrace and protection again and again.[5]

God's relationship to us as his bride is one of completely unconditional love—warm and tender in compassion, intimate in affection. Just as we are no longer only his servants but his friends, he is no longer only our master, but our husband. 'I promise that from that day on,' declares the Lord through Hosea, 'you will call me your husband instead of your master... I will accept you as my wife for ever, and instead of a bride price I will give you justice, fairness, love, kindness, and faithfulness. Then you will truly know who I am' (Hosea 2:16, 19–20).

God hungers for us. He was aware of us long before we were aware of him, and awake to our longing for love long before we were awakened to his presence in it. Song of Songs, a book that may be interpreted as reflecting the relationship between Christ and his church, beautifully captures this awakening. 'My bride, my very own, you have stolen my heart!' says the author. 'With one glance from your eyes and the glow of your necklace, you have stolen my heart' (Song of Songs 4:9). How is it possible that we should steal the heart of God, be the focus of his desire, the churning in his spirit?

Individually and as a community, God's yearning for us is so deep that he paid our dowry himself. We are bound to Christ and to one another not by a legal contract, but by a compassionate covenant—God securing his promise to save us by suffering with us in his Son, and dwelling in us by his Spirit.[6] We are 'the wife of the Lamb' (Revelation 21:9), brought by his love, bought with his blood. 'This metaphor confronts us with our responsibility to be single-minded in our devotion to God,' says Bruce Milne, 'and to recognize the gravity of giving our affection and loyalty to other things, not least our own ambitions and interest.'[7] There is a special knowing in the eyes of those who love. The only appropriate response to our groom is to return love with love as we are drawn into the divine intimacy of the triune God—chosen by the Father, purified in the Holy Spirit and sprinkled with the blood of Christ. This union was the purpose of all that Christ did and continues to do. 'Christ died for us, so that we could live with him, whether we are alive or dead when he comes,' says Paul (1 Thessalonians 5:10).

Pope John Paul II said, 'We are an Easter people and Alleluia is our song.'[8] When Jesus died, both his friends and his enemies, those who loved and those who hated him, believed his influence to be at an end. However, through his resurrection and ascension, the cross became a hinged door flung wide into heaven. As the bride of Christ, our hope of this heaven is grounded in conviction, not confusion. We adopt an eternal perspective on what we can now only partially see or experience. Peter writes to those who are suffering, 'But God shows undeserved kindness to everyone. That's why he appointed Christ Jesus to choose you to share in his eternal glory. You will suffer for a while, but God will make you complete, steady, strong, and firm' (1 Peter 5:10).

Whether we are undermined or undone, unfulfilled or unappreciated, we can remain joyful in hope, patient in affliction and faithful in prayer (Romans 12:12). Ours is the hope of heaven, the elation of eternity—not as the end of chronological time but in the person of Christ, not as a place set *aside* but a presence *inside*. In his prayers, Jesus reveals the essence of eternal life as an intimate knowing—the same 'knowing' used of sexual intimacy in marriage. 'Eternal life is to know you, the only true God,' prays Jesus, 'and to know Jesus Christ, the one you sent' (John 17:3). Heaven is not so much a place as a relationship—unceasing and uncompromised—not only elsewhere and otherwise, but also here and now.

God's compassion in Christ saturates the lives of those who experience it and reveals itself as the defining quality of Christian community. There is much in the world to draw our hearts astray from Christ, but much more in Christ to entice us to fidelity in mind and heart, body and soul. 'Our call is first to be the bride faithful,' says Francis Schaeffer, 'but also the bride in love.'[9] The celebration of communion, the Lord's supper, is surely the greatest rehearsal dinner in history. We are the betrothed of Christ honouring the dowry, his body and blood, already paid for us. We are lovestruck, demonstrating compassion and forgiveness among each other until he comes.[10] Our bridegroom will return to gather his bride and we will enjoy the fruition of Paul's words—that what we know in part, we will fully know, even as we are fully known.[11]

As we have seen, union with Christ inexorably involves us in community with each other. Although the church—believers together by its simplest definition—falls far short of the ideal, we must not despise what Christ so loves. We must, instead, be devoted to what we are destined to become one to another and all together in Christ. 'Christ loved the church and gave his life for it,' says Paul. 'He made the church holy by the power of his word, and he made it pure by washing it with water. Christ did this, so that he would have a glorious and holy church, without faults or spots or wrinkles or any other flaws' (Ephesians 5:25–27). We must strengthen in our resolve to exchange present realities for the coming reality of the kingdom in all its fullness. As Bruce Milne says, 'We are called to move in the direction of our destiny through daily repentance from sin and increasing conformity with the holy will of God.'[12]

Jesus began his ministry by quenching thirst at a wedding and will fulfil it by quenching thirst at his own. The book of Revelation closes with an invitation from the Spirit and the bride to the thirsty: '"Come!" Everyone who hears this should say, "Come!" If you are thirsty, come! If you want life-giving water, come and take it. It's free!' (Revelation 22:17). As in Jesus' parable of the wedding banquet, the Father has provided not only food but a feast, not just a sip but a surplus, and invited all comers.[13] As Matthew Henry says, 'There is enough and to spare, of everything that can add to our present comfort and everlasting happiness, in the salvation of his Son Jesus Christ.'[14]

Holiness is a defining quality of God's people. Our growing internal union with Christ reveals itself in a growing and visible external holiness. Our lack of internal holiness also reveals itself in moral failure and division. Perhaps the greatest blemish on the bride of Christ is our lack of compassion, our stubborn refusal to accept what Christ has offered and likewise to offer it to others. As we have seen, the affirmation of worth in God's image bearers is inherent to the worship of God himself. 'Compassion brings passion to the level of community and draws the energies of one's heart beyond itself,' says Paul Keenan.[15] As a truly compassionate community, we must embrace those who thirst both physically and spiritually and invite them to share in the hope of heaven here and now. Ours is the promise of a new heaven and a new earth, where justice will rule, beginning now.[16] God who has promised these things is faithful. Those who are gowned with the righteousness of Christ and set apart by the purity of the Holy Spirit will meet their bridegroom and will be like him when he returns. This hope encourages us to holiness—cleansed for compassion, set apart from all that soils and spoils—as we prepare for our wedding day.

*

HIV/AIDS education

Education has long been seen as the key to change in societies across the world, and education is therefore a vital element in the fight against AIDS and HIV. But who is to take the initiative to ensure that information about the disease is communicated effectively? Governments and international organizations the world over are working in conjunction with local partners to ensure that no one goes without being accurately informed about the impact of HIV and AIDS.

In October 2000, *Compassion* was part of an international conference entitled 'A Prescription for Hope', which directly addressed the issue of HIV and AIDS. The church has long been criticized for its lack of intervention in the AIDS pandemic, and the conference was held to appeal to the Christian world to wake up and take a leading role in fighting the disease. Education strategies that raise awareness about the disease, its causes, prevention and how to cope with it are being spearheaded by *Compassion* programmes across Africa.

The subject of HIV and AIDS is an uncomfortable one, but ignoring it will not make it disappear. Dr Adela Mareu is the director of *Compassion Tanzania*'s HIV programme and she has been working closely with staff across Tanzania to train five employees in each of *Compassion*'s projects as HIV/AIDS experts. As specialists, these employees seek to overcome the myths and taboos surrounding HIV and AIDS, to inform people accurately about the cause, effects and prevention of the disease and also to offer medical care and confidential counselling as well as practical aid and advice.

In the past decade, Uganda has halved its rate of HIV infection,[17] and education has played a major role in the reduction of the infection rate. While the AIDS epidemic has not reached levels in Tanzania as high as those in Uganda or other African countries, it is vital that prevention strategies are implemented before the situation becomes any more dire.

*

Group helps

Worship

I will rejoice in you and be glad (SF1 259)
O give thanks (SF1 395)
Rejoice, the Lord is King! (SF1 463)
This is the mystery (SF2 1060)
What a friend I've found (SF2 1109)

Word

Isaiah 52
Ephesians 5:21–33

Prayer

- Ask that communities will be receptive to the education they receive about HIV/AIDS.
- Ask that myths and taboos, which have prevented accurate distribution of information, will be shattered with truth about the disease.
- Ask that fathers will value their families and remain faithful to their wives to prevent the spread of HIV/AIDS.

Fellowship

Think of your faith community as the bride of Christ. What is Jesus' wedding vow to you? What are yours to him? Write them down.

- How deeply committed are you to one another?
- How devoted are you to what we are destined to become in Christ?
- How will you move together in the direction of your destiny?
- How does compassion figure in your marriage?

Witness

Think of yourselves as individuals and as a community. Explore these questions together:

- What is your tendency: to be without doing or to do without being? Give an example of each.
- What are you called to be?
- What are you called to do?
- Why is achieving balance vital for compassionate witness?

For personal reflection

You are the bride of Christ and it is your 25th anniversary. Christ has given you a gift in a box that you now hold on your lap.

- What's in the box? Is it something you expected or is it completely unexpected?
- How do you feel before you open it?
- How do you feel afterwards?
- What is its special significance to you alone?
- What will you do with it?
- How will you use it?

Explore these questions in your journal or with a close and trusted friend.

NOTES

1 Jean Fleming, *The Homesick Heart*, Navpress.
2 Ephesians 5:22–27; Revelation 19:6–9; 21:2, 9; 22:17.
3 Isaiah 62:4–5.
4 M. Henry, *A Commentary on the Whole Bible, Volume 3*, World Bible Publishers, p. 545.
5 Isaiah 54:5–6, 8.
6 Ephesians 2:11–22; 2 Corinthians 3:4–6.
7 B. Milne, *Know the Truth*, IVP, p. 212.
8 S. Ratcliffe, *Oxford Quotations by Subject*, Oxford University Press, p. 67.
9 R. Backhouse, *1500 Illustrations for Preaching and Teaching*, Marshall Pickering, p. 58.
10 1 Corinthians 10:16–23.
11 1 Corinthians 13:12.
12 Milne, *Know the Truth*, p. 282.
13 Matthew 22:8–9.
14 Henry, *A Commentary*, p. 708.
15 P. Keenan, *Heart Storming*, Contemporary Books, p. 15.
16 2 Peter 3:13.
17 *Guardian*: 'Famine in Africa'.

IN-DEPTH REFLECTION

Why partner with the church?

Compassion recognizes the importance of solidarity with Christians across the world and the strategic position of the church within the context of a local community. For this reason, all *Compassion*'s projects are run through local Christian partners. An understanding of regional culture, local beliefs and specific needs of a community are essential to effectively reach those in poverty. It is this fundamental knowledge that the church has and can utilize.

As we seek to advance the kingdom of God, we should seek to resource his church. *Compassion* works deliberately to equip the local church to fulfil its God-given role in ministering to needy children and families. This can be summed up in the word 'facilitation', an idea founded in scripture. The word in Greek means *paraclete*, which is a legal advocate or counsel for defence, an intercessor or a helper.[1] In the Bible, the Holy Spirit is the facilitator who intervenes to release God's power within his people. We in turn can release the potential in others. The Western world has access to finances and resources that can help to transform the vision, passion, knowledge and manpower of a church into an effective child development centre.

Successful development should not be dictated by those on the other side of the world, but worked out alongside the local community. The longevity and effectiveness is increased when local people have ownership of the project. God has provided even the poorest of the poor with resources and skills that they can utilize. Evidence of this can be found in the valuable participation of parents in *Compassion* projects. In the Philippines, uneducated mothers are taught how to screen children for health complaints.

IN-DEPTH REFLECTION: WHY PARTNER WITH THE CHURCH?

As they learn this skill, so they become passionate advocates for children's health within their own families and communities. In Honduras, *Compassion* projects run sewing classes for parents and, as a result, mothers now make school uniforms for the children. This not only has practical benefits for the project but is also a good way of introducing parents, many of whom are not Christians, to the church. Churches that were once unknown in their communities have become beacons of light in desperate situations as they reach out not only to the children but their families as well.

Some of the poorest and most threatening neighbourhoods in the world are impenetrable by those who do not live there. By partnering with local people, it is possible to gain access to these areas. In El Salvador there is a huge problem with gang violence in the capital, San Salvador. Tikal is one of the most dangerous areas in the city, where many inhabitants are gang members and assault, robbery, kidnapping, rape and murder are common occurrences. The *Compassion* project, 'Amigos de Jesus', works with the children living in this neighbourhood, registering many of the sons and daughters of gang members.

As the children are given skills and the chance to live alternative lifestyles, so they have a more hopeful vision of the future. These children are then like little pastors in their own homes, ministering to their parents. The influence of a child should never be underestimated, as many gang members have been touched by the love of Christ and broken their involvement with the violent groups. These reformed men and women pass on the wisdom of their experience through the *Compassion* projects, warning children about the dangers of the world and encouraging good decision making.[2] Their own powerful testimony allows them to talk with increased passion and authenticity and stand as a great witness for the changing power of Christ. Change can and will take place, even in the most impossible of situations, when faith is put into action.

Local Christians are great role models for the children they work with because they have empathy for their situation and can inspire concern and pride for the community where they live. A large number of formerly *Compassion*-sponsored children return to the communities in which they grew up, as teachers, doctors and nurses, through a desire to see further development take place. Permanent change for the better occurs when there is a continual regeneration rather than just a migration of those who have skills away from the area. It is incredible how much change can come through investment in the local community by the local community.

NOTES

1 *Ministry Insights, Principles of Child Development*, Compassion source, Gordon Mullinex, 2000.
2 Roberto Medrano, El Salvador Communications specialist.

CHAPTER SIX

Compassionate witness

SECTION ONE

Compassionate witness: in common unity

'God had only one son,' said David Livingstone, *'and he was a missionary.'* [1]

Those of us who have had the privilege of journeying with a loved one through the process of dying know also how precious last moments become. In these moments we often bear witness to a person's purest self and truest character. Hence, last words are often significant words. Those who witnessed Jesus' physical and emotional anguish on the cross also witnessed him forgive his enemies, welcome a thief into paradise and make arrangements for his surviving family. They also heard him commit his spirit to the Father as he submitted himself to the finality of death (or so they thought).

It is truly impossible to imagine how those who witnessed Jesus' death felt when he was raised to life again with a new but recognizable appearance. This extraordinary experience alone must have transformed all that Jesus taught them from black and white into glorious technicolour. But there was more to come. Jesus would say goodbye again, only this time he would go to glory and promise the coming of another just like him in return. These words too would reveal Jesus' truest character and deepest compassion. They would also have a dramatic impact. 'Go to the people of all nations and make them my disciples,' says Jesus. 'Baptize them in the name of the Father, the Son, and the Holy Spirit, and teach them to do everything I have told you. I will be with you always, even until the end of the world... But the Holy Spirit will come upon you and give you power. Then you will tell everyone about me... everywhere in the world' (Matthew 28:19; Acts 1:8). At the core of Jesus' final instructions to his disciples was the call to participate with him in witness through the power of the Holy Spirit.

The early Christian community wholly believed what Jesus said and waited in constant united prayer for the fulfilment of his promise.[2] They weren't so much praying for the Holy Spirit to come as preparing themselves for what the Holy Spirit would bring. 'It was a power that was both awaited in obedience and utterly unexpected in its energy and urgency,' says Janet Morley. 'It generated both a deep interior fire, and immediate, compelling and outrageous public witness.[3] These ten days of watchful prayer prefaced the great task of witness begun locally at Pentecost and more broadly through Stephen's martyrdom and Paul's ministry. Believers bonded together in community everywhere the gospel spread and took hold. They began to reflect God's universal compassion and fulfil his purpose to be a universal people drawn from every tribe, tongue, nation and race.[4] How humbling it is to acknowledge that we, today, are testimony not only to the Lord's answered prayer for future believers but also to the faithfulness of early believers in fulfilling their commission to spread the gospel and make disciples. It is now our turn to take the good news of Christ to the end of our street and the ends of the earth.

'Evangelism is not a professional job for a few trained men,' says Elton Trueblood, 'but is instead the unrelenting responsibility of every person who belongs to the company of Jesus.'[5] We are a compassionate community modelled after the triune God himself. Our call to witness is nothing less than triunitarian: to reveal the whole of God—Father, Son and Holy Spirit—through the whole of us. 'Those who deny the Trinity,' says J.I. Packer, 'have to scale down the Gospel too.'[6]

Christian faith is personal, but it is not private. We were created in God's image for community and as a community we witness to God's compassion in the world. We proclaim God's work in Christ both in what we say and in what we do. Sin produces division. It causes prejudice and friction, creates injustice and oppression, ravages marriages, families, churches, communities and nations. It produces exploitation of those who are weak by those who are strong and those who are poor by those who are rich. Internally we are at war with ourselves and estranged from God. No wonder the gospel of Christ is such good news. Evil is firmly and finally dealt with in Christ's death and resurrection. 'Even when we were God's enemies, he made peace with us, because his Son died for us,' says Paul. 'Yet something even greater than friendship is ours. Now that we are at peace with God, we will be saved by his Son's life' (Romans 5:10).

Someone once said, 'God does not expect us to be more than we are; He expects us to be all that we are.'[7] The gospel's only purpose is reconciliation. In Christ, sin and suffering have been accepted and atoned for, our fallen humanity has been reconciled and returned to intimacy, and our dignity has been restored. Compassionate witness is simply to make visible in the world what has already been accomplished in us. As God's love transforms us, we are filled with compassion and seek a reconciliation that extends to others inside and outside the Christian community. We don't just deliver the message; we are the message.

'There is one Christ in whom all believers hope,' says Matthew Henry, 'and one heaven they are all hoping for; therefore we should be of one heart.'[8] In the Holy Spirit, early followers became a reconciled, courageous and dynamic community. They communicated God's message in word and deed. They praised God, met together often and shared everything they had. They even sold their assets to give to those in need. Their compassion was so evident and so attractive that the community grew bigger by the day.[9] The apostles preached passionately and powerfully that the Lord was risen, a fact that would have seemed farcical or fanatical were it not for the wider witness of a compassionate community in action.

Compassion belongs in community and will always reveal itself there. *Suffering with* is not a personal talent, but a way of being together, a mutual communal vocation. Encouraged by the presence of Christ alongside us and the presence of the Holy Spirit in us we draw others away from aloneness and into community. We reflect God's unity in the way that we love each other and we witness to God's compassion in the way that we are together. To lack love destroys both our community and our witness.

Charles Spurgeon says, 'If you have not the spirit of God, Christian worker, remember that you stand in somebody else's way; you are a fruitless tree standing where a fruitful tree might grow!'[10] Bringing the whole of the gospel to the whole of the world is a fresh task for each generation, a task motivated by the Holy Spirit, compelled not by duty, but by love. We have come to the cross ourselves and experienced there the removal of all that separates us from God and the gift of peace with God. We are eagerly bound to share the message of the cross and confidently trust that the grace that saved us will save others also, however great the sin or deep the need.

Erin Majors says, 'A candle loses nothing by lighting another candle.'[11] To be compelled by God's compassion in witness is to live the whole of our lives in line with it. Early Christians knew their purpose. Plucked from darkness into light, they too helped to pluck others from darkness into light. How, then, are we to reveal God? 'Treat others just as you want to be treated,' says Jesus (Luke 6:31). Our gospel is not so much a social gospel as a communal one. We are a Christian community in witness to social communities through compassionate love. In fact, compassion is *the* defining quality of wanna-be disciples of Christ. As we compassionately suffer with others, they experience God's love in us and respond to it for themselves. 'Keep in step with God's love...' says Jude. 'Be helpful to all who may have doubts. Rescue any who need to be saved... have mercy on everyone who needs it' (Jude 21–23).

Jesus prayed that we would be possessed of such a unity as to bring others to faith. As a compassionate community, we are drawn into Jesus' own union with the Father and the Holy Spirit. Unity is a powerful experience and a powerful witness. 'No man is an island entire of itself,' said John Donne. Human beings are communal beings. We are an integral part of our environment and our environment is an integral part of us. We may feel isolated, but we do not experience life in isolation. Our environment shapes our experiences. We are not passive recipients of our surroundings and neither do we respond passively to them. Although we must accept that a change in the global environment of poverty and despair will not necessarily lead to changed lives, we must also accept that to leave the environment unchanged is grievous to God and can offer no hope to those who must endure it. In his humanity, Jesus becomes part of our environment and contributes to our experience of being human the compassion that brings ultimate transformation.

'In our era,' says Dag Hammerskjold, 'the road to holiness necessarily passes through the world of action.'[12] Our lips are the messengers of our hearts; whatever is there will come out. We must, however, do more than just preach the gospel. Proclaiming the good news always includes the practice of good deeds. 'We know what love is because Jesus gave his life for us,' said John. 'That's why we must give our lives for each other... Children, you show love for others by truly helping them, and not merely talking about it' (1 John 3:16, 18). Practical witness doesn't add to or detract from the gospel, nor is it secondary. Fulfilling our God-given responsibility to help people in poverty is integral to the gospel itself. It is a crucial test of how faithful we are to Christ's own mission to spread the good news among those who are poor, announce freedom for those imprisoned, restore sight to those who are blind and release everyone who suffers from their suffering.

*

Child soldiers

In the 1990s, more than two million children worldwide were killed in war, caught in the crossfire of a conflict they neither caused nor understood. It is perhaps most disturbing to learn that many of those brandishing the weapons are themselves children. Their innocence makes children easy prey for the military and rebels who seek to swell their numbers. Children may be snatched from their families and homes and forced to watch obscene acts of violence as a means by which to harden them to the realities of war. In some cases they must even commit atrocities against their own family to ensure that they will never be able to return to the once-safe community where they grew up.

In war-torn situations, children who have been orphaned become the most vulnerable. Educational and social services do not exist to provide for these children. Left to roam, or forced to go to work, they search for purpose and meaning in their life. This search can lead them in the wrong direction. At present there are 300,000 children worldwide serving as soldiers, many under the age of ten.[13] When the fighting ceases, these children must try to find a direction for their life outside the world of war. It is projects such as *Compassion* that find these children and help them to come to terms with the horror of their experiences.

*

Group helps

Worship

May your love (SF1 366)
Now thank we all our God (SF1 386)
We want to see Jesus lifted high (SF2 1105)
Ye servants of God (SF1 628)
You shall go out with joy (SF1 641)

Word

Isaiah 61:1–2
Matthew 28
Luke 4:18–19

Prayer

- Pray that children who have been abused as child soldiers will be provided with effective care and support to help them come to terms with their situations.
- Ask that *Compassion* projects will offer long-term support and stability to former child soldiers.
- Pray that children who have been child soldiers will be seen as victims and not punished as criminals.

Fellowship

Imagine yourselves as Mary witnessing the death of Jesus. Read and reflect on the following excerpt from *Amid the Ruins*.

- How was Mary's experience of motherhood and grief like and unlike that of other mothers?
- What do you think Mary was thinking and feeling at the cross?
- What impact did the gift of salvation from her own son make in her life and witness?
- Mary is the only person in the Gospels known to have witnessed the span of Jesus' life. From the poverty of his birth to the pathos of the cross and, undoubtedly, witness to post-resurrection events, Mary had much to ponder in her heart. How do you think this extraordinary experience equipped her to reveal God to others, and fulfil her part in the great commission?
- What can we take from Mary's own experience into ours?

> *Near the cross an anguished face*
> *Aching arms cannot embrace*
> *The babe who for his mother cried*
> *The man who for his mother died*
> *Where now the frankincense and gold*
> *Where the glory once foretold*

COMPASSIONATE WITNESS: IN COMMON UNITY

No star beyond the teary blur
All is woe and bitter myrrh

Sweet Mary, do you ponder this?
God did know a mother's kiss
Once a mother's heart did own
Called a mother's lap his throne
Once did trust a mother's love
Did once a mother's saviour prove
Near the cross beloved John
'Dear woman, here is now your son.'

Amid the ruins they whisper
'the end of the world will be like this.'
© RENITA BOYLE

Witness

Witness is to make visible in the world what has already been accomplished in us. Take a big piece of paper and draw the outline of a body on it. As a group, think about your faith community. What areas of division, prejudice, friction, conflict, hurt, injustice or lack of inclusion exist under the surface? Make a rip in the body for every divisive thing mentioned. How do these divisions show themselves in the body of Christ? Think about these areas and explore the following questions as a group:

- What does it mean to be reconciled?
- How do forgiveness and reconciliation relate to one another?
- To what extent do you believe that 'the only purpose of the gospel is reconciliation?'
- How will you work toward reconciliation as a body?
- How will you make visible what is being accomplished in you?

For personal reflection

Choose a quiet candlelit space in which to write in your journal. Reflect on the statement, 'A candle loses nothing by lighting another candle.' Who are the candles in your life? How is a candle lit? What happens when the flames of two candles meet? Where are candles most useful?

Think of yourself as a candle—lit or unlit, used or unused, in a drawer or as a focal point, where you've been or where you'd like to go. Using all your senses, write about the experience of being a candle.

NOTES

1. T. Castle, *A Treasury of Christian Quotes*, Hodder & Stoughton, p. 162.
2. Acts 1:14.
3. J. Morley, *Bread of Tomorrow*, SPCK/Christian Aid, p. 143.
4. Acts 15:14; cf. Revelation 5:9.
5. www.christianquotes.org.
6. J.I. Packer, *God's Words*, IVP, p. 55.
7. Source unknown.
8. M. Henry, *Concise Commentary on the Whole Bible*, Moody Press, p. 913.
9. Acts 2:44–47.
10. www.christianquotes.org.
11. www.christianquotes.org.
12. Source unknown.
13. *One, Compassion* source 2002.

SECTION TWO

Compassionate witness: in solidarity

Someone once said, 'There are two kinds of people: those who come into a room and say, 'Here I am' and those who say, 'Ah, there you are.'

The compassionate solidarity of God—Father, Son and Holy Spirit—cannot be disguised. God's own plan to save us involved him fully in our suffering. Throughout history he has consistently shown his solidarity, his compassion in suffering with us from among us. In Christ, our triune God experienced humanity in a deeply profound and permanent way. Jesus shared our flesh, vulnerabilities, temptations and, ultimately, our sin.

Like those who have borne faithful witness to Christ before us, we are entrusted to reveal Christ in this generation, to participate with him in his absolute commitment to mission. He is the Father's missionary to a lost world, and we are his. He enables us through the authority given him by the Father, ensures us of his continuing solidarity 'even until the end of the world' (Matthew 28:20) and empowers us through the indwelling presence of the Holy Spirit. He also calls us to go.

Relocation is a key principle in making disciples. Jesus showed his solidarity with us by coming, but first he obeyed the Father by going. 'He didn't commute to earth one day a week and shoot back up to heaven,' says John Perkins. 'He left his throne and became one of us so that we might see the life of God revealed in him.'[1] When was the last time we asked God about relocation—where exactly he wants us to go and witness, to reveal him to others? This thought is frightening to most of us. To consider relocation forces us to confront our own values, identify our own prejudices and acknowledge to what degree we are really prepared to follow Christ.

Habib Sahabib says, 'Blessed is he who hungers for friends—for though he may not realize it, his soul is crying out for God.'[2] Most of us will not be called to relocate physically, to uproot geographically and move in order to reveal him. However, we are all, without exception, called to relocate our priorities in Christ, to uproot our inner selves continually and move spiritually, emotionally and mentally nearer to those whom Christ would make our neighbours. As Henry Martyn says, 'The Spirit of Christ is the spirit of mission, and the nearer we get to him the more immensely missionary we become.'[3]

We may be the only witness for Christ that our neighbour, near or far, will ever know. This truth puts us in a place of both great honour and great responsibility. Jesus' bodily presence in the world changed it. Individually and as a community, we are now the body of Christ. Only we can offer what is most needed in our world—the incarnate love and compassion of Christ in us. 'The reconciliation we are powerless to bring, Christ can bring supernaturally through the presence of his body,' says John Perkins. 'Through his people, the church!'[4] Others will experience Christ first of all in our presence—the way we are in ourselves, the way we are with each other. Christ is our identity and our purpose. We don't just preach the gospel, we mirror the gospel; we don't just preach Christ, we mirror Christ.

There are no boundaries on what has become known as the great commission. Everyone everywhere needs the gospel. Jesus, however, in both word and deed, demonstrated God's consistent compassion for those deprived, despised and dispirited. This he did through his presence among them. His solidarity yielded such sensitivity that he met each person's individual need with an appropriate response. He healed those who needed healing, forgave those who needed forgiveness, inspired those who needed vision, challenged those who needed challenging and welcomed those regarded to be the least, including children.

Compassionate solidarity is not defining problems for others, or imposing solutions on those in need. It does not produce dependency but reflects the interdependency of compassionate community. Compassion *suffers with*. It is not patronage, but partnership—a mutual way of being, of giving and of receiving, core to the triune community of God himself. Witness is never about preaching alone but also about meeting the needs of the whole person.

Jesus revealed a true solidarity in his encounters with others. We observe this closely in his contact with the Samaritan woman at the well. Jewish people travelling from Judea to Galilee did their best to avoid Samaria or, rather, Samaritans. Such was their prejudice that they crossed the Jordan River to bypass the area and, when meeting Samaritans on the road, crossed to the other side lest even their shadows should meet.

In a typically unexpected move for those around him, Jesus cut a path through racial and religious prejudice, as well as Samaria, on his way to Galilee. He took a break from the midday heat at Jacob's well. There he asked a Samaritan woman for water. She was surprised that he would approach her, let alone talk to her. She was even further surprised when, in the course of their conversation, he uncovered her past and offered her a future—the overflowing life-giving water.[5]

The biggest surprise, however, is how much he revealed of himself to this seemingly disgraced and disgraceful woman—more than had as yet been revealed to any of his disciples. He was not merely the prophet she thought him, but the Messiah, the Christ, the Son of God, the Father, who would draw believers from every nation. She quite forgot her water jar, and her inhibitions, as she ran to tell the town's people about Jesus. As a result, Jesus was asked to stay on and many Samaritans put their faith in him. 'We no longer have faith in Jesus just because of what you told us,' they said to the woman. 'We have heard him ourselves, and we are certain that he is the Saviour of the world!' (John 4:42).

We do not know exactly what happened to the Samaritan woman, how the overwhelming experience of face-to-face grace ultimately reshaped her life and impacted those around her, but we do know that it did. Jesus demonstrated his solidarity with her by deliberately cutting through prejudice. How will we cut through our prejudices and preconceptions to reveal a truly involved, compassionate God rather than a distant, charitable deity? Jesus also demonstrated his solidarity in the way that he connected with the woman, engaging her in friendship over a shared need for water. How will we connect with others in a way that invites mutuality and leaves us open to receiving as well as giving?

As we have seen, we are image bearers of God, meant for mutually loving community. Satan wreaks havoc with this identity, constantly undermining our true worth, tempting us to erode our dignity with behaviours that lead to our own destruction as well as the destruction of those around us. Compassionate witness is God's means for respecting and restoring the dignity and worth with which he created us. To witness compassionately is to meet the deepest need of every human being to know that we are loved, made for love and can be loving. This is what the woman at the well needed to know. Jesus' witness affirmed her dignity and, in so doing, demonstrated his. Witness in solidarity not only demonstrates what God intends for us, but helps us all to become what God intended. Jesus met not only the woman's felt need for water but her deeper need for life—the ability to rise above her past in the present, to stop living in self-destruction and start living in dignity. 'Christ shows that the water of Jacob's well yields short satisfaction,' says Matthew Henry. 'Of whatever waters of comfort we drink, we will thirst again. But whoever partakes of the Spirit of grace and the comforts of the gospel, shall never want for that which will abundantly satisfy the soul.'[6]

William Booth didn't mince any words with believers who excused themselves from mission:

'Not called!' did you say? 'Not heard the call,' I think you should say. Put your ear down to the Bible, and hear him bid you... put your ear down to the burdened, agonised heart of humanity and listen to its pitiful wail for help. Go stand by the gates of hell and hear the damned entreat you... And

then look Christ in the face, whose mercy you have professed to obey and tell him whether you will join heart and soul and body and circumstance, in the march to publish his mercy to the world.[7]

God calls us to go even if he calls us to stay. If he isn't calling us to relocate physically, he is almost certainly calling us to relocate our prayers, money, time, skills and energies to people most in need of them, many millions of children among them. The Holy Spirit has gifted each of us to reveal God. We may do this in different ways, but we must all do it. If we can prophesy, serve, teach or encourage others, we should. If we can give, we should be generous. If we are leaders, we should do our best. If we are good to others, we should do it cheerfully.[8] To whom will we go to reveal God today?

*

The lure of the gang

Poverty destroys families as parents leave their children and search for work elsewhere. In El Salvador many parents have fled their families and gone to the USA in search of a better life and higher wages. Many lose contact with the children they leave behind. These children often join together to form a substitute family, which takes the form of a gang. However, the loss of love that they have experienced in their lives is rarely regained in the gangs they form, and life becomes, quite literally, a fight for survival.

Rival gangs control the streets of Soyapango in El Salvador. Participation in the gang lifestyle provides youngsters with the sense of belonging that they crave, and also the status that commands respect. In the eyes of society, these children are nothing, but once they have the power to kill, they become someone. It is impossible to ignore the threat of violence and death, and therefore by wielding weapons these youngsters find some identity in their communities.

In a country with very limited employment opportunities for

young people, the gangs are increasing in numbers. Between 25 and 50 thousand youngsters are already gang members. Very few of these will actually see life beyond the age of 30, dying in futile gangland battles.[9] The attraction of the gangs is an empty substitute for true identity and self-worth. It is the true identity and worth that an individual finds in Jesus Christ that *Compassion* seeks to bring to the children of El Salvador and other countries ravaged by this gang culture. By providing options and alternative lifestyles, projects are seeking to encourage young people to live outside the constraints and restrictions of circumstance.

*

Group helps

Worship

I love you with the love of the Lord (SF1 205)
I will sing, I will sing (SF2 855)
Jesus, lover of my soul (SF2 873)
Rejoice! (SF1 461)
Son of man (SF2 1006)

Word

Isaiah 52:7–10
John 4:3–40

Prayer

- Pray that God will protect *Compassion* projects from violent attacks and theft by gangs.
- Pray for children who are born into gangs, asking that God will help them to see a life outside the violence.

- Pray for strength and protection for those who reach out to the gang members.

Fellowship

Reflect on the following lyrics to an African hymn by creating a large group collage around its themes. Use magazines, newspapers, photographs, natural materials, paint, chalk and so on. Finish your time together by reading Isaiah 52:7–10.

> *The cross is the way of the lost*
> *The cross is the staff of the lame*
> *The cross is the guide of the blind*
> *The cross is the strength of the weak*
> *The cross is the hope of the hopeless*
> *The cross is the freedom of the slaves*
> *The cross is the water of the seeds*
> *The cross is the consolation of the bonded labourers*
> *The cross is the source of those who seek water*
> *The cross is the cloth of the naked.*
> FROM A 10TH-CENTURY AFRICAN HYMN [10]

Witness

Imagine yourself living in a community of great need. Perhaps there has been an earthquake or flood. Perhaps there is a continuing famine or civil war. Perhaps you are among those most in need in your own town or city. Explore the following questions together as a group:

- What needs do you see or experience as parent, child, male, female, elderly person?
- How do you feel about yourself because of your need?
- Where do you get help?
- What is the attitude of those who give you assistance?

Now think about Christian believers who have relocated into devastated communities around the world. Is God asking you to relocate? If not, how can you relocate your priorities among those in need at home or abroad?

For personal reflection

Think of yourself walking somewhere dark, enclosed and stifling. Suddenly the view opens up and you happen on some form of water—fountains, a puddle or waterfall, dew on the grass, an ocean or lake, a pool or well. Using all your senses, describe the water.

- Who, if anyone, do you meet by the water?
- What happens next?
- How do your internal feelings change?
- How might this experience change you for the rest of your life?
- If the water were to suddenly become a person, who might it be and why?

NOTES

1 J. Perkins, *With Justice for All*, Regal Books, p. 88.
2 T. Castle, *A Treasury of Christian Wisdom*, Hodder & Stoughton, p. 94.
3 Castle, *Treasury of Christian Wisdom*, p. 162.
4 Perkins, *With Justice for All*, p. 53.
5 John 4:1–25.
6 M. Henry, *Concise Commentary on the Whole Bible*, Nelson, p. 986.
7 www.christianquotes.com.
8 Romans 12:6–8.
9 El Salvador's teenage beauty queens live and die by gang law: Sandra Jordan, *Guardian*, 10 November 2002.
10 Taken from J. Morley, *Bread of Tomorrow*, SPCK/Christian Aid, p. 111.

SECTION THREE

Compassionate witness: in humble servanthood

'If you would win the world,' says Alexander Maclaren, 'melt it, do not hammer it.'[1]

The Christian community has a message of profound importance in a self-centred, self-seeking world: personal ambition isn't everything. In fact, personal ambition is nothing. The way of salvation and satisfaction is not self-interest, but self-denial and servanthood. We *find* ourselves in the *loss* of self to Christ. This is the gospel we are compelled to share with everyone around us, the commission we are bound to undertake. We are not saved *by* good works but *for* them; we are not saved by doing good, but in order to do good. 'God has shown us how kind he is by coming to save all people,' says Paul to Titus. 'He taught us to give up our wicked ways and our worldly desires and to live decent and honest lives in this world. We are filled with hope, as we wait for the glorious return of our great God and Saviour Jesus Christ. He gave himself to rescue us from everything that is evil and to make our hearts pure. He wanted us to be his own people and to be eager to do right' (Titus 2:11–14). Rescue from our wrongdoing is only half the good news. The other half is that we are rescued for a purpose —mutual love and service, nothing less than the restoration of God's image in us. In Christ we are called to live the life of the Tri-unity for all to see.

Compassionate submission to the Father was a prominent characteristic of Jesus' life. As has been noted, Jesus served with such compassionate solidarity that his life culminated in death on a cross.[2]

Just before his ascension, Jesus said, 'Go to the people of all nations and make them my disciples. Baptize them in the name of the Father, the Son, and the Holy Spirit' (Matthew 28:19). If we would exercise the triunitarian authority given to us in the great commission, we must first freely surrender to it. We can witness to Christ only in the measure that we have become Christ-like in the Holy Spirit. Although we can never imitate his deity, we can—through abiding compassion—imitate the servanthood that won our love.

A young salesman asked an elder salesman the secret of his success. 'You just have to jump at every opportunity that comes along,' said the elder salesman. 'How do you know when an opportunity is coming?' asked the younger. 'You don't,' replied the elder salesman. 'You just have to keep jumping.'[3] Jesus was singularly and lovingly devoted to the Father and to those among whom he was sent. He served those around him as well as those to whom he was specifically prompted by the Holy Spirit. Jesus did not serve people to serve his own purpose. Jesus instead served people out of compassion simply because it *was* his purpose. In encouraging us to do the same, Paul says, 'Be sincere in your love for others... Love each other as brothers and sisters and honour others more than you do yourself. Never give up. Eagerly follow the Holy Spirit and serve the Lord... Take care of God's needy people and welcome strangers into your home.' (Romans 12:9–11, 13). We just have to keep jumping.

Someone once said, 'It is impossible to live with our arms crossed when Jesus died with his arms open.' How do we proclaim the gospel? Jesus reached a hostile world through humility. He affirmed human dignity in his contact with people—often deprived and despised. Jesus took people by the hand, embraced children in his arms and looked people in the eye. He touched wizened and leprous limbs, blind eyes, deaf ears and dumb mouths. He felt heartache for those who were diseased and love for those who were questioning. Jesus was humble. He often wanted to serve unseen and was prepared to serve unthanked. He regularly sacrificed his privacy and his personal needs to serve. He didn't reject the crowds; nor did he resist those who came in person and, on top of all this, he sought other opportunities to serve also.

If Christ is not everywhere apparent among us, then we are not what God intended us to be. We must remember who we were and see ourselves in Jesus' miracles. We are the widows he honoured, the children he blessed, the tax collector made good, the leader whose daughter was healed. We are those who were lame that walk, those who were blind that see, those who were deaf that hear, those who were dead that rise! We are the good news in Christ.

God's love is universal. John reminds us, 'Everyone who has faith in [Jesus] will have eternal life' (John 3:16). We are to show justice, compassion and respect to everyone, but especially those who are most vulnerable. This is not exclusive to the Christian community. God will reckon harshly with those found wanting in compassion.[4] God knows those who are yet strangers to us. They must not be taunted, trampled or treated with contempt but tenderly nurtured to faith.

Jesus' deepest act of humility and service was extending forgiveness to his enemies by dying for them.[5] We must not take lightly what so heavily laid on Christ. Forgiveness is a vital first step in the process of peace. Responding to it is the second. We too were enemies but have now been given the ministry of reconciliation. 'God has done it all!' said Paul. 'He sent Christ to make peace between himself and us, and he has given us the work of making peace between himself and others' (2 Corinthians 5:18).

Someone once said that rough edges make us easier to get hold of but harder to embrace. Those among us who experience harsh realities also often experience hard feelings. Fear, suspicion, anger, bitterness and resentment make it easy to lash out at the very love we so long for. Jesus caught the attention of a hostile world through humble servanthood. He didn't come to condemn us but to save us—a motivation born completely of love and compassion. How much more effective our witness would be if we embraced this truth. Jesus established his kingdom first in the hearts of wounded people by affirming their humanity in the way he served. We must do more than preach; we must serve with the power of humility. Our actions must so pulse with servanthood that compassion emerges as the underlying theme of the whole of our lives. Servanthood is the precursor of salvation. As we help people at the point of felt need, the Holy Spirit opens the way to meet their deepest need.

Charity has been described as 'the art of doing unselfish things for selfish reasons'. This should not be true of us. Worship and witness come together in meeting the needs of those who are oppressed. Jesus conveyed God's priorities in his witness among those in greatest need. In carrying out the great commission, we must ask ourselves where the great omissions are. Sadly, many children still figure among 'the least of these' today—abandoned, untouched and untouchable, unloved and unwanted, unseen and unheard. We must take seriously the responsibility to sow the seed among this generation that grows secretly from the gentle but steady encouragement of servanthood. We must never forget that Jesus' twelve disciples were only the core of a growing community of men, women and children, which included those who had been excluded elsewhere.

Someone once said, 'Those who serve with humility walk comfortably with Christ.' Jesus was an eager servant to those around him. He often, though not always, met immediate need with an immediate response. We must not think, however, that Jesus' service evolved from a short-lived desire to help. Jesus was wholly surrendered to the Father's will and wholly given to compassion as prompted by the Holy Spirit. His service of others was primarily an act of worship to God himself, primarily a response of womb-stirring compassion. So must ours be. We are not a charitable institution but a compassionate community listening to the prompting of the Holy Spirit. We discover the rhythm of God's heart in the flow of compassion, in those increasingly less staccato moments when we choose to act beyond obligation or niceties. As we respond to others with the compassion of God—Father, Son and Holy Spirit—we discover that love gives just because it wants to, that our purpose is all of love and, as Philip Larkin says, 'What will survive of us is love.'[6]

*

Social needs

Nirun, Sutatip and their mother were quite happy living in the small shack they called home in northern Thailand. While the rain seeped through the makeshift roof and there was not much space to sleep, they enjoyed the strong sense of support from within the community. However, as illegal dwellers on the slum site, they had no rights as tenants, and when the government told them to move they had no choice but to go. The family were relocated to a government apartment with nine other people and, while the rain no longer seeps in through the roof, the support of the community has been lost.

Niran's and Sutatip's mother, Lila, describes how, before, 'we lived like a big family, like a community; when we moved up here we live like individuals'. And for the privilege of this new home the family have to pay rent, which Lila can barely meet with the sum that she gets paid as a banana seller. On occasions, she must find the extra cash from money lenders and sinks further into debt and despair.

Poor people the world over do not have the luxury of being able to choose where they live. This sense of powerlessness can be soul-destroying for parents who want the best for their children. Lila's delight remains in her children. Both are enrolled in the *Compassion* project. Lila does not have to worry about finding money for school fees, meals and clothing, and some of the weight of her life has been lifted. She can help them to build a life for themselves.

Group helps

Worship

I know you love to crown the humble (SF2 803)
How can I be free from sin? (SF2 779)
Jesus Christ (SF2 865)
One shall tell another (SF1 417)
The Spirit of the Sovereign Lord (SF2 1049)

Word

Psalm 130
Titus 2:11—3:7

Prayer

- Pray that the local churches across the world will be centres for reconciliation.
- Pray that the Holy Spirit will enable the local church to unite divided communities.
- Pray that children in *Compassion* projects will learn the importance of getting along with their neighbours.

Fellowship

As a group, identify and share a time when you served someone else without obligation or expectation.

- How did this experience differ from those times when your giving was less purely motivated?

- How is serving one another primarily an act of worship to God?
- How are we a compassionate community as opposed to a charitable institution?

Witness

Explore these questions together:

- How did Jesus demonstrate a holistic compassion—meeting the needs of the whole person?
- What are the implications of this for your group in the way you present the gospel and reveal God among yourselves?
- How will you improve your ministry to meet the needs of the whole person?
- How will you provide a place to belong?

For personal reflection

Write a piece of prose or poetry in which each line begins or ends with one of the following:

- Today I will serve…

- Jesus didn't come to condemn me but to…

- …what will survive of me is love.

- …we are a compassionate community.

NOTES

1 Source unknown.
2 Philippians 2:8.
3 M. Hodgin, *1001 Humorous Illustrations for Public Speaking*, Zondervan, p. 334.
4 Exodus 22:22–25.
5 Romans 5:6–8.
6 Philip Larkin, 'An Arundel Tomb', 1964.

SECTION FOUR

Compassionate witness: in obedient response

Archbishop Temple once said, 'The last place that gets converted on a man is his pocket.'

When it comes to the kingdom, Jesus has more to say about possessions than almost any other issue. His parables jangle with references to the stewardship of wealth. After telling the story of the rich farmer who built bigger storage barns but died before they were emptied, Jesus said, 'This is what happens to people who store up everything for themselves, but are poor in the sight of God' (Luke 12:21). He then admonishes his disciples not to worry about their needs: 'Sell what you have and give the money to the poor... Make sure your treasure is safe in heaven' (Luke 12:33). Jesus doesn't deny us our treasure but directs our choice of it. What good is a bulging bank balance and a bankrupt heart? If we store up treasure anywhere, it should be heaven. If we give to anyone, it should be those in greatest need.

Logan Pearsall Smith says, 'Those who set out to serve both God and Mammon soon discover there is no God.'[1] Jesus' teaching about wealth is clear. 'You cannot be the slave of two masters...' he said. 'You cannot serve God and money' (Luke 16:13). Having money and serving money aren't the same thing. Having money isn't evil; the love of money is.[2] How do we know when money becomes Mammon, a god in our lives? When our possessions usurp God's priorities; when we love things more than people. Walter Hilton once said, 'It is easier to renounce worldly possessions than it is to renounce the love of them.'[3] Sin doesn't come from what we have, but from who we are. Good and evil come from the heart. Our hearts will always reveal what we treasure.[4]

Compassionate witness comes from digging deep in Christ's person before digging deep in our pockets. The primary issue is not money but life, not what we own but who owns us, not what we have but who we become. If we are to know and express fullness of life in Christ, we must lose it in obedience to Christ. 'If any of you want to be my followers,' said Jesus, 'you must forget about yourself. You must take up your cross and follow me. If you want to save your life, you will destroy it. But if you give up your life for me, you will find it. What will you gain, if you own the whole world but destroy yourself? What would you give to get back your soul?' (Matthew 16:24–26).

A story is told of a pig and a hen who were walking down the road when they happened upon a poster for an upcoming harvest supper. It read, 'Ham and eggs will be served.' The hen said to the pig, 'It's so nice to be able to help out.' 'It's all right for you,' the pig replied. 'You'll be making a contribution, but I'll be making a sacrifice!'[5]

Irrespective of our earthly assets, our greatest capital is ourselves and we must invest ourselves in what has greatest eternal value. Jesus spoke of profit and loss, comfort and security in terms of eternity. Prestige, power and possessions, importance, ingenuity and influence are intoxicating but they are also temporal, detrimental, even devastating to the soul. How can a soul made for eternity be satisfied with the trappings of time? Eternal living is ultimately more lucrative and infinitely more lasting. Possessions perish but our identity, meaning and purpose are imperishable in Christ.

Jesus wasn't successful in worldly terms, yet his teaching, as affirmed by his personal integrity, remains the most potent and pertinent witness in the world today. His death became the means of reconciliation, his resurrection the means of ultimate deliverance. Jesus invested himself in us and did so to the point of death, even counting it a joy.[6] We are called to do the same.

There is an old proverb that says, 'A man of words and not of deeds is like a garden full of weeds.' Part of our identity in Christ is the responsibility to act as he would as a witness in the world. Activity, however, is not the same as action. Paul Tilloch says, 'The first duty of love is to listen.'[7] If we are to respond in obedience rather than rashly reacting, we must discover and accept our purpose and obey purposefully. Significant and enduring witness is possible only through intimate listening. Those who pause, ponder and pray before a single act will achieve more than the abundant activity of many. 'Faith never knows where it is being led,' says Oswald Chambers, 'but it loves and knows the One who is leading.'[8]

A story is told about a little boy who played the part of the innkeeper in the nativity play. He was so involved in the human drama of the story that when it came time for him to send Mary and Joseph to the stable, he said instead, 'Come back! You can have my room and I'll sleep in the stable.'

As we have seen, generosity comes from the heart, from the lived experience of being loved. God is lavish in his generosity and loves people who reflect this in their own giving. The Holy Spirit produces God's generosity in us. 'If we can give, we should be generous,' says Paul. 'If we are good to others, we should do it cheerfully' (Romans 12:8). How we give is as vital as what we give. 'What if I gave away all that I owned and let myself be burnt alive?' says Paul. 'I would gain nothing, unless I loved others' (1 Corinthians 13:3). We give ourselves, not just our things. Responding to Jesus without love doesn't count. 'Christianity,' says William Barclay, 'should be characterised by the open hand, the open heart and the open door.'[9] Well-chosen witness will communicate the extravagant love of the gospel effectively.

Jesus taught that poverty, though a physical reality for many, is a spiritual reality for us all. Our deepest hunger is heaven; our greatest thirst is glory. God created us in his image for the sheer delight of loving us. Only through Christ can we return to God; only through the Holy Spirit can we be full of him. This is the good news to which we are witness. There is a way for those who are heartsick to get home. Physical prosperity is one thing; spiritual prosperity is everything. Jesus himself is our buried treasure in return for which we will gladly give up all.[10] Those who hunger and thirst after righteousness are promised abundance. 'God blesses those people who want to obey him more than to eat or drink. They will be given what they want!' (Matthew 5:6).

Outward poverty exposes those who are impoverished to injury and wrong and makes justice impossible to seek and savour. Dignity is desired but denied, hunger is rarely satisfied, thirst rarely quenched. Paul reminds us that those who have been given a trust must prove faithful of having received it.[11] Christ has entrusted us with the greatest of all commissions. Although those who are poor need a share in our physical prosperity, they also need the spiritual prosperity brought by the gospel. Hope will be delivered, justice done, wrong righted and oppressors oppressed. Our lives are spent profitably if we invest them in those who are poor.[12]

God's compassion demands that we think beyond ourselves and provide for more than our own needs. We must make God's kingdom our first concern, sign the cheque for both our money and our lives and let God fill in the amount. As Bob Gass says, 'We want to be able to face God and declare that we have invested every ounce of energy, every talent, every penny entrusted to us to fulfil God's purposes on the earth.'[13] It is precisely this point that Jesus makes in the parable of the gold coins.[14] A hardened absentee king gives several servants a gold coin each to turn into profit for his return. Two do just that, are highly commended and are entrusted with more. One, however, is immobilized by fear of the king's reputation for injustice, so does nothing with what has been entrusted to him. His coin is taken by the king and given to the servant who turned the highest profit.

Jesus is not here suggesting that God is a hardened, unjust nobleman who must be obeyed with instilled fear. Neither is he building a case for capitalism or condoning oppression and unfair gain. Jesus is instead providing a contrast, pointing to the imminent arrival of God's kingdom, a kingdom both established in and reflective of God's justice and compassion. What God has entrusted to us has been entrusted in love and must be invested in love, a love so based on God's reputation for compassion that it casts out every fear we have. We are God's servants and we must maximize the potential of both the gospel and the gifts he has given to us. 'Most important of all, you must sincerely love each other, because love wipes away many sins,' says Peter. 'Welcome people into your home and don't grumble about it. Each of you has been blessed with one of God's many wonderful gifts to be used in the service of others. So use your gift well… Everything should be done in a way that will bring honour to God because of Jesus Christ, who is glorious and powerful for ever' (1 Peter 4:8–11).

Mignon McLaughlin says, 'We'd all like a reputation for generosity and we'd all like to buy it cheap.'[15] God's generosity cost him everything. We are witnesses to this abundant generosity—welcoming people into our homes and God's kingdom, sharing our own lives and God's love. True compassion will cost us everything. Through the compassion of the Father, we turn our backs on bitterness and revenge. Through the love of the Son, we serve others before ourselves. Through the compassion of the Spirit, we are sent out into the world.

✱

Alcohol abuse

Pequito had little to aspire to in his home town of Sula in Honduras. A life of pain and struggle faced the children of the town and the only escape for many people was found in drink. Pequito's father was one such man. Frustrated by the situation that imprisoned him, his drinking binges frequently led to outbursts of violence inflicted on both Pequito and his mother.

Home was clearly not a happy place for such a little boy and, without the opportunities to break the mould, it looked as if history would repeat itself through Pequito. However, Pequito was given the chance to break from the expectations and the struggle of life, in a *Compassion* project.

Pequito's father was astonished that someone should take an interest in the future of his son and the welfare of the whole family and he wanted to know why. Through close contact with the project workers and members of the church in the area, Pequito's father was introduced to Christ and, through this relationship with Jesus, a truly remarkable transformation took place. Pequito's father became a man who, in his own words, 'learned to love other people'. The family now have dreams and aspirations and they can see beyond the bottom of the next bottle and toward the future.[16]

*

Group helps

Worship

All I once held dear (SF2 646)
Be thou my vision (SF1 38)
I, the Lord of sea and sky (SF2 830)
Take my life, and let it be (SF1 496)
Will you come and follow me? (SF2 1120)

Word

Psalm 49
Matthew 16:24

Prayer

- Pray that parents of *Compassion* children who have drink and drug addictions will seek help.

- Pray that staff at *Compassion* projects will be equipped to help parents who are seeking to break addictions.
- Pray that children who suffer from violence at home will find places to offer them love and support.

Fellowship

Ask each person in the group to keep a record of everything they spend and what they spend it on for a week, including direct debits, credit cards, and so on. Do the same in regard to time and talents. Reflect on these questions as a group:

- What did this exercise reveal about your giving? Did it throw up anything unexpected?
- To what extent did you give to those who are most vulnerable?
- Are there things you now want to change about the way you give?

Witness

Ask each member of the group to choose for themselves a group of people whom they would ultimately like to make an impact on for Christ—children, young people, an ethnic or religious group, workmates, a specific group of people in a foreign country, and so on. Give the group six months to find out as much as possible about their chosen group, primarily through listening. Pray together that God would increase your love and compassion during this exercise and help you to discern how you might witness most appropriately.

For personal reflection

'There will your heart be also.' Write a piece of prose entitled, 'My life as a treasure chest'. Choose one of the pictures of yourself on the inside front cover of your journal from which to write. Explore these questions:

- What is inside you?
- How valuable is the treasure you contain?
- How often do you unlock yourself and share your treasure with others?
- Where did you find your treasure?
- What would you most like to see in the treasure chest of yourself?
- What do you possess that God treasures?

NOTES

1. J. Green, *Cassell Dictionary of Cynical Quotations*, Cassell, p. 106.
2. Luke 16:11; 1 Timothy 6:10.
3. A.P. Castle, *Quotes and Anecdotes: An Anthology for Preachers and Teachers*, Kevin Mayhew, p. 363.
4. Matthew 15:19; Luke 12:34.
5. R. Backhouse, *1500 Illustrations for Preaching and Teaching*, Marshall Pickering, p. 153.
6. Hebrews 12:2.
7. Castle, *Quotes and Anecdotes*, p. 312.
8. www.christianquotes.org.
9. Backhouse, *1500 Illustrations*, p. 196.
10. Matthew 13:44.
11. 1 Corinthians 4:2.
12. Isaiah 58:10.
13. B. Gass, *The Word for Today*, February–April 2004, UCB, p. 7.
14. Luke 19:12–26.
15. Green, *Dictionary of Cynical Quotations*, p. 37.
16. Original source *Compassion International It Works* trip.

SECTION FIVE

Compassionate witness: in hopeful expectancy

'Suffering comes in a cup,' says Matthew Henry, 'not a river, not a sea but a cup which we'll soon see the bottom of.'[1]

It is easy to lose sight of hope in suffering. How can we stand confidently in unseen future promises when we are barely able to make it through the day? We weren't created for pain but with purpose, to glorify God by revealing the whole of him in the whole of us. In so being, we bring others to our triune God—Father, Son and Holy Spirit.

John saw God's glory in Christ, even in his humanity. 'The Word became a human being and lived here with us,' says John. 'We saw his true glory, the glory of the only Son of the Father' (John 1:14). Through Christ, we are also God's children. We too are vessels for the overflowing capacity of God, even in suffering. 'God whispers in our conscience, speaks in our silence and shouts in our pain,' says C.S. Lewis. 'It is his megaphone to rouse a deaf world.'[2] When we reflect Christ in our suffering, we confront the world with the means of deliverance and hope. Like Jesus, we ask God to bring glory to himself through our suffering.[3] What will we pray when we don't know what to say? 'Father, reveal yourself.'

Graffito says, 'God is alive, he just doesn't want to get involved.'[4] Thankfully, this common perception is not true. The fall of humanity brought failure but God brings hope out of it. Jesus restores whatever lies in ruins, and does so to greater glory. 'I tell you for certain,' said Jesus, 'that a grain of wheat that falls on the ground will never be more than one grain unless it dies. But if it dies, it will produce lots of wheat. If you love your life, you will lose it. If you give it up in this world, you will be given eternal life. If you serve me, you must go with me. My servants will be with me wherever I am. If you serve me, my Father will honour you' (John 12:24–26).

Jesus reminds us that increase always involves sacrifice. A grain of wheat will only ever be a grain of wheat unless it dies to itself, allowing others like it to sprout and flourish. Christ did not need to become human to gain glory or have honour himself, to occupy praise or embody eminence. Neither, as a human being, did he need to suffer and die in order to procure peace with God for himself. Rather, our deliverance is owing to the sacrificial compassion of Christ. Through the dying of this one has come the living of all those who are like him. Out of a time of agony comes an eternity of salvation that is ours to experience and proclaim.[5] We now share with Christ in the principle of increase by sacrifice.

The Greek word translated 'witness' in the New Testament is strongly linked to the word 'martyr'. It describes a person who bears witness or offers testimony even to the point of death.[6] The 'hall of faith', as Hebrews 11 has become known, offers potted histories of previous saints and what they both achieved and endured because of their faith. Indeed, the chapter begins by defining faith as a hopeful expectancy and describes the faithfulness of our spiritual ancestors even though they never lived to see the promise of God fulfilled. 'Faith makes us sure of what we hope for,' says the writer to the Hebrews, 'and gives us proof of what we cannot see. It was their faith that made our ancestors pleasing to God' (Hebrews 11:1–2). Among these faithful are those whose witness led to persecution, even martyrdom. In Hebrews 11:35–40 we are presented with a moving description of what they endured and why.

These people were not fanatical in their faith, but faithful witnesses to the God of faith. Looking for a place to call their own, they sacrificed all for the hope of heaven and as a testimony to the generations of believers yet to come. Theirs was the principle of increase by sacrifice. Dietrich Bonhoeffer says, 'When Christ calls a man he bids him to come and die.'[9] Faithfulness to Christ necessarily leads to the death of our selfish nature as we take up our crosses to follow him. Like Christ, we are crucified, dead and buried. Like Christ, we are risen, reigning and glorified. We will share in the glory of Christ, because we have suffered with him. We too share God's compassion, not wanting to reach the goal of our faith in Christ without the company of those who have yet to find faith in Christ.

Here we are reminded that the philosophy of faith is not 'seeing is believing', but 'believing is seeing'. Jesus is the ultimate witness of God's compassion. He endured the shame of the cross, not to achieve glory but to bring others with him into glory. We must keep our eyes on Jesus who both leads us and makes our faith complete. The more we believe in him, the more clearly we see him. Jesus saw through the cross to the joy that would come. We are that joy, the reward of his sufferings. So also are those brought into the kingdom of God through our witness.

'Dear God,' wrote a child in a letter, 'I didn't think orange went with purple until I saw the sunset you made on Tuesday. That was cool.'[8] Suffering and joy seem completely at odds with one another. However, God will blend them perfectly to reveal the ultimate glory only hinted at in this life. We reflect God most when, in our own woundedness, we witness to the kingdom among those who are wounded—those who are poor in spirit but hungry for righteousness, those who are mourning, meek and merciful, those who are pure, peaceful and persecuted. If we allow God's grace to work in our own grief, we will reveal him to others who are grieving. Like the 'man of sorrows' who often wept, we will mourn with others and show compassion, *suffering with* them. In heaven, all those in Christ will be perfectly and eternally comforted. The deeper our despair, the greater our deliverance will be. There will be no more tears, a promise doubly sweet for those who have borne so many.[9]

What hope! Through the resurrection of Christ we will attain the fullness of life for which we were originally destined. Jesus said, 'I came so that everyone would have life, and have it fully' (John 10:10). Chronologically, time advances to a close. In Christ, however, time is no longer our enemy. Death, and all else that laid claim to us in sin, has no claim on us in eternity—an eternity that begins now. We will be fully reconciled to God, ourselves and each other, our world and God's time. We live today as if the good anticipated tomorrow were already ours. We live in hopeful expectancy that what John said of Jesus is increasingly true of us. We too will witness to the glory of God, even in our humanity.

We can witness in and to the world because Christ has overcome the world.[10] His presence in heaven and the Holy Spirit's presence in us are a pledge of greater power to do greater work. We are most effective when we use God's gifts with God's power. Paul prayed that the Holy Spirit would strengthen us with a might equal to the immeasurable riches of God's glory, his power working in us to do far more than we dare ask or imagine.[11] Hope matures within us as we mature in ourselves. 'We gladly suffer, because we know that suffering helps us to endure,' says Paul. 'And endurance builds character, which gives us a hope that will never disappoint us. All this happens because God has given us the Holy Spirit, who fills our hearts with his love' (Romans 5:3–5).

Emil Brunner once said, 'The church exists by mission as fire exists by burning.'[12] So deep is God's compassion that he rejoices in each person saved and grieves each that is lost. In the face of such overwhelming world deprivation, it sometimes seems that we expend ourselves for nothing. Jesus wasn't successful in worldly terms, but served faithfully the values of heaven. A teacher once asked her pupils what they wanted to be when they grew up. One boy said, 'I want to be possible.' 'What do you mean?' asked the teacher. 'My mother is always telling me I'm impossible,' he replied. 'So I want to be possible.'[13] God knows each child in the human flesh pile of every war, earthquake, flood and famine. From the cradle to the cross Jesus demonstrated God's compassion as a total and sustained *suffering with*—a constant, consuming commitment particularly to those who are oppressed. Poverty is an issue of personal, communal and spiritual importance to God, a priority of his heart's work. So must it be to us.

Just before being discovered by the Nazis, Anne Frank wrote in her diary, 'How wonderful it is that nobody need wait a single moment before beginning to improve the world!'[14] God leaves us in no doubt that we must improve the world for those who experience its harshest realities. However, we must also witness to what lies beyond and above this world. The absence of God is the greatest and most painful deprivation human beings can endure. Now is the day of salvation—not yesterday, not tomorrow. We can't act in the past, nor must we postpone action until tomorrow. Now is the day of our salvation and the day for us to bring salvation, the eternal presence of God, to others through our compassion. With so compassionate a God, so clear a directive and so great a need, what else could we possibly be waiting for?

✷

Words of encouragement

Ruth Coaquira is a doctor working with eight *Compassion* projects in the Bolivian city of Lapaz. Ruth not only works to minister to the needs of the children but also in educating their parents about the basic health and hygiene issues that can prevent common illnesses.

Ruth knows the importance of these practices because, not so long ago, she was one of those children in need of sponsorship. After her father lost his job as a miner, Ruth and her family were forced to move to the city in search of work. Their transition was made easier through the help of *Compassion*'s programme, which gave Ruth and her brother not only education but also extra food and supplies for the family.

By the time she was 15, Ruth had decided that she wanted to become a doctor and have a career in medicine. Her fulfilment of this dream is thanks in part to the support of her sponsor.

'My Dad... well, he didn't have much faith in me. He didn't think that I would make it'. Ruth was determined that this would not stand in her way and the words of encouragement she received from her sponsor really served to cement her desire. 'My sponsor said it's possible. You can do just about whatever you want. She completely changed my life.' And through Ruth hundreds of children in Lapaz have been offered a healthy future.[15]

∗

Group helps

Worship

At your feet we fall (SF1 28)
He is the Lord (SF2 755)
I give you all the honour (SF1 191)
Lift Jesus higher (SF1 326)
O for a thousand tongues (SF1 395)

Word

Hebrews 11
Revelation 1:4–8

Prayer

- Ask that God will inspire us to be more than just financial providers but also channels of love and encouragement to our brothers and sisters overseas.
- Pray for God to guide us as we seek to give to those who are in greater need than we are.
- Ask that God will give us a greater heart of compassion as we seek him.

Fellowship

The Greek word for 'witness' is strongly linked to the word 'martyr'. It describes a person who bears witness or offers testimony even to the point of death. Discuss how Jesus bore witness to the compassion of God even to the point of death, and what this means to you personally. What can we learn from his example?

Have each person in the group write their name on a piece of paper and put it into a hat. Have the group draw names and say this blessing to the person whose name has been drawn:

I pray that you will be blessed with kindness and peace from God, who is and was and is coming... May kindness and peace be yours from Jesus Christ, the faithful witness.
REVELATION 1:4–5

Witness

Ask the members of your group: Who do you *not* want to go to glory without? Pray for those who are mentioned and opportunities to reveal God to them in word and deed.

For personal reflection

Look at the photographs of yourself in the front of your journal.

- Who told you in word and deed that you were impossible?
- Who told you that you could be possible and how has Christ's compassion made you so?
- Whose possibility will you affirm today?

Reflect on this in your journal or discuss it with a close and trusted friend.

NOTES

1. M. Henry, *A Commentary on the Whole Bible, Volume 3*, World Bible Publishers.
2. www.christianquotes.org.
3. John 12:27–28.
4. J. Green, *Cassell Dictionary of Cynical Quotations*, Cassell, p. 104.
5. Romans 5:19.
6. W.E. Vine, *Vine's Concise Dictionary of Bible Words*, Thomas Nelson, p. 416. *Martus* or *martur* (3144).
7. R. Backhouse, *1500 Illustrations for Preaching and Teaching*, Marshall Pickering, p. 83.
8. S. Hample and E. Marshall, *Children's Letters to God*, Workman Publishing.
9. Revelation 21:4.
10. John 16:33.
11. Ephesians 3:14–21.
12. Backhouse, *1500 Illustrations*, p. 263.
13. M. Hodgin, *1001 Humorous Illustrations for Public Speaking*, Zondervan, p. 173.
14. A.P. Castle, *Quotes and Anecdotes: an Anthology for Preachers and Teachers*, Kevin Mayhew, p. 164,
15. Original source *Compassion International It Works* trip.

IN-DEPTH REFLECTION

How can we be changed?

When considering how we can make an impact on the hurting world we see on our doorsteps, perhaps we put a little too much emphasis on what we give financially. Indeed we do have the valuable financial resources to make an impact but we need to consider other ways in which we can give and, indeed, how we too may receive.

If compassion literally means coming alongside those who are suffering, then it implies a solidarity between us, not a one-way channel of support and resources. While we can never presume to understand completely what it is like to live as another individual, we are still able to share in their lives.

Financial giving is in many ways the easiest way to impart support to our brothers and sisters across the world, but through a one-to-one relationship with a child in desperate need we can offer more than just a flow of money. We can offer ourselves through correspondence, the building of relationships and prayer support. It takes time to write a letter, time to pray for a child in need and only a few seconds to write a cheque, but we should never underestimate the value of the prayers and the letters.

As children survive in environments where they are regarded as vermin and treated as such, we can show them their true worth. Letters bringing words of encouragement and support from the other side of the world are precious. Children can see the face and love of God through these situations and, indeed, learn of their own self-worth. This provision for the child is a continuation of the holistic development that *Compassion* practises.

We should never under-estimate, either, how we can be touched by those in need. We might be financially better off than many across the world, but material wealth is not directly proportional to spiritual wealth. Jesus tells us that when we give we can expect to receive. Indeed, we too can be blessed by the children in *Compassion* projects. Jesus said, 'When you give a feast, invite the poor, the crippled, the lame and the blind. They cannot pay you back. But God will bless you and reward you' (Luke 14:13). Children who, despite their tough existence, have a real and loving relationship with their heavenly Father and incredible faith can reach out to us in our spiritual poverty.

While the children in the developing world are prisoners of poverty, we are in many ways prisoners of our own consumer society. The Ugandan bishop, Festo Kivengere, commented that he finds it 'more difficult to minister to those who are suffering from prosperity. With prosperity comes a kind of deadening façade that numbs the sensitivity'.[1] We get caught up in the trappings of the world, placing too much of our trust and faith in financial policies, property, governments and our own strength, when we should be putting our greatest trust in God. It is this unfailing trust that our brothers and sisters across the oceans can show us.

Giving is never a one-way process. We are a bridge of hope to children and they in turn are a bridge of hope to us. We are not born to live in isolation or on our own understanding, but as part of a larger network, and we should be seeking to make full and ready use of the multitude of gifts with which the Lord has provided us. One of the smallest bones in the body is found in the ear, but without it the whole of the auditory sense will not work. In the same way we should value even the smallest, most vulnerable child in God's kingdom.

To support a child in desperate circumstances is a command from God, but it is equally an opportunity and a wonderful chance to have our own lives impacted from a distance. It's a chance to be a facilitator and a link in a chain of events that can see God's world transformed, and to stand in solidarity with those on the other side of the world. In short, showing compassion is meeting with God.

NOTES

1 Taken from *The Compassion Project*, *Compassion International* 1998, p. 107.

Bibliography

Richard Backhouse, *1500 Illustrations for Preaching and Teaching*, Marshall Pickering, 1991.

John Bickerseth and Timothy Pain, *The Four Faces of God*, Kingsway, 1992.

Stuart Briscoe, *Bound for Joy*, Regal, 1975.

Clive Calver, et al., *Dancing In the Dark* seminar notes, Spring Harvest, Lynx Communications, 1994.

Tony Castle, *A Treasury of Christian Wisdom*, Hodder & Stoughton, 2001.

Anthony P. Castle, *Quotes and Anecdotes: An Anthology for Preachers and Teachers*, Kevin Mayhew, 1979.

Ronald Dunn, *Don't Just Stand There, Pray Something!*, Alpha, Scripture Press, 1992,

Charles Elliott, *Praying the Kingdom*, Darton, Longman & Todd, 1985.

Leith Fisher, *The Widening Road: from Bethlehem to Emmaus*, Scottish Christian Press, 2003.

Leith Fisher, *Will You Follow Me?*, Scottish Christian Press, 2003.

Bob Gass, *The Word for Today*, UCB, August–September 2003.

Jonathon Green, *Cassell Dictionary of Cynical Quotations*, Cassell, 1994.

S. Hample and Eric Marshall, *Children's Letters to God*, Workman Publishing.

BIBLIOGRAPHY

Matthew Henry, *Concise Commentary on the Whole Bible*, Moody Press, 1983.

Michael Hodgin, *1001 Humorous Illustrations for Public Speaking*, Zondervan, 1994.

David Hubbard, *The Practice of Prayer*, IVP, 1983.

Selwyn Hughes, *My Favourite Stories about Children*, CWR, 2001.

Paul Keenan, *Heart Storming*, Contemporary Books, 2002.

Peter Kreeft, *Making Sense out of Suffering*, Servant Books, 1986.

Herbert Lockyer, *All the Prayers of the Bible*, Zondervan, 1959.

Eric Marshall, *Kids Talk about Heaven*, Kyle Cathie, 2003.

Paul Mason, *Out of the Mouths of Babes*, Monarch Books, 1999.

Bruce Milne, *Know the Truth*, IVP, 1982.

Janet Morley, *Bread of Tomorrow: Praying with the World's Poor*, SPCK, 1992.

Henri J. Nouwen et al., *Compassion*, Doubleday & Co., 1982.

John Perkins, *With Justice for All*, Regal Books, 1982.

Susan Ratcliffe, *Oxford Quotations by Subject*, Oxford University Press, 2003.

William Strange, *Children in the Early Church*, Paternoster Press, 1996.

M.C. Tenney, *12 Questions Jesus Asked*, Victor Books, 1985.

Sammy Tippit, *The Prayer Factor*, Scripture Press, 1989.

Elmer Towns, *The Names of the Holy Spirit*, Regal, 1994.

William E. Vine, *Vine's Concise Dictionary of Bible Words*, Thomas Nelson, 1999.

❧ barnabas

Resourcing children's work in church and school

Simply go to **www.brf.org.uk** and visit the barnabas pages

BRF is a Registered Charity

A Browse our books and buy online in our **bookshop**.

B In the **forum**, join discussions with friends and experts in children's work. Chat through the problems we all face, issues facing children's workers, where-do-I-find… questions and more.

C **Free** easy-to-use downloadable **ideas** for children's workers and teachers. Ideas include:
- Getting going with prayer
- Getting going with drama
- Getting going with the Bible… and much more!

D In **The Big Picture**, you'll find short fun reports on Barnabas training events, days we've spent in schools and churches, as well as expertise from our authors, and other useful articles.

E In the section on **Godly Play**, you'll find a general introduction and ideas on how to get started with this exciting new approach to Christian education.

Compassion
Releasing children from poverty
in Jesus' name

Compassion began its ministry in Korea in 1952. Now, over 50 years on, *Compassion* works in 23 of the world's poorest countries, helping over 600,000 children through sponsorship. *Compassion* links one child with just one sponsor with whom they can develop a personal friendship through letter-writing.

The work of *Compassion* is:

Child-focused

Compassion's holistic approach to child development equips individuals physically, socially and spiritually, empowering them to become adults who can make an impact on the world around them.

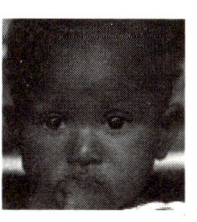

Church-based

Compassion works exclusively through local Christians, enabling them to become advocates for children and agents for change in their communities.

Christ-centred

Compassion seeks to reflect the character of Christ in every way to pursue the mission Christ gave to the church.

For more information about the work of Compassion, visit **www.compassionuk.org**